MW01121417

The International Recording Industries

The recording industry has been a major focus of interest for cultural commentators throughout the twenty-first century. As the first major content industry to have its production and distribution patterns radically disturbed by the Internet, the recording industry's content, attitudes and practices have regularly been under the microscope. Much of this discussion, however, is dominated by US and UK perspectives and assumes the 'the recording industry' to be a relatively static and homogeneous entity.

This book attempts to offer a broader, less Anglocentric and more dynamic understanding of the recording industry. Its starting premise is the idea that the recording industry is not one thing but is, rather, a series of recording industries, locally organised and locally focused, both structured by and structuring the international industry. Seven detailed case studies of different national recording industries illustrate this fact, each of them specifically chosen to provide a distinctive insight into the workings of the recording industry. The expert contributions to this book provide the reader with a sense of the history, structure and contemporary dynamics of the recording industry in these specific territories, and counteract the Anglo-American bias of coverage of the music industry.

The International Recording Industries will be valuable to students and scholars of sociology, cultural studies, media studies, cultural economics and popular music studies.

Lee Marshall is a Senior Lecturer in Sociology at the University of Bristol. His research interests focus on popular music, intellectual property and celebrity. Previous publications include *Bob Dylan: The Never Ending Star* (Polity 2007), *Bootlegging: Romanticism and Capitalism in the Music Industry* (Sage 2005) and *Music and Copyright* (co-edited with Simon Frith, Edinburgh University Press 2004).

Routledge Advances in Sociology

10. Self-Care
Embodiment, personal autonomy and the shaping of health consciousness
Christopher Ziguras

11. Mechanisms of Cooperation
Werner Raub and Jeroen Weesie

12. After the Bell
Educational success, public policy and family background
Edited by Dalton Conley and Karen Albright

13. Youth Crime and Youth Culture in the Inner City
Bill Sanders

14. Emotions and Social Movements
Edited by Helena Flam and Debra King

15. Globalization, Uncertainty and Youth in Society
*Edited by Hans-Peter Blossfeld, Erik Klijzing, Melinda Mills
and Karin Kurz*

16. Love, Heterosexuality and Society
Paul Johnson

17. Agricultural Governance
Globalization and the new politics of regulation
Edited by Vaughan Higgins and Geoffrey Lawrence

18. Challenging Hegemonic Masculinity
Richard Howson

19. Social Isolation in Modern Society
Roelof Hortulanus, Anja Machielse and Ludwien Meeuwesen

20. Weber and the Persistence of Religion
Social theory, capitalism and the sublime
Joseph W. H. Lough

21. Globalization, Uncertainty and Late Careers in Society
Edited by Hans-Peter Blossfeld, Sandra Buchholz and Dirk Hofäcker

22. Bourdieu's Politics
Problems and possibilities
Jeremy F. Lane

The International Recording Industries

Edited by Lee Marshall

Routledge
Taylor & Francis Group

LONDON AND NEW YORK

First published 2013
by Routledge
2 Park Square, Milton Park, Abingdon, Oxon OX14 4RN

Simultaneously published in the USA and Canada
by Routledge
711 Third Avenue, New York, NY 10017

Routledge is an imprint of the Taylor & Francis Group, an informa business

British Library Cataloguing in Publication Data
A catalogue record for this book is available from the British Library

Library of Congress Cataloging in Publication Data
The international recording industries/edited by Lee Marshall.
    p. cm. – (Routledge advances in sociology; 75)
    Includes bibliographical references and index.
    1. Sound recording industry. 2. Music trade. I. Marshall, Lee.
    ML3790.I582013
    384 – dc23
    2012010478

ISBN: 978-0-415-60345-4 (hbk)
ISBN: 978-0-203-83466-4 (ebk)

Typeset in Times New Roman
by Florence Production Ltd, Stoodleigh, Devon

Printed and Bound in the United States of America
by Edwards Brothers Malloy

Contents

Figures

Tables

Contributors

Martin Cloonan is Professor of Popular Music Politics at the University of Glasgow. His books include *Popular Music and the State in the UK* (Ashgate 2007) and *Dark Side of The Tune: Popular Music and Violence* (with Bruce Johnson, Ashgate 2008). His recent research has concentrated on the live music industry and future research will include a history of the UK's Musicians' Union. Martin is chair of the anti-censorship organisation Freemuse (www.freemuse. org) and manages the band Zoey Van Goey (www.zoeyvangoey.com).

Hugh Dauncey is Senior Lecturer in French Studies at Newcastle University. His research focuses on public policy dimensions of popular culture in France, particularly sport and music. He has co-edited collaborative volumes on the 1998 World Cup, the Tour de France, popular music in France, and, with Philippe Le Guern, *Stereo: Comparative Perspectives on the Sociological Study of Popular Music in France and Britain* (Ashgate 2010). He is currently completing a monograph on the social and cultural history of cycling in France, to be published by Liverpool University Press. In 2003 he was appointed Chevalier de l'Ordre des Palmes Académiques by the French state, in recognition of his services to French culture.

C. Michael Elavsky is Assistant Professor in the Department of Media Studies at Pennsylvania State University. His research addresses a wide range of issues including media studies, new media, pedagogy, the cultural industries and music as cultural/political communication.

Pekka Gronow is Adjunct Professor of Ethnomusicology at the University of Helsinki. He has published a number of books and articles on the history of the recording industry and is currently the coordinator of The Lindström Project, an international research project that attempts to document the global history of the Carl Lindström Company (Odeon, Parlophon, Fonotipia etc.) from 1904 to 1945. He has previously worked as an archivist and was responsible for the mass digitisation of the Finnish radio sound archives.

Philippe Le Guern is Professor in Popular Culture and Music Studies at the Université de Nantes, teaching in the Department of Communication Studies and the Department of Philosophy. He is a member of the Centre Atlantique de Philosophie and associate member of the Centre de Recherche sur la Littérature et les Arts (CRAL) at the EHESS. He has edited a number of studies on popular culture which cover fan culture, music and everyday life, Bourdieu and popular culture, including *Les cultes médiatiques. Oeuvres cultes et cultures fans* (PU Rennes 2002), *Sociologies des musiques populaires Réseaux*, vol. 25, 141–2 (La Découverte 2007) co-edited with Simon Frith, *Stereo: Comparative Perspectives on the Sociological Study of Popular Music in France and Britain* (Ashgate 2011) co-edited with Hugh Dauncey, and recently *Musiques et technologies numériques* (Réseaux 2012). He is currently the principal investigator in a French national research council project on the effects of digital technologies on work in cultural industries. He also works to encourage dialogue between French and British researchers studying popular music.

Adriana Helbig is Assistant Professor of Music and an affiliated faculty member in Cultural Studies, Women's Studies, Global Studies, and at the Center for Russian and East European Studies in the University of Pittsburgh. A member of the graduate faculty, she teaches courses on global hip-hop, world music, music, gender, sexuality, music, technology and cultural policy. She is the co-author, with Oksana Buranbaeva and Vanja Mladineo, of *The Culture and Customs of Ukraine* (Greenwood Press 2009).

Sam Howard-Spink is Clinical Assistant Professor of Music Business at New York University's Department of Music and Performing Arts Professions, in NYU Steinhardt. A music industry journalist since 1997, his current research interests are focused on the political economies of music, networks, globalisation and the BRICs. At NYU Sam teaches Emerging Models and Markets for Music and Interactive, Internet, and Mobile Music, and founded the NYU Music Video Games Research Project. His Portuguese needs work.

Dave Laing is Visiting Research Fellow at the Institute of Popular Music, University of Liverpool. He was formerly Reader in Music at the University of Westminster. His books include *The Sound of Our Time* (Sheed and Ward 1969), *One Chord Wonders* (Open University Press 1985) and *Buddy Holly* (Equinox 2010). He has co-edited three encyclopedias including *The Encyclopedia of Popular Music of The World* (Continuum 1999). He is an advisory editor to the journal *Popular Music* and associate editor of *Popular Music History*.

Lee Marshall is a Senior Lecturer in Sociology at the University of Bristol. His research interests centre on issues concerning authorship, stardom and intellectual property, with a particular interest in the music industry. His first book, *Bootlegging: Romanticism and Copyright in the Music Industry* (Sage 2005), won the Socio-Legal Study Association's early career book prize. His second book, *Bob Dylan: The Never Ending Star*, was published by Polity in 2007. He is currently researching contemporary developments within the music industry.

Tuulikki Pietilä is a Social Anthropologist and an Academy Research Fellow in the Helsinki Collegium for Advanced Studies. She has published a monograph on trade and gender in Kilimanjaro (*Gossip, Markets, and Gender: How Dialogue Constructs Moral Value in Post-Socialist Kilimanjaro*, University of Wisconsin Press 2007). Currently, she is studying South-African music and music industry, on which she has published a number of articles.

John Williamson is a part-time Lecturer and Honorary Research Fellow in the Department of Music at the University of Glasgow. While simultaneously managing Belle and Sebastian and working as a freelance journalist, he completed a Ph.D. on *Intellectual Property, Rent-Seeking and Entrepreneurship in the Music Industries* at Queen Margaret University in 2009.

Masahiro Yasuda is Associate Professor at Kyoto Seika University, teaching Cultural Sociology and Popular Music. He gained Master's and Doctoral degrees at the Centre for Mass Communication Research, Leicester University. Writing (and translating) extensively on local music scenes and globalisation, ICT's impacts on culture industries, and popular music pedagogy, he is currently researching the networking of the local blues scene in Kyoto.

1   Introduction

Lee Marshall

The recording industry has been a major focus of interest for cultural commentators throughout the twenty-first century. As the first major content industry to have its production and distribution patterns radically disturbed by the Internet, the recording industry's content, attitudes and practices have regularly been under the microscope. Underpinning most of this speculation and analysis, however, is not only a belief that the interests of 'the recording industry' are synonymous with the interests of the major record labels, but also that 'the recording industry', or even 'the majors', are entities with consistent goals and practices regardless of specific locality.

This book attempts to offer a better understanding of the recording industry as a whole. Its starting premise is that the recording industry is not a homogeneous entity, having instead different contours in different localities. As well as being a global industry, the recording industry is actually a series of recording industries, locally organised and locally focused, both structured by and structuring the international recording industry. At the heart of the book, therefore, are case studies of seven national recording industries, each specifically chosen to provide a distinctive insight into the workings of the recording industry. The aim of the book is to provide the reader with a sense of the history, structure and contemporary dynamics of the recording industry in these specific territories.

The book has two complementary rationales. The first, already stated, is to provide a more sophisticated account of the recording industry than is often witnessed in contemporary analyses. The record industry has been 'big news' over the last decade or so, but the overwhelming focus of analysis has been on the major record labels Universal, Sony, Warner and EMI with their headquarters in Los Angeles, New York, New York and London, respectively. Obviously, the major labels are important – they are called majors for a reason – but focusing too much on the fortunes of these global companies not only overlooks large portions of the recording industry (the vast majority of recording companies are not major labels) but also risks affording the majors a greater coherence than they actually have. The fortunes, strategies and effects of how, say, Warner operates in Finland may not be the same as in Hong Kong. By looking at the recording industry at a more local level we should be able to better understand the interplay of global and local forces that inflect the current tribulations in the recording industry.

The second rationale is the desire to counter the Anglo-American bias of coverage of the music industry. This has been something of a weakness within the study of popular music for many years, but it is particularly acute in studies of the music industry. The fact that there is little English-language work available on the French music industry (which has the third largest recorded music market in Europe) hinders attempts to fully understand the record industry. This is even more apparent in the case of Japan, which has had the second largest recorded music market in the world for many years (likely to soon become the biggest) and historically has contained many features that could soon become more prominent elements of the US and UK industries (such as 360 contracts and tight integration between TV and music companies). The subjects of this book may be far-flung, but they are not trivial; the 7 case studies include 3 of the 10 largest record markets in 2010 and 4 of the top 20.

'The record industry' has thus tended to be overly homogenised in scholarly and media accounts of the music industry. As we move in to the twenty-first century, however, it seems that the local is becoming an even more important part of the recording industry. While globally the value of the recorded music market has fallen by roughly 40 per cent over the last ten years, this fall has dispro-portionately affected 'international repertoire'. Sales from 'domestic repertoire' (i.e. releases by artists from that specific country) have been less badly hit. The table below compares the market share of domestic repertoire from various countries in 1995 (around the peak of the recorded music market), 2000 (when steady decline begins to set in) and 2010.

This is a selective list in order to give a sense of the range of countries that have experienced a relative growth of domestic repertoire. This trend has not occurred everywhere; some territories have witnessed a decline in local repertoire (for example, Hong Kong has declined from 54 per cent in 1995 to

Table 1.1 Percentage of the overall value of recorded music accounted for by domestic repertoire, 1995–2010

	1995	*2000*	*2010*
Canada	10	12	27
Czech Republic	29	43	51
Denmark	30	31	57
Finland	37	38	51
France	47	51	60
Hungary	27	38	38
Japan	76	78	81
Norway	19	20	46
Portugal	21	21	35
South Africa	20	23	45
South Korea	57	63	72
Sweden	31	30	49
Switzerland	6	8	15

Sources: IFPI *Recording Industry in Numbers* 1999, 2003, 2011.

25 per cent in 2010, while Mexico's domestic repertoire has declined from 63 per cent to 43 per cent). Some countries' local repertoire has virtually disappeared (Singapore, from 41 per cent to 1 per cent; Bulgaria, from 84 per cent to 4 per cent). To explain the situation in individual territories requires detailed analysis of specific circumstances (the *raison d'être* of this book) but, on the whole, there does seem to be an overall trend of local repertoire increasing its market share in the first decade of the century. It is, of course, an increased share of a smaller market, but the figures suggest that music fans have been more loyal to local artists than global hits (a plausible, but partial, explanation is that listeners are more likely to illegally download music from international mainstream artists such as Lady Gaga). This implies that local artists and, therefore, local industries with knowledge of local music scenes, will become increasingly important.

An important caveat needs to be added to this discussion, however: the data refers to physical product only, not digital. Obviously, this becomes more significant as time goes on and, without detailed analysis, it is difficult to accurately predict the effects of this exclusion. It is plausible, however, that large numbers of local artists are selling music digitally, and, therefore, the overall proportion of local repertoire would still increase (though, counter to this, the vast majority of iTunes' sales come from major hits rather than the long tail; firm prediction is thus very difficult).

This caveat highlights a theme that recurs throughout this book – that the 'official' data produced by the local recording industry associations and the IFPI covers only a portion of the record economy in a particular country. Virtually every case study author makes this point. There are a variety of explanations for why this data can only be partial (discussed in Chapter 3) but the most significant one here is that they only account for record purchases that go through 'official' accounting channels, and many forms of music consumption remain at the perimeter of the official industry. By this I do not just mean 'piracy' (which is discussed below) but, rather, forms of local, small-scale musical economies beyond the scope of the 'legitimated' global industry.

One way to conceptualise this is to conceive of the international recording industry as a series of concentric circles. At the centre is the hegemonic mainstream, the centres of the record industry's power, in territories such as the US, UK, Japan, France and Germany. In these countries, the legitimated industry is extremely important and connected to many forms of musical activity. Next comes what I am referring to as the integrated countries, such as Belgium, Finland, Canada and Singapore. These countries share many similar characteristics with the hegemonic mainstream and their musical economies are thus very tightly integrated with the legitimated industry, although extrinsic companies tend to dominate the intrinsic ones. The outermost concentric circle contains the periphery nations, such as Ukraine. In these countries the legitimated industry enjoys far less influence, with global record labels being just a small part of the local music economy, or not having a presence at all.

This is a crude schema and it has limitations. First, it can be hard to map certain countries on to it, especially those such as Japan and South Korea in which there

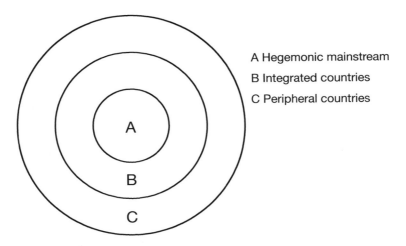

Figure 1.1 The international recording industry

is a very powerful and legitimated industrial structure that does not necessarily correlate to the four major labels prevalent in the West. Second, it risks over-emphasising the power and influence of the legitimated industry at the centre. Even within the hegemonic mainstream there is a great deal of economic activity that occurs outside of the main record labels. However, the concentric circles in Figure 1.1 do give some sense of how the legitimated industry becomes less influential the further one moves away from the centre. As you move towards the periphery, informal economies and local, small-scale economies become more prevalent. This does not make them any less significant – indeed, by keeping money in the local economy rather than seeing it flow to the hegemonic centre, these informal economies can actually be more significant for the domestic economy – it is just that the legitimated industry becomes an increasingly smaller part of the musical economy, and, as such, the power of the major labels to assert their practices diminishes.

The most manifest example of this concerns discourses of piracy. Piracy has, of course, been front and centre in debates about the recording industry within the hegemonic mainstream in the last decade (Chapter 8 on France outlines one of the most significant national responses to illegal downloading) but this kind of piracy is qualitatively different from more conventional forms of piracy that have long obsessed the legitimated industry. In the years BN (Before Napster), the majors' focus was on 'hard' piracy in territories some distance from the hegemonic mainstream and, although piracy closer to home has been the most pressing issue in recent years, more conventional forms of fights against piracy remain. Four of the countries studied in this book have been placed on the United States Trade Representative's Special 301 'watch list' or 'priority watch list' for failing to implement or enforce intellectual property protection to a standard satisfactory to the US and its content industries, opening up the possibility of US trade sanctions as a retaliatory measure.

Considered from a different perspective, however, piracy is merely a matter of legitimation. Some forms of music consumption are defined as legitimate while others are determined to be illegitimate. Looking at the issue this way is important because it emphasises that piracy, rather than being any kind of legal absolute, is an ideological construction that requires continual maintenance. The perspective that copyright infringement is important enough to warrant trade sanctions from the US Trade Representative, or for the French state to cut off an individual's access to the Internet, requires persuasion and reiteration from those whose interests it serves. Seen from this perspective, the current crisis of the recording industry is actually a crisis of legitimation: record labels have been unable to persuade consumers that copyright is worth upholding (this is not the same as consumers believing that authors should not be recompensed, merely that copyright is not an effective way to achieve that goal).

For this book, however, the point I want to raise relates to piracy in the peripheral countries, not the hegemonic mainstream, for the question of legitimation in these territories becomes even more acute given that what is occurring can be considered as a form of cultural imperialism, or the importation of Western ideas of intellectual property and authorship into settings where it conflicts with existing social and musical practices. It thus becomes even harder for the legitimated industry to persuade, say, Czech consumers, that the intellectual property rights of some multinational companies are something that they should be concerned about. This is particularly so when the practices of intellectual property enforcement (such as maintaining CD prices at an artificially high level to prevent the sale of cheap imports in the hegemonic mainstream) contradict the material conditions experienced by music consumers (low wages), or when they contradict the experiences of sharing and community that are more explicit elements of 'non-Western' musical practices.

Thus, when considering the case studies it is important to maintain a critical perspective towards discussions of 'piracy' and not merely to adopt the perspective of the legitimated industry. We need to pay attention to the power dynamics in the relationship between companies based in the hegemonic mainstream and the local recording industries in integrated and peripheral countries. This is the bigger lesson for our understanding of the international recording industries: we need to consider how the peripheral countries look from the hegemonic mainstream, but also consider how the hegemonic mainstream looks from the peripheral countries.

Looking at the case studies in this collection, it is clear that it is not so much a geographical comparison as a historical one. The historical development of the recording industry in each nation is, of course, tied to the broader dynamics of the global record industry, but they are more closely related to the economic and political history of the individual country. To understand the international recording industries involves having an understanding of things like communism, apartheid, colonialism and the Second World War, the material circumstances that they generated and the musical cultures to which they gave rise. The recording industry does not exist within a vacuum. This is why musical consumption is so often a question of legitimation – musical cultures give rise to musical industries, not vice versa.

The structure of the book

The book is structured into two parts. The first part contains three chapters that contextualise the case studies in Part II. The first of these chapters, by John Williamson and Martin Cloonan, problematises the way in which 'the music industry' is often assumed to mean 'the recording industry' rather than recognising the recording industry as just one part of the overall music industry. Interestingly, the impetus for their approach came from their experience of the industry in Scotland, where the majors have no presence and play little part in the local music economy. It is a polemical piece and actually argues against the need for any new books on the record industry! However, while agreeing with the political and analytical points made by Williamson and Cloonan (and one can see evidence supporting their arguments in many of the case studies, particularly when considering how musicians can make a living in the various countries), I do think that the recording industry remains important enough to study. Indeed, just as they correctly argue for a more sophisticated understanding of 'the music industry', I would argue likewise for 'the recording industry', which is one of rationales for this volume.

The other two chapters in Part I offer a history of the recording industry. Chapter 3, by Dave Laing, runs from the start of the recording industry up until 1999, paying particular emphasis to its global dimensions. Chapter 4 considers the downturn in the recording industry since 1999. Both chapters offer a broader context in which to understand the patterns and practices described in the case studies.

The second part of the book contains seven case studies, arranged alphabetically. Although the choice of countries may appear somewhat arbitrary, each of them is also representative of certain types of record market. First, there are two countries from the hegemonic mainstream, Japan and France. As mentioned earlier, despite their size and importance there are relatively few English-language accounts of either market. While the structure of Japan's music industry (and those of Eastern Asia generally) are quite distinctive from those of Western Europe and North America, the structure of the French recording industry will be familiar to anyone with knowledge of the UK or US industries. That does not make France uninteresting, however: first, there are issues concerning language and cultural identity that make it different from the anglophone mainstream markets while, second, its government has been the most proactive in developing legislative responses to the problem of online piracy, developing a 'three strikes' policy that many other countries are now beginning to adopt.

As well as Japan and France, a third major market is included in the case studies: Brazil. However, whereas the legitimated industry is very well established in the first two markets, Brazil is a much more bifurcated situation. There is an established official industry, but great swathes of Brazilian music production and consumption are not accommodated by it and, as such, Brazil has found itself a central focus of anti-piracy rhetoric and action. The bifurcated nature of the Brazilian market can also be seen in the study of South Africa, with a relatively secure legitimated industry accounting for a part of the market, but large parts are left to more informal, local markets. In both cases, the dramatic wealth discrepancies of the national population structure the record markets.

The remaining three case studies are of three small European nations. In one sense, Finland is included for its typicality: it is a small, stable market which has been affected by the downturn although, as Pekka Gronow shows, the major labels have still been able to remain profitable during this time. However, its ordinariness makes Finland a good study for considering the majority of small markets in Europe; for example, the problems presented by language barriers, or the way that the international labels arrived first through licensing agreements with local labels and then through takeovers are representative of large numbers of the 'integrated countries' mentioned above. It also demonstrates that, despite the global downturn, indigenous industries have a certain level of insulation from the crises affecting the majors. For example, unlike in the US and the UK, music retail in Finland has remained sustainable.

The final two studies move further away from the hegemonic mainstream. The Czech Republic has probably straddled the boundary between 'integrated country' and 'peripheral country' for many years, with the legitimated industry seeming at some points ready to firmly establish itself while, at other points, the decline in music retail and the continuing cultures of piracy making it seem like the Czech recording industry will remain on the periphery – where it would sit alongside Ukraine, a country firmly established as being on the perimeters of the global recording industry. With the fall of communism, both the Czech Republic and Ukraine went through major transformations roughly a generation ago, involving the privatisation of previously nationalised industries. However, while their recording industries have developed along different trajectories, the practices and attitudes of the communist past still linger, most obviously in the way that surreptitious copying remain primary ways for people to share music. However, whereas sharing was once a means to subvert communist censorship, it is now a means of subverting intellectual property laws, a further example of how musical culture shapes musical industries.

Note

During the time that this book was being written, Universal Music Group agreed to purchased the recorded music division of EMI (in November 2011). The 'big four' is thus likely to become a 'big three'. However, discussion in the book will continue to refer to the four major labels for two reasons. First, the takeover remains subject to regulatory approval, and recent history suggests that this is by no means guaranteed (see Chapter 3). Second, the case studies all refer to periods of activity during which there were four major labels. Adding any discussion of a big three would have been merely speculative.

Part I

Context

2 Contextualising the contemporary recording industry

John Williamson and Martin Cloonan

In 2004 we presented a conference paper entitled 'The music industry doesn't exist and if it does it doesn't matter' (Williamson and Cloonan 2004). Needless to say, our intention was to be somewhat polemical. An updated and more considered version of our paper was later published as 'Re-thinking the music industry' (Williamson and Cloonan 2007). Our purpose in both cases was to provoke debate and to move analysis of 'the music industry' away from a focus on the recording industry (and in particular the major record companies) towards one that highlighted both the diversity of those firms whose work involves the making and distribution of music and the new type of businesses which emerged in the music industries in the period post 1999.[1]

We suggested that the term 'music industries' (plural) rather than music industry (singular) was more helpful when reflecting these changes and argued that more attention be paid to the live music and music publishing industries, not least their place in the '360-degree' type companies which have emerged in the early part of the last decade, of which Sanctuary Music Group and Live Nation are the most significant. While the terminology is not the main issue, we were pleased to see similar arguments appearing both in the media (Sandall 2007; Hunter-Tillnet 2010) and from within the industries themselves which recognised the strength of our case – if often only implicitly.

More importantly, the recording industry and its lobbyists also lessened their claims to be 'the music industry'. The UK recording industry's representative body, the British Phonographic Industry (BPI), no longer talks of itself in terms of representing the UK music industry, branding itself the 'British Recorded Music Industry' (www.bpi.co.uk), while the International Federation of the Phonographic Industry (IFPI) issued a document in 2007 talking of the position of the recording industry as part of a 'broader music industry' (IFPI 2007) which 'shows music to have an economic importance that extends far beyond the scope of recorded music' (ibid.).

While such recognitions further vindicated our original points, here we wish to move our analysis forward and will do this in two parts. The first will revisit our original arguments and note that while they were initially open to accusations of overstatement, they actually *understated* the extent of the structural changes in the music industries in the period since the late 1990s. It will highlight the most significant economic and cultural shifts in the music industries in the period under consideration by examining the headline changes in the most significant of the music industries – recording, live music and music publishing. In doing so, we will note that as the recording industry has declined in both economic value and political clout, other sectors have grown as the music industries have shifted their focus from the sale of physical products to intangible ones, selling various combinations of services, experiences and rights in an attempt to resolve what Styven calls the 'intangibility dilemma' (2007: 67). In this sense we regard the current volume as something of an obituary for the recording industry as significant in and of itself. In reality, its significance was only ever as part of a broader set of music industries within which it was economically dominant for a comparatively brief period.

Having outlined the changes across the music industries, the second part will examine the companies that dominated the music industries in 2011. While some of these are the same names that have been prominent in the past, we will note that they are considerably different in nature from their previous incarnations and that they are adopting new strategies and structures to ensure their survival. At the centre of these cultural shifts is copyright, the intangible product that the companies in the music industries have used as the basis of their continual reorganisation – the one that facilitates the strategies of rent collection and value skimming that are now central to their businesses. We will return to this later, but first we need to look back.

REVISITING 'RETHINKING THE MUSIC INDUSTRY'

Starting points

We wish to begin by retracing our original steps and the work that prompted this research. Our worldview is inevitably influenced by both geography and lived-in experience of working in the music industries. We both live and work in Glasgow, Scotland, a city with a remarkable music scene (see Porter 2004; Glasgow City of Music 2008; Phelan 2010). One of us is a full-time band manager and part-time academic; the other reverses these roles.[2] We have worked together on a number of projects, of which a report on 'the music industry' in Scotland (Williamson *et al.* 2003) is perhaps the most important in shaping our subsequent thinking. As residents of a (stateless) country that has a vibrant musical culture but no major record company presence, undertaking the report brought home to us the inadequacy of accounts of 'the music industry' which centred on the major record companies. Such accounts – to misquote Morrissey – said nothing to us about our lives. It was this feeling that informed our original thinking.

Without wishing to repeat ourselves, we will note the main points of our argument (if only for the benefit of new readers). We began by noting that a number of commentators from within the music industries, media, government and academia routinely equated 'the music industry' with the recording industry and in particular with the four major record companies (EMI, Universal, Sony/BMG and Warner Brothers). We argued that this was too simplistic and that, in order to develop a more sophisticated analysis, a move from talking of a music industry (singular) to 'music industries' (plural) was helpful.

We justified this on a number of grounds related to history (we didn't think notions of a singular industry made sense historically), geography (it is only in a very small number of large cities where the major recording companies have/have had a significant economic impact), inequality and conflict (both of which talk of a single, seemingly united, industry belief), education (we thought that our students deserved better) and policy (where politicians wanted a simple definition of a complex amalgam of industries). In doing all this we were conscious of writing at a time when elements within the recording sector were presenting that sector *as* 'the music industry' as part of a self-interested attempt to extend the period for which sound recordings remain in copyright.[3] In short, our stance was above all a political one.

While the most significant changes in the music industries in the last decade (declining CD sales, large increases in ticket prices fuelling a rapid growth in the live music industry and the extraction of substantially more income from the exploitation of copyright) first became evident in the early part of the 2000s, it was only subsequently that their real impact became apparent. This took various forms across the various music industries, but was most notable in the reorganisation of music industries' companies; conflict and litigation around illegal downloading; attempts to establish new and sustainable pricing models and sources of revenue; and jostling for political influence in the ongoing debates around copyright and ticket sales. Chapter 4 in this volume will discuss some of these changes in more detail. In this chapter we will consider how the changes have contributed to the shift in power from the recording industry to the live music and (music) publishing industries.

The recording industry: a short-lived phenomenon

In 2008, for the first time in living memory, it was reported that British consumers spent more on live music than they did on recorded music (Page and Carey 2009). They did the same thing in 2009 and 2010, with the gap between the value of live music and that of recorded growing (Page and Carey 2010, 2011). While always treating such figures with a degree of scepticism, in reading such analyses it was hard for us not to feel somewhat vindicated in our original contention that an analysis of 'the music industry' which over-privileged the recording sector was too simplistic to capture the reality of the situation. Although a relatively short-lived phenomenon proves little, there are grounds for arguing that the economic dominance of the recording sector, which would now appear to have ended not just in the UK but globally, was only ever something of an historical blip. Space limits a full discussion of the circumstances that facilitated this, but relevant factors include the comparative lack of alternatives for emerging acts, the relative power of the recording sector vis-à-vis the live sector and the relative lack of competition for young people's leisure spending.

Moreover, it is entirely plausible to argue that, historically, for most musicians, *performance* has been the source of the majority of their income, whether achieved through playing live themselves, or having their work performed (in either recordings or in concerts). As David (2010: 129) argues, 'for the vast majority of musical artists the primary source of income is, will be, and always has been, live performance.' Only a comparatively small number of musicians have ever made the majority of their income from recorded music and it seems that they may have been the beneficiaries of a particular set of circumstances, alluded to above, which are unlikely to be repeated. Even major songwriters such as Paul McCartney get the vast majority of their income come from live work. As early as 2002 he earned $64.9 million from concerts compared to $2.2 million from both recordings and publishing (Connolly and Krueger 2006). The same source notes that in 2002, of the thirty-five top-earning acts in the USA only four made more from recordings than performance (cited in David 2010: 128).

Our original article observed that, in spite of several years of declining sales, the recording industry was still the largest part of the wider music industries at the time of writing, and responsible for around 70 per cent of music revenues in 2004 (Williamson and Cloonan 2007: 314). More presciently, it observed that 'this percentage is likely to decline substantially in the coming years, largely as a result of the growth of the live music industry and the exploitation of publishing and synchronisation rights' (ibid.). However, it is oversimplifying matters to suggest that the declining significance of the recording industry is purely a result of the growth of other areas. In the period since 1999, both of the other major music industries have seen a growth in their revenues, but this too may be a short-lived phenomenon.

Nevertheless, these businesses, which are selling experiences (live) and rights (publishing), are fundamentally different and unlikely to suffer the spectacular decline seen in the sales of recorded music, which at this point in time appears to be both permanent and irreversible. While the demand for a product that has been indelibly linked to particular technological developments may vanish, the nature of the entertainment and rights' industries may be the basis of their longevity and survival. This means that to work out fully the implications of the changes in the period, it is necessary to examine both the reasons for the decline of the recording industry (and why this differs from previous downturns) and the growth of the other music industries.

With the exception of the period between 1921 and 1935 when the combination of the growth of radio and the Great Depression meant that record sales dropped in the USA every year between 1921 and 1935 (Gronow and Saunio 1998: 38), the recording industry has never declined so much in value over such a lengthy period of time as it has since 1999. This was confirmed in 2011 when the recording industry's international representative body, the IFPI, reported that trade revenues to record companies fell by a further 8.4 per cent to $15.9 billion (IFPI 2011: 7) and that physical sales of recorded music had declined by 14.2 per cent. While their report was keen to highlight some positives – the continuing growth of the digital download market, subscription services and revenues from performance rights – this could not disguise the continuing year-on-year decline of the recording industry. Given that worldwide sales at their peak in 1999 were worth $27.3 billion (IFPI 2000), the scale of the recording industry's decline is apparent. Indeed, were it not for the growth of revenues from digital sales ($4.6 billion in 2010) and performance rights ($0.85 billion), the picture is even less encouraging for the recording industry: sales of physical product have declined from $27.3 billion in 1999 to $10.4 billion in 2010.

There are a number of reasons for such a dramatic decline, which can be loosely rounded up under a number of headings. The most central was the failure of the major record companies, while enjoying a boom period, to deal adequately with technological change. That the decline in global revenues coincided with the advent of Napster, and the widespread availability of free digital music files on peer-to-peer websites is no coincidence, but this alone fails to explain the long-term decline. Indeed, it can be argued that previous technological advances in the recording industry (most notably the advent of the CD, the first consumer digital product) have actually worked to the benefit of the recording industry.

However, our argument is that it is not so much technological change itself, but rather the clumsy and ill-considered responses to them from both the record companies themselves and their representative bodies that have ended the recording industry as we previously knew it. This, of course, is at odds with the version of the industries themselves, which use the value-laden term 'piracy' to effectively blame consumers for their problems. Eleven years after the advent of large-scale peer-to-peer music sites, the IFPI's chairman and Chief Executive, John Kennedy, maintained that 'digital piracy remains a huge barrier to market growth' (IFPI 2010: 3). These responses included miscalculations, which have had a disastrous impact from both a public relations and economic perspective.

The public relations failings are evident from the vast amounts of time and money that the record labels have spent on litigation and lobbying. The former originated with legal cases against the manufacturers of MP3 players (Diamond Rio) and the operators and facilitators who made sharing MP3 files possible (Napster, Audiogalaxy, Kazaa and Limewire among them) but moved on (in the USA and some other countries) to action against consumers in the form of individual file-sharers. These cases were often indiscriminate in their targets and included cases filed against the dead (Orlowski 2005) and 12-year-old children. Those sued were often forced into large out-of-court settlements, which often hugely over-valued the music they were alleged to have downloaded.

Suing consumers often formed part of a two-pronged attack on 'piracy' by the record companies' trade associations, which also included lobbying governments to intervene by creating new and more punitive laws covering such file-sharing. It is difficult to estimate the extent and cost of such lobbying, but when EMI threatened to leave the IFPI in 2008, it claimed that it was spending $250 million per year on 'anti-piracy' activity through trade organisations (Gallo 2008). Assuming the other major record companies made similar contributions, this would suggest that the recording industry was spending in excess of $1 billion per year fighting piracy, a campaign that seemed to have little or no success in solidifying the sales of their recorded music.[4]

While litigation and lobbying tend to have an indirectly negative effect on the public perceptions of the recording industry, the declining income has been the result of a combination of factors and is not – as suggested by the recording industry organisations – merely caused by illegal downloading. The limited success (or out and out failure) of the majority of the responses supported by the recording industry (their own music download sites,[5] mobile phone ringtones, legitimate digital music retailers[6] and, more recently, streaming services built around the advertising/subscription model[7]) suggests that there is unlikely to be a significant upturn in their fortunes in the coming years. This is compounded by the pricing response of the labels, which has seen the retail price of CDs drop from an average price of $14.19 in the USA in 2001 (IFPI 2007) to as low as $8.99 for physical versions of major new releases in 2011.[8]

Digital distribution has also put a downward pressure on prices, and, as with the physical products where deals with major retailers have put increasing pressure on smaller, independent retailers, record companies have opted to collaborate with major retailers such as Amazon.com in an effort to bolster sales if not revenues. When Kanye West's 'My Beautiful Dark Twisted Fantasy' topped the US charts in 2010, the majority of sales were digital downloads (Caulfield 2010) with most of these through a $3.99 deal on Amazon, during a week when there was a further $3 discount on offer across the site in general which could be used towards the purchase of the album. When The Decemberists topped the Billboard chart in 2011, 65 per cent of their first week sales of 94,000 were purchased from Amazon.com at $3.99 (Caulfield 2011).

The combination of the availability of free music (and the emergence of a generation no longer used to paying for music), the expenses associated with unsuccessfully fighting it, and the reduced revenues from lower sales and prices have weakened the recording industry to a point where, far from being the most significant part of the music industries, it is now seemingly the weakest. The failed attempts to respond to new technology and retain control over distribution have resulted in a cycle of job cuts, mergers and consolidation, and the introduction of deals that rely on more than just recording rights as a concession to the '360-degree' models pioneered by independents and companies from outside the recording industry.[9] These new contractual terms, along with the reduced amount of money and personnel that labels have to spend on marketing new music, make them a less attractive proposition for both established and unknown artists, with important examples of the former opting to release their own music.[10]

The live music industry

As previously noted, the most apparent shift in the music industries in the period since our article was written is the acceleration of the shift in the balance of power between the live and recording industries. While the majority of media coverage has focused on the decline and problems of the recording industry, live music (and the companies involved) have become much more significant in the context of the wider music industries. Our argument here is that the growth of the live music industry is pivotal not only to an economic shift in the study of the music industries, but also an ideological one.

The evidence to support the growth of the live music economy since the mid-1990s comes from a myriad of sources, albeit ones that tend to focus on the top end of the global touring market. Krueger noted that in the period between 1996 and 2003, the average price of a concert ticket in North America rose by 82 per cent (2005: 1), while trade publication, *Pollstar*, claimed that for the same market between 2005 and 2007 there was a compound annual growth of 12.5 per cent in the value of ticket sales (cited in Live Nation 2008: 3). By 2009, the same source estimated that the value of concert ticket sales in North America was $4.5 billion (cited in ibid.: 8), while in the UK the PRS for Music, which collects royalties on behalf of songwriters, estimated that concert ticket sales (combining the primary and secondary ticketing markets) generated just over £1 billion (Page and Carey 2010: 4). The same research also highlighted that in 2009, the threatened tipping point, where revenues outstripped those of the recording industry had also been reached, at least in the UK.[11]

Further evidence of this shift in the balance of power can be seen in the size and main activities of the largest companies (see Table 2.1[12]) involved in each of the industries.

While Universal, Sony, Warner and EMI have constituted the 'big four' record labels for a number of years, the latest addition is Live Nation Entertainment, a firm formed as a merger between the world's biggest concert promoter, Live Nation, and the world's biggest ticket agency, Ticketmaster, and which derives its income primarily from live music. It reported a turnover of $5.6 billion in 2010 (Live Nation 2011: 46), which is almost the equal of the largest record company, Universal Music Group (which had a turnover of around $6.4 billion in the same financial year[13]) and considerably greater than that of some of the other major record labels that have dominated academic discourse around the music industries. By way of comparison, the turnover of Warner Music Group in the same financial

Table 2.1 Largest music industries' companies by turnover, 2010

Company	Turnover ($bn)	Main activities
Universal Music Group (UMG)	6.4	Recording, publishing, merchandising, management
Sony Corporation (Music Division)*	6.29	Recording, publishing
Live Nation Entertainment (LNE)	5.06	Concert promotion, venue ownership, ticketing, sponsorship, management, merchandising
Warner Music Group (WMG)	3.51	Recording, publishing, merchandising, management
EMI	2.6	Recording, publishing

* Sony Corporation (Music Division) comprises Sony Music Entertainment (their global recording arm, with worldwide subsidiaries), Sony Music Entertainment Japan and their 50 per cent share of Sony/ATV Music Publishing.

year was $3.51 billion (Live Nation 2011: 41) while EMI generated around $2.6 billion in the same period (see Peoples 2011), suggesting that the major operators in the live music industry are now worthy of the same type of detailed study that Negus applied to the recording industry (1992, 1996).[14]

A number of caveats can be added to this appraisal of the growth of the live music industry, not least surrounding the sustainability of such rapid growth in a period of economic recession. Live Nation has already been forced into reducing ticket prices at some of its larger shows, warning shareholders that 'during past economic slowdowns and recessions, many consumers reduced their discretionary spending and advertisers reduced their advertising expenditure. This may result in reductions in ticket sales, sponsorship opportunities and our ability to generate revenue' (2011: 28). Leaving aside wider economic conditions, it seems unlikely that a boom, which has been based on increased ticket prices, can be maintained in times of economic adversity, but what is certain is that demand for live music will remain and that a long-term decline of the type witnessed in the recording industry is extremely unlikely.

The economic supremacy and expected long-term viability of the live sector can be attributed not only to economic factors (live music has become increasingly important for musicians as their main source of income) but also ideological ones. This can be seen in the changing conceptions of what is the ultimate popular music experience. Here we can see a shift from artefacts to experiences: the former in the shape of the single from the mid 1950s to 1960s, the album from around 1967 on, and subsequently with developments in sound carriers (vinyl, tape, eight-track, CD) and players (various configurations of hi-fi often designed to get the best out of the new sound carriers). In this sense, the MP3 stands out as a new format whose proponents do *not* claim that it is superior as a sonic experience, just more convenient.

Put simply, the point here is about the changing ways in which we listen to music. Despite important developments in both technology and venues, which have made the sound at gigs better, it is apparent that many musical events work not on the principle of a great aural experience but on precepts of *being there*. As Walter Benjamin would have recognised, the prime experience here is aura, rather than necessarily aural.

A guide to the live sector spoke of it 'selling a unique experience' (Kemp *et al.* 1–19). During interviews with concert promoters carried out as part of a team of which one of us (Cloonan) was a member,[15] they continually expressed the view that live music was the last bastion of authentic musical experiences. Thus, Edinburgh promoter Mark Mackie told us that the 'live music experience that you can't replicate is what people are buying into' (Mackie 2008) and Geoff Ellis, promoter of Scotland's major festival, T in the Park, suggested that live music was strong 'because you can't download that experience; you can't buy a DVD or watch it online' (Ellis 2011). This can be seen as being in marked contrast to the experience of recorded music where, while no two listening experiences are ever exactly the same, they can be similar enough to have the hallmarks of replication. This is not the case with live music which, even with shows that feature the same set nightly, can be of significant difference due to factors such as size of and lay-out venue, how musicians play, audience reaction, and so on. It is such factors that give promoters an ideological advantage in claiming 'uniqueness' but a business headache in ensuring that shows are at least similar enough to mean that they work on a practical level for musicians, audiences, venues and promoters. Thus, an ideological victory may come at an economic price. However, as live music and music publishing both pre-date the recording industry, so they are likely to outlast it.

Music publishing

The third of the major music industries, publishing, has also grown substantially in value since 1999. It is the most reliant on increasing the revenues generated from ownership of intellectual property rights around pieces of music (songs, rather than recordings) and this has been increasingly viewed as a potential replacement source of income for writers and record companies in the light of declining revenues from recordings. This is visible in the results of the collection societies, which are responsible for gathering mechanical and performing royalties for songwriters, composers and publishers. Synchronisation rights – where master recordings are used to accompany films and advertisements – have also grown exponentially as a source of revenue for music publishers in recent years. In addition, business-to-business revenue has formed an increasing part of the music industries' overall income (Page and Carey 2009, 2010, 2011).

Until recently in the UK, PRS for Music continually reported rapid growth in both their revenues and distributions to members. At the time of writing, their most recent financial results showed a slight year-on-year decline,[16] which was largely down to an 8.8 per cent drop in the royalties collected from recorded media (PRS for Music 2011: 1). In previous years, the growth in revenues collected by the organisation was the result of the increased revenues from broadcasting, online, public performance and international collections offsetting the lower sums raised from the manufacturing or downloading of recorded music. Despite PRS for Music revenues increasing from £255 million in 2001 (North 2002: 7) to £611.2 million in 2010 (Plunkett 2011), a small decline in the last year was still attributed by PRS for Music chief executive, Robert Ashcroft, to: 'the loss of high street outlets, the slowdown in physical musical sales as well as the challenges capturing the full value of music usage online' (PRS for music press release, 28 March 2011). In addition to the PRS for Music results, PPL (which collects performance rights for performers and record companies) announced in early 2011 a year-on-year growth of nearly 50 per cent in its international revenues (PPL press release, 24 January 2011). The US collection societies have also had a period of exceptional growth in the last decade. ASCAP (American Society of Composers, Authors and Publishers) and BMI (Broadcast Music Inc.) both announced revenues of just under $1 billion in 2010,[17] with the latter boasting, 'over the last ten years, our revenues have increased by more than 70%' (BMI 2010: 1).

The slight decrease in PRS for Music revenues in 2010 cannot disguise the huge increases that revenues from the live music and music publishing industries as well as ancillary industries such as music sponsorship, which rose in North America from $1.09 billion to $1.17 billion in 2011 (IEG 2011), have increased substantially in the last decade in the same period as sales in the recording industry have declined.

Summary

In summary, the changes visible across the different music industries in recent years sit comfortably with the arguments in our original paper. To view them as a single industry where recording provides the majority of income for artists is even more of an anachronism now than it was at the time we first put our views forward. We would maintain that, when viewed holistically, the music industries are still an important source of revenue within the creative economy despite the collapse of the recording industry and the recent economic downturn. There is certainly no evidence of the crisis in the 'music industry' as the record labels, lobbyists and media would have had us believe, merely a radical revision of the revenue sources and company types at work in the business around popular music.

MAKING SENSE OF THE COMPANIES IN THE MUSIC INDUSTRIES

In the remainder of the chapter we update of our original thesis, arguing that the continuing growth of the music industries reflects the success of both artists and the companies in the music industries in finding alternative sources of income in the light of decreasing sales of recorded music. By doing so, we suggest that the revenues (if not the profitability) of the music industries have continued to increase. We will argue that this has been achieved by a significant change in the nature of the companies at the centre of the music industries, both *strategically* and *structurally*.

The nature of these companies has moved towards the type of 360-degree model pioneered by Sanctuary (see Williamson 2010), which sees all of the largest companies attempting to generate revenue from a wide range of activities across the music industries. While Universal, Sony, Warner and EMI (previously viewed as the four major record companies) always had diverse interests and could not be viewed solely as record companies, each now has an increasingly diverse range of income sources beyond sales of recorded music, including interests in management, live revenue and merchandising. Similarly, Live Nation, which began as a concert promoter and venue owner, also owns artist rights in recordings, management, merchandising and the online activities of artists signed to them. This new type of company, which in many ways is something of a throwback to the type of integrated type of music companies of the 1960s and 1970s,[18] means that not only has what the companies do (and how they behave) fundamentally changed, but the way in which they are structured has too: each of the companies is in a continual state of restructuring.

As a result of this change in the nature of these companies, it is more appropriate than ever to characterise their assets in terms of their ownership of various intellectual property rights across a range of artist activities and their activities as a consequence of the need to maximise their income from these interests. This is most visible in two areas: the attempts of the various trade bodies to lobby for the extension of the duration of copyright and the attempts of the rights' collection societies to increase the amount they collect in revenues from copyright.

Strategies (1): lobbying for copyright extension

Clear examples of this come in the way in which the trade organisations for the recording industry – for example, the BPI in the UK and the Recording Industry Association of America (RIAA) in the USA – have had varying degrees of success in trying to extend the period of copyright protection on the sound recordings owned by their members. Tellingly, BPI now defines its role as to 'lobby Government and, where possible, work collaboratively with other organisations to implement BPI policy and ensure the future survival and growth of the music business',[19] listing the key areas of its lobbying as being 'copyright extension, reducing copyright infringement, copyright in the digital age and education and skills' (ibid.).

Another inevitable consequence of the contested nature of copyright is the advent of yet more lobbying bodies for the rights' industries. UK Music, which was launched in 2008, is an example of this. Its founding members included many of the other trade organisations such the Association of Independent Music (AIM), BPI, British Academy of Composers and Songwriters (BACS), Musicians' Union, Music Publishers' Association (MPA), PRS for Music and Phonographic Performance Limited (PPL). Although it claimed that it 'represents the collective interests of the UK's commercial music industry'[20] such claims were initially somewhat undermined by the lack of presence of any representatives of the live music industry (for example, the Concert Promoters' Association (CPA)). This was an especially glaring omission given that, according to PRS for Music's own research (Page and Carey 2010), live music is the largest part of what they would term the 'UK's commercial music industry'. The enmity between the live industry and the other sectors is perhaps related to what Paul Latham, CEO of Live Nation UK, described as the 'bounty-hunting' (Ashton 2010) of key UK Music funder PRS for Music in their attempts to increase the amount of revenue collected from live performance. As the lobbying activities of UK Music prioritise the expansion of copyright and increase of revenues from it, it is worth noting that this is not necessarily in the interests of all the music industries. The decision of the CPA and others from the live sector to join UK Music in May 2011 may simply paper over existing cracks. However, it also brought belated recognition from UK Music that '*for the first time*, the UK's entire commercial music industry will be represented by one umbrella body' (UK Music 2011, emphasis ours).

In the USA, in the wake of the World Intellectual Property Organisation (WIPO) allowing its members to revise and extend national copyright laws to cover the Internet and computer networks, new legislation in the form of the Digital Millennium Copyright Act (1998) and the Sonny Bono Copyright Term Extension Act (1998) served to widen the scope of copyright in a manner that Frith and Marshall (2004: 4) describe as benefiting 'corporate interests at the expense of those of both artists and consumers'. The latter extended the protection of sound recordings in the US to ninety-five years, and in doing so, offered encouragement to music industries' lobbyists in other parts of the world, including the European Union, where the term remains shorter.

By way of contrast, the position of the UK government has wavered between supporting the position of the Gowers' Commission (2006), which argued for no change in the term length and a compromise, which moved towards EU Commissioner Charlie McCreevy's position that advocated parity with the US term of ninety-five years. The campaign for term extension itself provided considerable evidence of the influence of music industries' lobbyists on politicians. A report by the House of Commons' Culture, Media and Sport Select Committee (2007)[21] rejected the findings of Gowers, while Pete Wishart, SNP MP for Perth and North Perthshire, introduced an unsuccessful Private Members' Bill in the House of Commons proposing an unspecified extension of term. Ultimately, the arguments for term extension were won by the lobbyists and the UK was one of the EU countries which voted for term extension, a decision that was announced in September 2011 (European Union 2011) despite opposition from countries such as Sweden and Belgium, in addition to a number of eminent academics.[22]

Strategies (2): extending the scope of copyright

In recent years, it has been not only the length, but also the scope of copyright on music, which has been extended, a result of both the gradual introduction of new rights and the more aggressive pursuit of existing ones. This has seen the growing importance of neighbouring[23] rights, described by Frith and Marshall as 'a right related to the original composition but subsisting in the recording itself rather than the underlying musical work' (2004: 8), which benefits both performers and producers (usually the record company) rather than the composer. This has gradually introduced a new income source for the record companies, with the most recent IFPI figures indicating that revenues from these performance rights have grown from zero in 2003[24] to $851 million in 2010 (Smirke 2011), growing globally by 4.8 per cent in 2010 and making up almost 5 per cent of all the recording industry's revenues (ibid.).

As well as new types of rights allowing the collection societies more sources of potential revenue, they have also become much more rigorous in the collection of income from broadcasts and public performances. In the period between 2003 and 2010, PRS for Music's revenues from broadcasting and online uses of music have increased from £84.6 million to £173.2 million, while public performance income has increased from £98 million in 2003 to £151 million (2010). Indeed, the organisation has been the subject of much criticism and adverse press coverage over their tactics in seeking licence payments from small businesses to this end. After a consultation with the Federation of Small Businesses, whose members had become increasingly irked by PRS for Music collection strategies, it was announced that there was to be a reduction in tariffs for small businesses (PRS for Music press release, 18 February 2009). However, the trade-off seems to have been a more aggressive pursuit of businesses and an interpretation of what constitutes a 'public performance', which is primarily geared towards raising revenue rather than upholding the spirit of the legislation (for example, PRS launched a court case against the garage chain, Kwik Fit, claiming that the music played by mechanics' radios was a public performance as customers may hear them (BBC 2007)).[25]

It is thus worth restating how the music industries have changed strategically in recent years, with the emphasis now placed increasingly on the collection of rents that are generated from the ownership of intellectual property rights rather than the selling of physical objects. These rents are of increasing importance for the music industries (particularly for the major record companies) as their traditional sources of income have dried up. This strategic change has been achieved in two ways. The first is by presenting a united front through the use of large-scale lobbying organisations – the type described by Pinnock as 'professional rent-seekers' (2007: 283) whose aims are to 'strengthen copyright legislation, introduce levies and tax benefits and to avoid anti-trust investigations' (ibid.: 284). The second is the collection of an increasing number of what Caves calls small 'lumps of rent' (2000: 297) from different sources (ibid.: 298–301) as pursued by what he terms the 'copyright collectives' (ibid: 302).

Such strategic changes have been accompanied by structural reconfigurations. To adapt to these new strategies, the companies involved in the music industries have had to undergo another substantial series of organisational and structural changes. While it could be argued that copyright has always been integral to the music industries[26] and that the major companies have been in a perpetual state of restructuring, described almost two decades ago by Negus as having 'arrived at their current form as a result of a complex history of acquisitions and mergers, technological changes, and booms and slumps connected to wider changes in the world economy' (1992: 3), our point is that the emphasis on the former and the importance of the latter have increased still further as a result of the changes in their activities and strategies since sales of recorded music began to decline.

Conclusion

This chapter has attempted to use our previous work (Williamson and Cloonan 2004, 2007) as a basis for painting a revised and updated picture of the music industries as we described them four years ago. We have argued that by studying them in terms of their component parts (notably recording, live music and publishing) it is easier to draw meaningful conclusions as to their strategies and structural changes than when they are presented as a homogeneous group with similar outlooks. It is for this reason that we view the continued use of the term 'music industry' increasingly untenable: not only is it used by lobbyists to hide major differences and conflicts within this supposedly unified entity, but it comes at a time when this type of political bartering (or rent-seeking) is ever more important to the turnover of the largest transnational corporations at work in the music industries. In short, the term serves political expediency rather than analytical ends.

In our view, all this makes it even more important for academics studying the industries to challenge the claims and worldviews of the 'music industry' organisations. We have attempted to do this by examining economic changes in each of the major parts of the music industries and by separating the rapid decline in the value of the recording industry from the parallel growth of both the live music industry and the copyright-driven publishing industry. This shift has resulted in a number of important changes in the nature of the five major companies that dominate the music industries. In recent years, each has made moves towards the 360-degree model with interests being acquired in aspects of recording, live performance, publishing, management and other parts of the music industries, and in doing so have increased their number of potential sources of revenue.

We have subsequently observed that this has increased still further the importance of intellectual property rights to the major companies, especially for those who previously traded primarily in tangible objects (records, CDs etc.). In doing so, the companies have become increasingly reliant on lobbying (through industrial organsiations) and rent-collection (through their collection societies), making the politics of the industry organisations and structure of the individual music industries' companies all the more integral to understanding how the music industries work.

However, no matter how fundamental the strategic and structural changes across the music industries have been in the last decade, what Negus described as 'a conflict between commerce and creativity' (1992: 152) remains at the heart of their activities. The most notable part of the recent changes is to highlight the failure of the music industries in purely commercial terms since 1999. With the major music companies all losing huge amounts of money, their individual and collective actions embody the very kind of inequality and conflict, with the inevitable political and policy-making consequences, that we used as our initial justifications for pluralising 'the music industry'.

Notes

1 1999 is suitable starting point for an analysis of the decline of the recording industry as it was the year in which the file-sharing service, Napster, was launched and also the peak of recorded music sales. Sales have declined in every year since.
2 John Williamson manages Belle and Sebastian and Martin Cloonan manages Zoey Van Goey.
3 For further discussion of the attempts of the record companies to extend the copyright term on sound recordings see Williamson *et al.* (2011).
4 An independent inquiry commissioned by UK Prime Minister David Cameron (Hargreaves 2011) noted that despite various claims from the record industry about

the impact of illegal downloading 'we have failed to find a single UK survey that is demonstrably statistically robust. For many surveys, methodology is not available for peer review' (ibid.: 69). It concluded that at around 0.1–0.5 per cent of overall economic activity illegal downloading was 'neither negligible nor overwhelming' in its economic impact (ibid.: 73). It found that across the globe prosecution had little overall impact (ibid.: 78) and called for a policy of education, enforcement and growth of legitimate markets (ibid.: 81).

5 MusicNet and PressPlay – the two digital retailers created by the major labels in 2002 offered a limited selection of tracks and heavily managed the right to use tracks on mobile devices. In spite of the development costs, these services failed and were dropped with the advent of iTunes and its model, which involved the sale of individual tracks as well as album bundles.

6 Both SkySongs and Nokia's Comes With Music service in the UK closed in 2010.

7 While the likes of Spotify, which reached 1 million subscribers in 2011 has attracted a large number of users, it too is a loss-making business and is widely considered that the royalties they pay are negligible in terms of replacing other means of paying for music as a revenue stream (see Halliday 2011).

8 For example, the price of the Fleet Foxes album *Helplessness Blues* on Amazon.com on week of release (April 2011).

9 The '360-degree' deal where artists sign over multiple rights (e.g. recording, concert promotion, publishing, merchandising) to the one company came to the fore in recent years as a tactic employed by Live Nation. However, it has antecedents in earlier attempts by managers (and others) such as Col. Tom Parker to exert control over every aspect of an artist's earnings.

10 For example, on the expiry of their deal with EMI, Radiohead have subsequently released two albums, *In Rainbows* and *The King of Limbs* online themselves, minimising the chances of pre-release leaks and increasing the share of revenue to the band.

11 Page and Carey estimated the value of the UK's live music industry in 2009 to be £1.537 billion (2010: 2) compared to the £1.356 billion (ibid.) generated by the UK recording industry.

12 Compiled by John Williamson from Annual Reports of Vivendi, Sony, Live Nation, Warner Music Group and EMI for year ending 2010.

13 Converted from €4.49 billion (Vivendi Annual Report 2010: 3).

14 Evidence of this beginning to happen can be seen in the AHRC-funded research conducted by the Universities of Edinburgh and Glasgow (www.gla.ac.uk/departments/livemusicproject).

15 This research was entitled Promoting Live Music in the UK – An Historical, Cultural and Institutional Analysis – and was funded by the UK's Arts and Humanities Research Council. The project team was Matt Brennan, Martin Cloonan, Simon Frith and Emma Webster. See note 15 for details of project website.

16 Collections dropped from £618.2 million in 2009 to £611.2 million in 2010 (Plunkett 2011).

17 ASCAP collected $995 million (ASCAP 2010) and BMI $917 million (BMI 2010).

18 For example, EMI had interests in records, publishing, television/cinemas, retailers and recording studios before selling the majority of their shares in them to concentrate on recordings (see Frith 1981). For earlier examples of diverse interests in the music-related entertainment industries, see the profile of the Grade family offered by Davies (1981).

19 Available online at: www.bpi.co.uk/category/policy-and-lobbying.aspx (accessed 25 May 2011).

20 Available online at: www.ukmusic.com (accessed 28 April 2011).

21   Chaired by John Whittingdale, one of the MPs most vocal in his support of the music industries.
22   Available online at: www.cippm.org.uk/copyright_term.html (accessed 30 September 2011).
23   These have been slowly introduced by national legislatures – the majority of income currently comes from Europe, with the USA a slow adopter.
24   They first featured as part of the IFPI's Recording Industry in Numbers in 2004.
25   PRS for Music has decided that a shared radio in an office with two workers constitutes a public performance (personal communication, May 2011; see also online at: www.prsformusic.com/users/businessesandliveevents/musicfor businesses/officesandfactories/Pages/officesfactories.aspx (accessed 10 October 2011).
26   It was identified as such by Frith (1987) and Fabbri (1991).

Bibliography

ASCAP (2010) *Annual Report*. New York: ASCAP.
Ashton, R. (2010) Live Nation Chief Slams PRS 'Bounty Hunters', *Music Week*, 16 September. Available online at: www.musicweek.com/story.asp?storycode= 1042544 (accessed 16 September 2010).
BBC (2007) Kwik-Fit Sued over Staff Radios. Available online at: http://news. bbc.co.uk/1/hi/scotland/edinburgh_and_east/7029892.stm (accessed 25 May 2011).
BMI (2010) *Annual Report*. New York: BMI.
Caulfield, K. (2010) Kanye West, Nicki Minaj Score Big Debuts on Billboard 200, *Billboard*, 1 December. Available online at: www.billboard.biz/bbbiz/content_ display/industry/news/e3ie805375f7f1dfebf863c22981624a761 (accessed 7 December 2010).
Caulfield, K. (2011) The Muscle Behind the Decemberists' Number 1? Amazon and NPR, *Billboard*, 27 January. Available online at: www.billboard.biz/bbbiz/industry/ record-labels/the-muscle-behind-decemberists-no-1-npr-1005014252.story (accessed 28 January 2011).
Caves, R. (2000) *Creative Industries*. Cambridge, MA, and London: Harvard University Press.
Connolly, M. and Krueger, A. (2006) *Rockonomics: The Economics of Popular Music*. Amsterdam: Handbook of Arts and Culture.
Crosley, H. and Peters, M. (2008) Live Nation, Jay-Z Deal Imminent, *Billboard*, 2 April 2008. Available online at: www.billboard.biz/bbbiz/content_display/genre/ news/e3i83144a3e9301e87b2ec5fe1129792408 (accessed 27 January 2011).
Culture, Media and Sport Committee (2007) *New Media and The Creative Economy*. London: HMSO.
David, M. (2010) *Peer to Peer and the Music Industry*. London: Sage.
Davies, H. (1981) *The Grades*. London: Weidenfeld & Nicolson.
Ellis, G. (2011) *Interview with Martin Cloonan*, Glasgow, 14 March.
EMI (2011) *Annual Report 2010*. London: EMI.
European Union (2011) Directive of the European Union and of the Council amending Directive 2006/116/EC on the Term of Protection of Copyright and Certain Related Rights. Brussels: European Union.
Farndon, L. (2011) EMI Tycoon Guy Hands Himself £12 Million Payday, *Daily Mail*, 7 January. Available online at: www.dailymail.co.uk/money/article-1345175/EMI-tycoon-hands-12m-payday.html (accessed 10 January 2011).

Fabbri, F. (1991) Copyright: The Dark Side of the Music Industry, *World Beat*: 1(1): 109–14.

Finch, J. (2010) EMI Crashes £1.75 Billion into the Red, *The Guardian*, 4 February. Available online at: www.guardian.co.uk/business/2010/feb/04/emi-music-announces-massive-loss (accessed 27 January).

Frith, S. (1981) *Sound Effects*. London: Constable.

Frith, S. (1987) Copyright and the Music Business, *Popular Music*, 7(1): 57–75.

Frith, S. and Marshall, L. (eds) (2004) *Music and Copyright* (2nd edn). Edinburgh: University of Edinburgh Press.

Gallo, P. (2008) EMI to exit IFPI, *Variety*, 9 January. Available online at: www.variety.com/article/VR1117978756.html?categoryId=16&cs=1 (accessed 2 July 2008).

Glasgow City of Music (2008) *Application Dossier*. Glasgow: Glasgow City of Music.

Gowers, A. (2006) *Gowers' Review of Intellectual Property*. London: HMSO.

Gronow, P. and Saunio, I. (1998) *An International History of the Recording Industry*. London: Cassell.

Halliday, J. (2011) Spotify Reaches 1 Million Paying Subscribers, *Guardian Online*. Available online at: www.guardian.co.uk/technology/2011/mar/08/spotify-hits-1-million-paying-subscribers (accessed 8 April 2011).

Hargreaves, I. (2011) *Digital Opportunity: A Review of Intellectual Property and Growth*. London: Intellectual Property Office.

Hunter-Tilney, L. (2010) The Music Industry's New Business Model, *Financial Times*, 10 September 2010. Available online at: www.ft.com/cms/s/2/92d98d1c-bae9-11df-9e1d-00144feab49a.html#axzz1PiuAbDjG (accessed 12 September 2010).

IEG (2011) *IEG International Sponsorship Report*. New York: IEG.

IFPI (2000) *The Recording Industry in Numbers (1999)*. London: IFPI.

IFPI (2007) *The Broader Music Industry*. Available online at: www.ifpi.org/content/library/the-broader-music-industry.pdf (accessed 23 September 2007).

IFPI (2010) *Digital Music Report*. London: IFPI.

IFPI (2011) *The Recording Industry in Numbers*. London: IFPI.

Kemp, C., Chamberlain, R. and Stone, R. (2008) *Music Event Management and Promotion*. Kings Ripton, Cambs.: Elm.

Krueger, A. (2005) The Economics of Real Superstars: The Market for Rock Concerts in the Material World, *Journal of Labour Economics*, 23(1): 1–30.

Leaver, A. (2010) A Different Take: Hollywood's Unresolved Business Model, *Review of International Political Economy*, 17(3): 454–80.

Live Nation (2008) *Annual Report 2007*. Los Angeles: Live Nation.

Live Nation (2011) *Annual Report 2010*. Los Angeles: Live Nation.

Mackie, M. (2008) *Interview with Emma Webster*, Edinburgh, 1 July.

Negus, K. (1992) *Producing Pop*. London: Edward Arnold.

Negus, K. (1996) *Popular Music in Theory*. Cambridge: Polity.

North, A. (2002) *The Value of Music: The Draw of Live Music*. London: Performing Right Society.

Orlowski, A. (2005) RIAA Sues the Dead, *The Register*, 5 February. Available online at: www.theregister.co.uk/2005/02/05/riaa_sues_the_dead (accessed 19 January 2012).

Page, W. and Carey, C. (2009) *Adding Up the UK Music Industry for 2008*. London: PRS for Music.

Page, W. and Carey, C. (2010) *Adding Up the UK Music Industry for 2009*. London: PRS for Music.

Page, W. and Carey, C. (2011) *Adding Up the UK Music Industry for 2010*. London: PRS for Music.

Peoples, G. (2011a) Top Warner Execs 2010 Pay Increased Despite Revenue Drop. *Billboard*, 20 January 2011. Available online at: www.billboard.biz/bbbiz/industry/record-labels/top-warner-execs-2010-pay-increased-despite-1004139709.story (accessed 27 March 2011).

Peoples, G. (2011b) RIAA Weighs in on Flap over Executive Salaries. *Billboard*, 23 May. Available online at: www.billboard.biz/bbbiz/industry/record-labels/riaa-weighs-in-on-flap-over-executive-salaries-1005198182.story (accessed 25 May 2011).

Pham, A. (2011) Major Labels, Music Publishers Lining up Behind Apple's iCloud, *Los Angeles Times*, 2 June. Available online at: http://latimesblogs.latimes.com/entertainmentnewsbuzz/2011/06/major-labels-music-publishers-apple-icloud.html (accessed 3 June 2011).

Phelan, G. (2010) Soundtrack to Glasgow. *Sydney Morning Herald*, 18 June. Available online at: www.smh.com.au/travel/soundtrack-to-glasgow-20100618-ylzb.html (accessed 20 June 2010).

Pinnock, A. (2007) The Grampian Hills: An Empirical Test for Rent-Seeking Behaviour in the Arts, *Cultural Trends*, 16(3): 277–94.

Plunkett, J. (2011) Music Royalties Fall for the First Time, *The Guardian*, 28 March: 26.

Porter, H. (2004) Glasgow: A Scene Gets Heard, *Time*, 22 August.

PRS for Music (2011) *2010 Financial Results Briefing Paper*. London: PRS for Music.

RIAA (2007) *The CD: A Better Value Than Ever*. New York: RIAA.

Smirke, R. (2011) IFPI 2011 Report: Global Recorded Music Sales Fall 8.4%; Eminem, Lady Gaga Top International Sellers, *Billboard*, 30 March. Available online at: www.billboard.biz/bbbiz/industry/global/ifpi-2011-report-global-recorded-music-sales-1005100902.story (accessed 4 April 2011).

Smith, E. (2011) Live Nation CEO Pay Doubles to $15.9 Million. *Wall Street Journal*, 15 April. Available online at: http://online.wsj.com/article/SB10001424052748704495004576265412740068244.html?KEYWORDS=live+nation (accessed 28 April 2011).

Sandall, R. (2007) The Day the Music Industry Died, *The Sunday Times*, 7 October. Available online at: http://entertainment.timesonline.co.uk/tol/arts_and_entertainment/music/article2602597.ece (accessed 7 October 2007).

Sony Corporation (2010) *Annual Report*. Tokyo: Sony Corporation.

Styven, M. (2007) The Intangibility of Music In the Internet Age, *Popular Music & Society*, 30(1): 53–74.

UK Music (2010) *Liberating Creativity*. London: UK Music.

UK Music (2011) *Live Music Industry Unites, Joins UK Music*. Available online at: www.ukmusic.org/news/post/144-live-music-industry-unites-joins-uk-music (accessed 3 June 2011).

Vivendi (2011) *Annual Report*. Paris: Vivendi.

Warner Music Group (2011) *Annual Report*. New York: Warner Music Group.

Williamson, J. (2010) Disorganisation and Finance in the Music Industries. Musselburgh: Queen Margaret University, unpublished Ph.D. thesis.

Williamson, J. and Cloonan, M. (2004) The Music Industry Doesn't Exist and If It Does It Doesn't Matter. Paper presented at IASPM UK and Ireland Conference, Limerick.

Williamson, J. and Cloonan, M. (2007) Rethinking the Music Industry, *Popular Music*, 26(2): 305–22.

Williamson, J., Cloonan, M. and Frith, S. (2003) *Mapping the Music Industry in Scotland: A Report*. Glasgow: Scottish Enterprise.

Williamson, J., Cloonan, M. and Frith, S. (2011) Having an Impact? Academics, the Music Industries and the Problem of Knowledge, *International Journal of Cultural Policy*, 17(4): 459–74.

3 The recording industry in the twentieth century

Dave Laing

Writing in 1987, Simon Frith argued that 'to analyze the music industry though its history means focusing on three issues', which he defined as 'the effects of technological change', 'the economics of pop' and 'a new music culture' (Frith 1987: 55–6). Frith's article made clear that by 'music industry' he meant the record industry, and this chapter is a further schematic, interpretive sketch of the record industry in the twentieth century. It benefits from the wealth of academic and journalistic research that has taken place in the twenty-five years since Frith's pioneering article, and in particular it attempts to take a global perspective.

The chapter follows Frith in conceptualising the industry's history as composed of the development of specific practices and institutions and their interweaving in a variety of ways at different points in the chronology. However, these are demarcated and defined in a different manner. As Fernand Braudel wrote in his history of capitalism and civilisation, 'can "true" growth . . . be anything but growth which links together, irreversibly, progress on several fronts at once, creating a mutually sustaining whole which is then propelled onto greater things?' (1984: 539).

The principal strands involved in the process are:

*   technological innovation (from Edison's cylinder to Frauenhofer's MP3);
*   intellectual property law and disorder (from the 1909 US copyright law to tape piracy);
*   the changing hierarchies of consumer media (print to online);
*   musical and demographic trends (dance crazes to youth cultures);
*   wider economic forces from the micro (the firm) to the macro (the global economy including the rise of consumerism).

While the present chapter is centrally concerned with the corporate structures of record companies, both 'majors' and 'indies', it necessarily engages with the shifting influences cast by these other strands. This chronological diachrony of the industry's fortunes in the twentieth century is divided into five sections, each covering approximately two decades.

Phase 1: early years to 1920

The 'invention' of an effective means to record sound by Thomas Edison occurred in 1877. However, it was not until the closing years of the nineteenth century that the provision of music in the home became the primary use of this new technology. During the first part of the new century, the nascent recording industry was dominated by three US companies and their foreign affiliates. The prominent place of Edison's National Phonograph Company, Columbia and Victor was due to their possession of the key patents for both hardware (gramophones and phonographs) and software (cylinders and discs). The era was also notable for the rapid global spread of the new industry, with both local or national and international (classical) music offered for sale. In this period, too, sound recordings were recognised as a new form of copyright work in international and, in some instances, national law.

Recent scholarship on this era has focused mainly on three issues. The first is the revolution in listening introduced by the invention of recording (e.g. Sterne 2003; Kittler 1999; Weheliye 2005). This has been described by some authors as a kind of Kuhnian paradigm shift, or Foucauldian change of episteme. Sterne, for example, places the phonograph at a pivotal point in a history of 'audile technique' and acoustic space, of sound and listening, while Weheliye sees a privileged relationship between African-American cultural formation and sound recording.

The second issue is the process by which music became the primary commercial use of sound recording, a topic that has been under-explored since 1954, when Roland Gelatt published the first edition of his general history of the field. Edison's famous 1878 list of possible uses of his invention mentions 'reproduction of music' only in passing, as one of ten ways in which it could benefit humanity (Gelatt 1977: 29). Some scholars have emphasised the extent to which the phonograph was 'a by-product of research on the telephone and telegraph' (Weheliye 2005: 26), that is, of contemporary business and government communication systems.

Perhaps as a consequence, the principal applications of the new technology in the late nineteenth century were as office machinery (e.g. dictaphones – Edison's first company was the *Speaking* Phonograph Company) (Kenney 1999) and as public entertainment among the sideshows of fairgrounds. The latter included some musical recordings, but the eventual settlement of the phonograph as a mode of domestic entertainment aligned it with such items as the piano, musical box and the player piano, the last of which rivalled the phonograph in popularity in the United States in the first two decades of the twentieth century (Siefert 1995; Brooks 1978). As such, its trajectory owed more to the changing structure of musical entertainment (its increasing privatisation) than to innate technical characteristics.

The third main issue in recent research concerns the competition, and differentiation, between the companies established in the United States and elsewhere by the principal patent owners. American writing on the early history has been distorted by 'the cult of Edison in phonographic historiography' (Sterne 2003: 28), which tends to forget that Edison's foray into recorded music ended in 1929 due to his stubborn commitment to cylinders rather than discs (e.g. Welch and Burt 1994). In contrast, both Victor and Columbia were more adventurous in repertoire acquisition, and Tim Brooks has argued persuasively that the latter was the first 'promoter of musical recordings, much to the disgust of Edison and other traditionalists' (Brooks 1978: 2).

By the end of this period, especially in the US, the original patents were beginning to fall into the public domain, leaving scope for new entrants to the market, as manufacturers of phonographs but also as specialist creators and distributors of recorded music itself (Koenigsberg 1990). According to Gelatt, there were 6 new phonograph and/or record firms in America in 1914, rising to 18 in the following year and 46 in 1916. By 1919, there were almost 200 companies in the US recorded music industry. A similar process had already occurred in Europe, where registration and protection of patents across numerous polities was more complex and enforcement was weaker.

The legal status of sound recordings was not established in the United States until the adoption of a new copyright act in 1909. As Lisa Gitelman (1999) has argued, the novelty of the new medium was interpreted as a form of 'writing', its 'mechanical reproduction' of a musical work comparable to a printed score. The new law also mandated a royalty rate payable to music publishers and composers for every cylinder, disc or piano roll sold, in return for a compulsory licence that enabled fledgling record companies to record songs without seeking permission from the powerful publishers (Sanjek 1988: 22–3). Other national laws generally followed the United States in granting compulsory licences in one form or another.

Another important facet of the early period was the swift international expansion of the recorded music industry. In this, it was typical of many manufacturing industries based in the European metropoles of global or regional empires or countries such as the US with a regional sphere of influence. According to Geoffrey Jones, the Gramophone Company 'was part of the first phase of British multinational investment, which occurred in the last two decades of the nineteenth century . . . [Its] wide network of foreign factories included ventures in Austria, France, Germany, India, Russia and Spain was not uncommon among early British multinationals' (Jones 1985: 77).

Underpinning this expansion was a 1901 cartel agreement between the British Gramophone Company and the US-based Victor, which divided the world market between the two companies (and provided for an exclusive exchange of matrices from each other's catalogues). Gramophone had the British Empire, Europe, the Middle East, Japan and Russia (Jones 1985: 81). Fred Gaisberg was a key figure in Gramophone's initial international growth. In 1902 he travelled with recording equipment to India, China and Japan. 'The object,' he wrote in his diary 'was to open up new markets, establish agencies, and acquire a catalogue of native records' (quoted in Moore 1999: 103). India became the hub for Gramophone's activities in other parts of South Asia. Recordings by Malaysian, Burmese and Afghan artists were made there and copies were manufactured in Mumbai and Delhi to ship back to the musicians' countries of origin. In Africa, Gramophone set up a South African branch in 1904 and made its first foray into West Africa (Sierra Leone, Nigeria, Gold Coast – now Ghana) in 1912 (Stapleton and May 1987: 259–64).

US-based companies followed the Monroe doctrine in regarding Latin America and the Caribbean as within their natural sphere of activity. Some tracks by local acts were made in such countries as Trinidad, Argentina and Colombia, but many were also made in New York, with artists from many nations travelling north. Lack of local studios meant that many Caribbean artists recorded in the United States, France or Britain until the 1940s.

The cartel deal did not, of course, prevent companies other than Victor and Gramophone competing with either. In the Middle East, for example, Egyptian music appeared in the catalogues of Gramophone, Odeon and the Lebanese company Baidophon before 1910.

Studies by Gronow and Englund of Scandinavia and Farrell of India have provided pictures of national markets at this early stage of the industry's development. Farrell showed how some music was liberated from its social context so that 'recorded sound brought many forms of classical music out of the obscurity of performance milieus such as the *cakla* (courtesan's quarter) and on to the mass market' (Farrell 1998: 58). In the four Scandinavian countries, the Gramophone Company was responsible for about half of the recordings of 'a wide variety of local content' made between 1899 and 1928 (Gronow and Englund 2007: 301).

This summarised the repertoire status in this first phase. While the technology and the new medium were swiftly globalised, for the most part the music that was marketed was entirely local. Very little European or American music was exported to other parts of the world. To that extent, musical and demographic trends played a limited role in these formative years for the industry. The most crucial factors were technological innovation and ownership of new technologies. The owners of sound recording and reproduction patents became the first generation of major record companies.

Phase 2: 1920–39

In this second period of the industry's evolution, there were critical developments in almost all of the strands noted earlier. In technology, the recording industry adopted the electrical system of sound recording pioneered by the US film business, a system neatly defined by Gronow and Saupio as 'microphone recording' (1998 [1990]: 37–8). Popular entertainment media was fundamentally restructured by the introduction of radio as a broadcasting system, much of whose output consisted of (live) music. For most of this period, radio was a rival to records as a means of supplying music for consumption in the home. It had a vital economic advantage in that this music was supplied free of charge. Here, as with many innovations, the timing of its regional and global introduction was staggered over three decades. While the first American radio stations were in operation at the start of the 1920s, there were no stations in parts of Asia and Africa until the 1940s.

From a global perspective, the most important musical trend was the installation of American dance and vocal music as the principal genre of international popular repertoire for record companies in Europe, Latin America and the Pacific Rim, a process crucially led by the international distribution of film musicals emanating from Hollywood. Within the United States itself, in contrast, new specialist markets were opened up, providing a range of European and Asian ethnic musics for immigrant communities, blues for African-Americans and country music for the rural white working-class.

In the field of intellectual property, a relatively minor lawsuit in England inaugurated what, much later, became an important new income stream for the record industry. In 1934, record companies sued the Carwardine coffee house in the city of Bristol. The enterprising owners were entertaining customers by playing records and the companies successfully claimed that this infringed their performance right, a right that had not previously been recognised in national law or international conventions. The case established the right for copyright owners in sound recordings to be paid when their recordings were played in public and led to the formation of Phonographic Performance Ltd (PPL). PPL soon had licensed the state broadcaster BBC and numerous cafés, offices and factories that used recordings in this way.

In the same year, an international convention on this performance right was drafted by the industry's first trade association, the International Federation of the Phonographic Industry (IFPI). This body had been formed in 1933 initially to counter the activities of BIEM, an alliance of music publishers founded to enforce a uniform pan-European rate for 'mechanical royalties', paid to publishers and composers by record companies that released versions of their songs (Laing 2009: 586–7).

Finally, and most importantly, this was the period of economic crisis, first in the early 1920s and then the great Depression, originating in the Wall Street Crash of 1929 but rippling out across the globe. The consequent loss of spending power, plus the attractions of radio, caused a massive decline in record sales in the United States. A market of 140 million units in 1929 had shrunk to 33 million by 1939.

The impact of these changes, notably the Depression, was dramatic. The record industries of North America and Europe underwent numerous mutations between 1920 and 1939. Of the 'big three' US companies, one (Edison's) was closed down and the others ended the period as subsidiaries of broadcasting companies. In Europe, the two biggest companies, Columbia and the Gramophone Company, merged to form Electric and Musical Industries (EMI) in 1931. In a process of consolidation that would be repeated in the industry throughout the twentieth century, Columbia had already bought out several European competitors, including Lindstrom (Germany) and Pathé (France). The merged EMI was the owner of 50 factories. Of these, 7 were in Asia, 3 in Latin America and 2 in Australasia. The remainder (38) were in Europe (many of which were soon closed), where it was by far the largest record company. EMI also had continued access to the full US repertoire of both Victor and Columbia.

The US Columbia Company made massive losses in the early 1920s after overestimating the rate of growth of the market and was purchased by its European counterpart. After EMI was formed, the US branch of Columbia was sold to Grigsby-Gronow, a phonograph manufacturer. Soon afterwards that company off-loaded Columbia on to the American Record Corporation (ARC). This was a newcomer to the industry which had already bought the Brunswick and Vocalion labels. It was owned by Herbert Yates, a producer of B-movies, and it had a strategy to beat the Depression. ARC issued records at very low prices, hoping to bring back former record buyers. Eventually, though, ARC was itself acquired, in 1938 by Columbia Broadcasting System (CBS), one of the big three radio networks in the United States.

The third giant of the American industry, Victor, was sold to a consortium of bankers in 1927. Two years later, Victor was bought by Radio Corporation of America (RCA).

The Depression did not wholly deter new entrants to the industry. In Japan, which was insulated from the worst effects, import duties led local companies to form joint ventures with Victor, Columbia and Polydor so that foreign titles could be manufactured in the country. However, nationalist policies caused foreign companies to divest their Japanese interests in 1938.

The Germany-based Küchenmeister radio, gramophone and film company built a strong presence in Central and Northern Europe in the 1920s, but succumbed to the Depression, although its German label Telefunken and Czech label Ultraphon survived. In Colombia, a radio station owner founded Discos Fuentes and in Greece, a former engineer for the Lindstrom group launched Minos to release local music. But by far the most important of the new entrants was Decca, formerly a British gramophone manufacturer. In 1929 its chairman, Edward Lewis, was, like ARC, determined to undercut his rivals on price. By the end of the 1930s, the UK market was in effect a duopoly of EMI and Decca.

Lewis also entered the US market, the first foreign record company to do so since Germany's Lindstrom group had set up Okeh there in 1918. He hired Jack Kapp, a former Brunswick executive who in turn signed Bing Crosby and other Brunswick stars to make Decca singles that retailed for 35 cents in competition with full-price new recordings from Victor and Columbia at 75 cents. Marc Huygens *et al.* have argued that Kapp's innovation was a crucial 'new strategy from a new entrant' that was the catalyst for a restructuring of the industry, in the form of differential pricing (Huygens *et al.* 2001:1004).

Outside Europe and North America, small markets for recorded music in the French and British empires continued to be controlled by EMI and other companies based in the metropoles. Artists were brought to European studios and copies of their master recordings and others made in the Caribbean, Africa and Asia were manufactured in Europe and shipped back to retailers in the colonies. In 1930, HMV was reported to have sold over 180,000 units of its West African series of recordings.

In a pioneering account of the recording industries of Africa, Ronnie Graham wrote of this period, 'Lacking access to capital, African businessmen failed to capitalise on the opportunities opening up to the major European recording companies' (Graham 1988: 17). An exception to this rule was South Africa, with its relatively large white mercantile class. There, an important label, Gallo, was founded by a record store owner in 1930.

To summarise this phase: rather than new technologies or legislative changes, wider economic forces, in the form of the global Depression, were the most important influence on the industry's evolution, followed by the dominance of the new medium of radio. These strands combined to force a realignment of the corporate structures of the record industry.

Phase 3: 1940–59

The third period of the twentieth-century industry's development saw further changes and fundamental developments across the field as a whole. If the Depression had been the overdetermining factor in the industry's evolution during the 1930s, now a combination of new formats, demographic changes and economic growth contrived to transform the industry, notably in the period following the Second World War.

The almost simultaneous launch of 33 rpm long-playing records by CBS and of 45 rpm single by RCA in 1948–49 was the greatest change in playback technology for more than fifty years. It should be noted, however, that the rise to prominence of vinyl took longer in some countries than others. EMI, in particular, was very slow to adopt the LP format and in North America and Western Europe singles continued to be issued as 78s as well as 45s until the late 1950s. In Asia, meanwhile, IFPI reported that shellac discs accounted for 90 per cent of its members' sales as late as 1957.

Many histories highlight the introduction of vinyl discs as the most significant feature of this era, but while this was a necessary precondition for the industry's growth during the 1950s, it was not a sufficient one. An equally vital factor, for the US in particular, was the introduction of a vibrant independent label sector that brought innovation in terms of repertoire and significant competition for CBS, RCA and Decca. Of the dozens of new labels of the 1940s and 1950s, at least twenty could claim to have made their mark on popular music history.

Aside from aesthetic and cultural changes, the primary exogenous factor that enabled this indie revolution was the increase in disposable income resulting from full employment in the war economy, while the key endogenous development was the lower cost of entry to the industry due to the availability of cheap pressing plants, increased opportunities for local radio airplay and the growth of the jukebox market that accounted for a large proportion of vernacular record sales.

The necessity of employing black workers in the war economy and further job opportunities in Northern and West Coast cities after 1945 created a new consumer group for blues and R&B, serviced by a series of small but dynamic record companies, among them Specialty, Modern, Atlantic (see Gillett 1974), Chess (see Cohadas 2001), Vee Jay and Sun (see Escott and Hawkins 1991). Valuable interviews with founders of such labels can be found in Broven (2009). The niche markets of folk and jazz also supported new companies such as Folkways (see Goldsmith 1998, Olmstead 2003), Elektra (see Houghton 2010) and Vanguard (all folk), and Prestige, Blue Note (see Cook 2001) and Riverside (all jazz). Crucially, these companies found imaginative solutions to the problem of manufacturing and distribution outside the networks controlled by Columbia, RCA Victor and Decca (Ennis 1992: 178). The prolongation of the economic boom into the post-war period was also hospitable to new companies entering the mainstream of the industry, notably Mercury and Capitol. The overall growth of the record market attracted investment in new labels from entertainment industry firms such as the film studios Warner Bros and MGM and the giant booking agency MCA.

Among the majors, the 1907 cartel arrangement between RCA and EMI was dissolved in 1952 when the American company extended its licensing deal for five years on reduced terms before it moved its foreign licence to Decca. This move was precipitated by an anti-trust action brought against record companies by the US Department of Justice.

At this time, CBS changed its international licensee to Philips of the Netherlands, providing the latter with the springboard it needed to expand its record industry activities throughout Europe and parts of Africa. The Philips electrical company had entered the record industry by the acquisition in 1942 of Decca's Dutch licensee HDD. EMI's loss of access to the majority of US repertoire led the company to seek replacements, by licensing releases from independent companies and in 1955, by purchasing Capitol.

Elsewhere in Europe, some independent companies were set up in the 1950s, though by no means in the quantity seen in the US. Some began as distributors of US jazz titles but rapidly branched out into national popular and pop styles. Among these were Sonet and Metronome (Sweden), Vogue and Barclay (France), Hispavox (Spain) and Dischi Ricordi (Italy).

In Eastern Europe, the policy of nationalisation followed by the Soviet-dominated regimes extended even to the record industry. The East German industry was centralised into the Amiga label, in Hungary there was Hungaraton (1951), in Czechoslovakia, Supraphon, in Bulgaria Bulgaraton and Jugoton was founded in Jugoslavia.

A generational shift in the audience – the emergence in advanced capitalist economies of the so-called boomer group of 'teenagers' – led to rapid growth in the size of the industry. Their discretionary spending power in an age of full employment in North America and Western Europe caused the value of recorded music sales in the United States to almost treble between 1954 and 1959. The rise of rock 'n' roll as a global genre was linked to the context where 'post-war prosperity and the growth of higher education extended young people's dependence on their parents but enabled them to begin seeking out alternatives to the dominant conventions governing sex, love, gender, race and class' (Walser 1998: 353).

The impact of the new independent labels in America precipitated the first analytical distinctions between their status and that of what came to be called the 'majors'. In 1970, the first edition of Charlie Gillett's magisterial *The Sound of the City* was the first book to deal directly with record companies as carriers of the new music, and in the following year Peterson and Berger unveiled their four-firm thesis that linked the rise of the indies to the rise of rock 'n' roll by showing that the number of companies responsible for US hits expanded dramatically in the late 1950s (Peterson and Berger 1975). They were also, no doubt, subliminally responding to the antipathy to large record companies that was part of the politicisation of rock culture in the 1960s, when RCA was lambasted for its involvement in weapons technology and CBS recuperated anti-capitalist feeling by notoriously running an advertising campaign titled 'The Man Can't Bust Our Music'.

The four-firm thesis did not export well, however. Although in France, for instance, indie labels Barclay (Eddy Mitchell) and Vogue (Johnny Hallyday and later Françoise Hardy) signed new pop acts, in Europe as a whole, there was no significant rise in the number of independents, nor in their market shares, either as importers of rock 'n' roll, or as enablers of local versions of the genre. Instead, EMI and Decca competed to license the new American music, sometimes on a hit-by-hit basis: Decca created a London American label in Britain for this purpose.

With the important exception of the Americas, the Second World War, like the First World War, had disrupted the international activities of major record companies. EMI was the most affected, with its London headquarters cut off from European and Asian branches. While many of these were re-established after 1945, the Chinese revolution led by Mao Tse Tung caused EMI to shift its operations to the British colony of Hong Kong in 1949.

In Central and Latin America, entrepreneurs set up labels in smaller countries such as Nicaragua, Ecuador, Uruguay and Bolivia, where Discos Mendez was an offshoot of a radio station. A similar process occurred in Haiti in the 1950s, where recordings made at a radio station were issued by a local record importer, who later moved to New York after falling foul of the dictator 'Baby Doc' Duvalier, 'giving the incipient recording industry a transnational structure in its earliest years' (Averill 1997: 23). In Jamaica, whose unique sound system-led industry was already in place by the mid-1950s, working-class families were acquiring record players and 'all gramophone owners were equally eager for something to play'. Chris Blackwell's R&B label and Edward Seaga's WIRL were among the companies set up to satisfy that demand (Bradley 2000: 42–5).

In Africa, the proliferation of new labels owned by Greek entrepreneurs in Leopoldville (later Kinshasa), the capital of the Belgian Congo (later Zaire) was atypical of a region where companies from the metropoles of the colonial powers still dominated.

More than most, this phase exemplifies the definition of 'true' growth quoted from Braudel at the opening of this chapter. The remarkable expansion of recorded music in the 1950s was the product of 'progress on several fronts', notably those of musical and demographic trends (rock 'n' roll and the teenage audience), new technologies (vinyl and transistors) and corporate developments in the rise of the indies. Behind them all was, too, the post-war consumer boom in Western capitalist economies.

Phase 4: 1960–83

In this fourth phase, there was an intensification of the dominant trends of the previous phase. New technologies, this time tape-based, were applied to the distribution of recorded music; the growth of youth audiences for post-rock and soul continued in a context of general prosperity in the developed world until economic growth was abruptly halted by the slump that began at the end of the 1970s. In the corporate dimension of the industry, further consolidation occurred as major record companies were integrated into conglomerate transnational companies.

By the end of the 1950s, 33 and 45 rpm vinyl discs had displaced 78 rpm shellac records as the primary format in almost all regions of the world, and the production of stereo discs was becoming widespread (in contrast, the attempt to market quadraphonic records in the early 1970s was an abysmal failure). Next came a new technology, that of tape recording. German firms had pioneered the use of magnetic tape in the 1930s and one of the fruits of victory in the Second World War was the confiscation of this technology by the US.

Initially, the format was reel-to-reel, an improved method of recording and editing performances, but cumbersome as a playback format. For that purpose, the insertion of tape into a plastic cassette housing proved to be a great success. The Dutch electronics (and record) company Philips exhibited its prototypes at the Berlin Audio Fair in 1963 and led the way with pre-recorded tapes and tape-decks for consumer use soon afterwards. In the US, a variation was the eight-track cartridge, used mainly in cars during the 1960s and 1970s.

In the most developed nations of North America, Western Europe and the Pacific Rim, the cassette became a popular alternative to the disc, with many consumers using both formats and hardware manufacturers redesigning their music systems to incorporate cassette decks. Sony's 1979 launch of the Walkman portable player was a crucial stage in sustaining the longevity of the cassette as a music format (Nathan 1999: 150–5).

In other parts of the world, the cassette had a revolutionary impact on the dissemination of recorded sound. In many countries with very low average incomes, disc players had remained the preserve of the middle classes, but cassette technology enabled the 'proletarianisation of popular music culture' (Stokes 2004: 234). The relatively low price of cassette players enabled much wider sections of the population to enjoy music in a domestic setting, but the technology also dramatically lowered the cost of entry to the record industry. In his classic study of the cassette culture of North India, Peter Manuel noted that by the mid 1980s, over three hundred small producers were issuing recordings of regional folk, devotional and popular genres (Manuel 1993).

The impact was felt from China to Peru and from Algeria to Namibia. Cassette technology marked a return to a premise of the early cylinder industry, that consumers could make their own recordings on blank media. In doing so, it had a consequence unintended by Philips. It massively increased the incidence of unauthorised copies of commercially issued recordings and returned 'piracy' to the centre of record industry concerns and the agendas of international intellectual property forums. Piracy severely curtailed the income that professional musicians could expect from their cassette recordings even as the vendors of unauthorised tapes claimed to be providing a service to low income music-lovers. A typical case was highlighted by Chris Waterman in his study of the Nigerian Juju culture (Waterman 1990: 151–4).

In Europe and North America, the 'threat' to the industry came less from the commercial piracy of cassettes than from so-called 'home taping'. This term, and its more legalistic equivalent, 'private copying', referred to the actions of consumers who taped albums or radio broadcasts for use by themselves or their friends or fellow music enthusiasts. Co-ordinated by IFPI and music publishers' bodies, the music industry lobbied national governments for legislation to introduce a novel 'levy' or 'royalty' on the sale of media capable of being used to make private copies. The campaign enjoyed considerable success: despite energetic opposition from consumer groups, tape manufacturers and blind people's organisations, by the end of the century almost all European Union members had a levy in place, although the governments of both the US and Britain refused to follow suit. On the international legislative front, the start of this era saw the introduction of the Geneva Convention of 1971, which required governments to enact laws to criminalise the piracy of sound recordings.

A decade earlier, the Rome Convention (1961) set a global minimum period of copyright protection of twenty years for sound recordings, broadcasts and films (Gronow and Saupio 1998 [1990]: 138–40). To join the convention, governments had also to grant performance rights to producers of sound recordings, guaranteeing them royalties when their tracks were broadcast or used in discotheques and retail premises. The refusal of successive US legislatures to grant this right has meant that it is one of the few countries (along with North Korea and Iraq) where radio stations still do not pay royalties to labels or recording artists.

The 1960s was the most important decade since the 1910s in terms of the growth in the global reach of the major record companies. While the US-based majors had entrusted licensees with their international marketing in the 1950s, they moved to set up wholly owned overseas branches in the following decade. CBS set up offices in the UK in 1963, and soon afterwards in France and Germany. RCA took a similar approach, as did some independents such as A&M and Atlantic.

The motive for this expansion was twofold. By the late 1950s, both CBS and RCA had noted that European markets were expanding swiftly. In its annual report for 1956, CBS stated: 'not only from Maine to California, but from Sweden to South Africa, Brazil to Japan, record sales increased. Sales by Columbia's globe-girdling network of subsidiaries and affiliates increased 50 per cent over the preceding year. In established markets such as Europe, record sales established new high levels.' The following year RCA pinpointed the contribution of record sales to the company's increased profits by its licensees in Australia, England, Germany, Sweden, Venezuela and South Africa (quoted in Zolov 1999: 23). It should be noted also that the consumer electronics divisions of these labels were already building television receiver assembly plants around the world. To that extent, recorded music was something of an afterthought in the global expansion strategies of CBS and RCA.

Second, following the international success of the Beatles, Rolling Stones and others, American companies were driven to seek to sign European artists with sales potential in North America. The US firms also sought to grab a share of local sales by local acts, especially in non-anglophone markets such as Germany, Italy, France and the main countries of Latin America.

A feature of this era was the emergence of the first continental European major since the demise of Odeon in the 1920s. PolyGram was the product of a merger in 1972 between Polydor (owned by the German conglomerate Siemens) and the record division of Philips. Following the purchase of British Decca in 1979, the company had strong branches across Europe, to add to Philips's presence in parts of Latin America (where Elemco of Brazil was purchased in 1967), Africa (notably Nigeria) and North America, where the company acquired Mercury (1971) and MGM (1972). In Asia, PolyGram went from a situation where one manager looked after its interests in Asia, Australasia and Eastern Europe in 1970, to the mid 1980s when branches in Hong Kong, Singapore and Malaysia were overseen from a fully staffed Far East and South East Asia division.

In a countervailing trend, new generations of independent labels flourished in both the 1960s and 1970s. With its slogan 'The Sound of Young America', Berry Gordy's Tamla Motown company pioneered black pop – African-American music for integrated teenage audiences (see George 1986) – and was followed by such labels as Stax (see Bowman 1997) and Philadelphia International (see Cummings 1975). In Britain, such companies as Island, Virgin and Chrysalis marketed the new rock music and in the late 1970s Rough Trade (see Young 2006), Stiff, Mute, Factory, Beggars Banquet and others embodied the DIY ethos of punk and 'new wave'. Gronow and Saupio add that in many parts of Europe, small labels grew up to release either conservative or folk-rock versions of indigenous musics, including twelve companies in Austria (1998: 165).

The new majors were beginning to turn their attention to continental Asia, a region where only EMI had previously been active. South-East Asia in particular was renowned as somewhere with little copyright protection, and in 1970 IFPI opened its first regional office in Hong Kong. Its specific aim was to 'combat piracy' and this move marked a major strategic innovation for the organisation, which henceforth would increasingly see anti-piracy work as its principal *raison d'être* (Laing 2004).

The wave of decolonisation in Africa and elsewhere led in some cases to the formation of new national labels. This was particularly the case in francophone nations, where socialist governments established state-owned companies on the Soviet model, such as Syliphone in Guinea. Elsewhere in Africa, local entrepreneurs entered the industry, such as the Tabansi label in Nigeria and Syllart, operated by the Senegalese producer Ibrahim Sylla.

For a brief period of the 1970s, Kenya attracted investment from foreign majors as PolyGram (which bought local label Associated Sound at the beginning of the decade), EMI (1977) and CBS (1978) who formed partnerships with local entrepreneurs, intending to use the country as a hub from which to sell local music throughout East Africa (Wallis and Malm 1984: 92–5). Their timing was poor. Within a few years, a global oil crisis provoked a global recession, hitting Africa hardest.

> The resulting scarcity of foreign exchange to finance imports began to debilitate the pop music industry, which is dependent on equipment manufactured in the industrialized West. At the same time, an epidemic of music piracy, fuelled by the proliferation of cheap cassettes and recording machines, raced across the continent, purloining profits and dampening artistic spirits
>
> (Stewart 1992: 5)

The majors pulled out, never to return.

The global recession coincided with the first fall in the value of recorded music sales since the 1930s. In North America and many parts of Europe, the value of sales did not return to their 1978 levels until the middle of the 1980s. The situation in the United States was typical. Between 1978 and 1979, sales dropped by 15 per cent, from $4.1 billion to $3.7 billion. There was a slight increase in the following 2 years, only to be followed by a further decline to $3.6 billion in 1982.

Among the majors, EMI was the most exposed to the recession. The company had unwisely spent its windfall from the mega-sales of the Beatles on investments in film production and the wider entertainment industry and a loss-making medical scanner. Its profits fell by over 200 per cent between 1977 and 1979, and it was acquired by another British company, Thorn Electrical Industries (Pandit 1996). The music company was to remain a division of Thorn-EMI until 1996 when a demerger made EMI once again a 'stand-alone' music company (Southall 2009).

During this phase, the industry was fundamentally restructured to produce many features of the corporate and regulatory systems that persist in the twenty-first century. Major record companies became genuinely global in their strategic operations, assisted by innovations in intellectual property regimes that were hospitable to their interests. At the same time, though, technological innovation, in the form of the cassette tape, both strengthened their power and undermined it.

Phase 5: The digital apotheosis, 1983–99

The last period of the twentieth century could reasonably be called the age of the Compact Disc, encompassing the highly successful launch of this first digital playback technology and its swift rise to become the dominant recorded music format just as global sales of recorded music went into what became a seemingly permanent decline in the mid-1990s.

Digital technology was already in use in some recording studios in the 1970s (Pohlmann 1989: 6) but the CD was jointly developed by Philips and Sony, two of the leading record-player manufacturers with interests in the record industry, although Sony's was limited to the Japanese market until the end of the 1980s (Nathan 1999: 137–46). The new disc was launched in late 1982 in Japan and the United States, and early the next year in Europe. Global sales were only 5 million units in 1983 but they swiftly rose to 400 million in 1989, higher than those of the vinyl LP, whose peak year had been 1978 when 942 million LPs were sold worldwide.

The rapid growth was assisted by the fact that PolyGram and Sony's partner CBS Records were enthusiastic supporters, although EMI was sceptical about the new format and slow to adopt it, as it had been with vinyl over thirty years earlier. However, the principal attraction for consumers was the 'replacement factor'. The major record companies were swift to issue large numbers of catalogue albums on CD, so that consumers could acquire the CD versions of their favourite vinyl or cassette albums.

As with earlier innovations, the timing of the acceptance of the CD varied according to a country's level of economic development. In the 1980s, take-up of CDs outside the most developed countries was limited to a small elite, with the cassette remaining the format of choice for the majority of the population. Both Philips and Sony unsuccessfully offered digital alternatives to the analogue cassette in the early 1990s, with the digital compact cassette (DCC) and MiniDisc.

Record companies also capitalised on the novelty and modernity of the CD by setting its retail price significantly above that of the LP and by persuading music publishers and many recording artists to accept lower royalty rates because of the cost of launching the format. As a result, major record companies enjoyed super-profits in the CD boom years. This was most evident with classical recordings, of which the majors had massive back catalogues. However, their insistence on premium pricing created a gap in the market that was filled in 1988 by the Hong Kong based label Naxos, which sold new recordings at less than one-third of the prices charged by the majors.

> The packaging was crude and the artists unheard of, but the performances were acceptable and sometimes accomplished . . . Over the next six years, Naxos breached the industry's price codes in all major territories and repertoire, trimming profits to a trickle.
>
> (Lebrecht 1996: 312)

The CD boom made major record companies desirable properties and in the late 1980s and 1990s, almost all the majors changed hands (MCA Records had four owners in less than ten years). The sequence of events was:

1986   Bertelsmann of Germany buys RCA Records from General Electric.
1988   Sony Corp of Japan buys CBS Records for $2bn.
1990   Warner Communications (owner of Warner Music Group) merges with Time.
1992   Matsushita of Japan buys MCA Records.
1997   MCA sold to Seagram of Canada and renamed Universal.

1998   PolyGram sold by Philips to Seagram and merged with Universal.
2000   Universal sold by Seagram to Vivendi of France, creating Vivendi Universal
2000   Time-Warner merges with online company AOL.

The management-speak buzzword associated with most of these transactions was 'synergy'. The addition of a record company to a media or consumer electronics group was supposed to add extra value by the creation of new products or marketing campaigns through collaboration between different divisions of a conglomerate. This also meant, however, that music divisions usually contributed only a small part of the conglomerate's turnover. In 1992, music sales represented between 8 per cent (MCA/Matsushita) and 28 per cent (Thorn-EMI) of parent companies' turnover (Burnett 1996: 58).

Another feature of this trend was the 'invasion' of a US-owned industry by foreign firms. Although there had been sporadic acquisitions by EMI and Philips in earlier years, the totemic American companies RCA and Columbia/CBS were now (and were to remain) in foreign hands. As well as an economic impact, this produced a culture shock as Japanese and German executives assumed control of US companies (see Negus 1996).

In keeping with these multi-billion dollar transactions, this was also the era of the businessman (there were no women involved) as superstar. In earlier phases of the industry, the 'record men' whose A&R skills had built independent labels, from Sam Phillips to Chris Blackwell, had been fêted, but now almost every CEO was treated as a putative 'master of the universe', to quote a hubristic phrase used of himself by Jean-Marie Messier of Vivendi Universal. Messier's high-flying career ended abruptly in 2002 when he was dismissed. He and ex-Seagram chief Edgar Bronfman Jr. were convicted by a French court of corporate fraud, and the company paid $50 million to the United States Securities and Exchange Commission to settle a similar charge. Each man has been the subject of a biography – Johnson and Orange's 2003 book on Messier and Fred Goodman's 2010 version of the career of Bronfman, who went on to engineer the buy-out of Warner Music Group from Time AOL.

Admiring profiles in business magazines of PolyGram's Alain Levy or BMG's Michael Dornemann were matched by muckraking works such as *Hit Men* by Fredric Dannen, Ronin Ro's account of the career of Suge Knight of rap label Death Row and CBS Records chief Walter Yetnikoff's autobiography. With its subtitle *Confessions of a Music Mogul in an Age of Excess* the latter was more like a rock star biography than the career memoirs of the head of CBS Records. It makes an instructive comparison with the anecdotal but precise autobiography of Clive Davis, Yetnikoff's predecessor (Davis 1975).

Takeovers and acquisitions at lower levels in the industry 'food-chain' also reached a peak in this era. Almost all the medium-sized international record companies were swallowed up by the majors. Indeed, some observers saw the biggest of these deals – EMI's purchase of Virgin Records in 1992 – as in effect a merger of two majors. Other important deals were PolyGram's absorption of

A&M and Island in 1989 and MCA's 1988 purchase of Motown in partnership with Boston Ventures, the first incursion of a venture capital firm into the record industry, something that would become more frequent in the twenty-first century.

Within the United States, the rising genres of hip hop and new age had been pioneered by new independent labels, operating under the radar of the majors. But major companies tried to move in as soon as each genre showed commercial potential. BMG cornered the new age market by buying Private Music (1984) and Windham Hill. In the rap and hip hop field, Def Jam was founded in 1984 but by 1995 it was majority owned by PolyGram. Priority (1985) was bought by EMI and La Face (1991) was financed and distributed by BMG. This last was a common method for majors to operate in the 1990s, especially in the United States: BMG also funded so-called 'boutique' labels Imago for Terry Ellis, a founder of the Chrysalis label in Britain and Zoo for Lou Maglia.

Locally owned companies with a significant national presence were also of strategic importance for majors seeking to expand their global market share. As the company most dependent on the success of its anglophone artists, Warner was especially assiduous in buying up significant local labels in such countries as France (Carrere and Erato), Sweden (Metronome), Italy (CGD) and Finland (Fazer). EMI purchased Minos (Greece) and Hispavox (Spain). BMG completed the purchase of the long-established Ricordi of Italy in 1994, although it was more interested in the company's massive music publishing catalogue.

The collapse of state-controlled economies in Eastern Europe in the early 1990s provoked a rush to take a stake in these markets. By definition, the majors had no previous experience in Hungary, Russia, Poland and the rest, so they sought local experts from either the now privatised state monopoly companies or from young entrepreneurs who had conducted music business activity with varying degrees of legality under the communist regimes. In Hungary, EMI hired the former chief of Hungaraton and in the Czech Republic it bought the Monitor label in 1994, five years after it was founded. Among the entrepreneurs were concert promoter Laszlo Hegedus in Hungary and jazz musician Martin Kratochvil of Bonton in the Czech Republic. Hegedus became PolyGram's partner in Hungary while Sony bought 51 per cent of Bonton in 1998 and the remainder in 2003.

In Asia, BMG, MCA and Sony set up branches or licensing agreements across the region in the early 1990s. Warner and PolyGram had established a presence there in the previous phase of the industry's development (Laing 1998).

Despite the establishment of the World Trade Organisation (WTO) with the express purpose of dismantling barriers to global trade, the expansion of trans-national companies continued to be impeded in a diminishing number of countries that had bans or restrictions on foreign ownership. For instance, Venezuela did not lift such restrictions until the late 1990s, so that the leading locally owned label Rodven was the distributor for EMI, BMG and PolyGram. As soon as foreign ownership was permitted, however, PolyGram bought Rodven for $57 million.

China was the most important 'protectionist' country in this era. The history of record companies in China since liberation in 1949 has been complex, but it can be said to have had three phases – strict state control through the China Record Company and regional monopolies until the 1990s when first foreign Chinese-owned companies from Taiwan and Hong Kong set up branches, followed by the slow movement towards the admission of transnational majors under pressure from the free trade and anti-piracy requirements of membership of the WTO (in the Trade-Related Aspects of Intellectual Property Rights or TRIPs section of the WTO treaty). China joined the WTO in 2001, but a decade later it had still not opened its market fully to foreign companies.

Major record companies increased their investment in music publishing in this period. Because of the automatic payment of a mechanical royalty whenever a sound carrier was sold, the exponential growth in record industry turnover produced a proportionate increase in publishers' revenues. Before the 1980s there had been occasional forays by labels into the publishing sector: EMI bought several British publishers in the 1950s and the Columbia Pictures catalogue in 1976, while Philips had purchased the venerable Chappell catalogue in 1968 only to sell it to raise cash in the early 1980s.

Now, every major company looked to publishing for a parallel source of income and a reliable source of profits from broadcasting, live music and synchronisation (film and advertising) fees. EMI bought SBK Songs, which included the former CBS Songs catalogue, and half of Jobete, the publishing subsidiary of Motown Records. Warner Music purchased Chappell and that catalogue's former owner, Philips/PolyGram, felt compelled to re-enter publishing through the acquisition of Dick James Music (holder of Elton John and early Beatles songs) and part of Andrew Lloyd Webber's Really Useful Group. Sony Music made a massive investment in ATV Music, publishers of many other Lennon–McCartney songs, which had been bought at auction in 1984 by Michael Jackson. BMG took a different strategy and purchased numerous small catalogues all over the world, culminating in the Ricordi acquisition.

The majors took much less interest in the third pillar of the music industry – live concerts and festivals. However, Sony and BMG made some attempts to invest in venues and almost all big labels bought up merchandising companies that sold T-shirts and other artist-branded paraphernalia.

In 1995 IFPI statistics surprisingly showed that the CD-inspired growth in world sales of sound recordings had come to a halt. The most widely accepted explanation was that the phase of consumers replacing vinyl albums with CDs was now over. Few pundits referred to the incipient online music world, which record companies, large and small, ignored or dismissed until the rise of Napster at the very end of the century (Alderman 2001). If anything, it was seen as a new variant of piracy, and issues involving copyright on the Internet were a main preoccupation of two new global conventions, the World Performances and Phono-grams Treaty, and the World Copyright Treaty. Both conventions were agreed in 1996 by governments meeting under the auspices of the World Intellectual Property Organisation (WIPO) (May 2007: 66–7).

Technological innovation was a primary factor in the evolution of the industry in this fifth phase. The CD produced super profits for major companies and triggered a swift sequence of mergers and acquisitions, fuelled in part by the newly discovered economic significance of the so-called 'creative' or 'cultural' industries as a whole. In the music media sector, the rise of MTV was emblematic of the new centrality of music videos to the marketing and identity of artists and bands. At the level of musical trends, the global and 'glocal' spread of rap and hip hop represented perhaps the most complex globalised instance of the adoption of an American genre by youth on every continent.

Concluding remarks: what is a major?

In a corporate publication of the early 1970s, EMI stated that the numbers of record companies throughout the world 'multiply, although many of the newcomers do no more than produce recordings for larger companies to manufacture and distribute on a royalty basis' (EMI 1971:10). This succinct definition, if uttered *de haut en bas*, sums up a widespread understanding of the distinction between majors and independents in the record industry. In the 1990s, drawing on the then fashionable ecological approach to business systems, Robert Burnett presented the distinction as one between generalists at the core of the industry and specialists at the periphery. He defined the latter as those firms that 'concentrate on a limited product or genre', while the former offer 'mass products for a mass audience or a wide range of products for different groups of consumers' (Burnett 1996: 78).

Both these definitions seem historically limited in that most major companies in the global record industry have now 'outsourced' both manufacturing and distribution, and many independent labels compete for the 'mass audience'. Nevertheless, the element of control by the majors implied by both approaches remains. In recent terminology, companies such as Universal, EMI, Sony and Warner are 'system integrator' firms at the apex of extended value chains, exerting pressure on the smaller companies that supply them with manufacturing and distribution services (Nolan *et al.* 2007).

Both older approaches are also lacking an international dimension, particularly in their understanding of the dynamics of the relationship between independent and major labels. One frequently found feature of the international expansion of major companies throughout the century was their reliance on local market knowledge not available inside the firm. This intelligence could be acquired in three main ways: using talent scouts, forming a licensing relationship and partly or fully acquiring the share capital of local companies.

The 'talent scout' option was necessary in the infancy of the industry, since there were no local labels in existence. The Gramophone Company's Fred Gaisberg typically used the company's appointed dealers in hardware to source popular singers and instrumentalists in countries as disparate as India and Italy. A similar procedure was followed internally by US record companies in the 1920s when they decided to exploit the immigrant, African-American and rural white markets.

The advantage of licensing deals was that they enabled record companies to sell their 'international' repertoire in alien national markets. The licensee could be relied on to create marketing strategies for the media and retail systems peculiar to their national economy. The licensing arrangement was the basis of the creation of a global (or at least international) market through the Gramophone Company–Victor concord of 1901. It remained a favourite strategy of majors throughout the first half of the century.

The principal disadvantages of licensing were both financial and corporate. A typical licensing deal returned a relatively small amount of the wholesale value of sales while access to the intellectual capital possessed by the licensee was both indirect and temporary – if the licence agreement ended, the major lost the licensee's local knowledge. In larger overseas markets, therefore, there was an inexorable impetus towards ownership of the market share of the licensee and its embodied experience of musical tastes and marketing methods. So began a familiar sequence of licensing, followed by a joint venture with licensee, then the purchase of part or whole of the licensee's company, and finally the transformation of that company into the national office of the major.

The introduction to this chapter introduced the idea of the 'interweaving' of the different strands that combine to produce the history of record companies and the record industry. Another way of expressing this is through the concept of conjuncture, which introduces a different qualitative measure of historical time: a conjuncture, at least in the definition advanced by Louis Althusser, following historians of science, is a moment where something fundamentally different occurs, a break, or turning-point, or, in a recent modish phrase a 'tipping point' (Gladwell 2000). Although few recognised it at the time, the end of the twentieth century marked a conjunctural moment for this industry, as combination of falling revenues and the emergence of the Internet (Napster was launched in 1999) precipitated it into an uncertain and perilous twenty-first century future.

Bibliography

Alderman, J. (2001) *Sonic Boom: Napster, P2P and the Future of Music*. London: Fourth Estate.

Averill, G. (1997) *A Day for the Hunter, A Day for the Prey: Popular Music and Power in Haiti*. Chicago: University of Chicago Press.

Bowman, R. (1997) *Soulsville U.S.A.: The Story of Stax Records*. New York: Schirmer Books.

Bradley, L. (2000) *Bass Culture: When Reggae Was King*. London: Viking.

Braudel, F. (1984) *Civilisation and Capitalism. 15–18th Century. Vol. 3. The Perspective of the World*. London: Collins.

Brooks, T. (1978) Columbia Records in the 1890s: Founding the Record Industry, *ARSC Journal*, 10: 5–36.

Broven J. (2009) *The Record Makers and Record Breakers. Voices of the Independent Rock 'n' Roll Pioneers*. Chicago, IL: University of Illinois Press.

Burnett, R. (1996) *The Global Jukebox: The International Music Industry*. London and New York: Routledge.

Cohadas, N. (2001) *Spinning Blues into Gold. Chess Records: The Label that Launched the Blues*. London: Aurum Press.

Cook, R. (2001) *Blue Note Records: The Biography*. London, Secker & Warburg.

Cummings, T. (1975) *The Sound of Philadelphia*. London: Methuen.

Dannen, F. (1990) *Hit Men. Power Brokers and Fast Money inside the Music Business*. New York: Times Books.

Davis, C. (1975) *Clive: Inside the Record Business*. New York: Morrow.

EMI (1971) *World Record Markets*. London: Henry Melland.

Ennis, P.H. (1992) *The Seventh Stream: The Emergence of Rock 'n' Roll in American Popular Music*. Hanover, NH, and London: Wesleyan University Press.

Escott, C. and Hawkins, M. (1991) *Good Rockin' Tonight: Sun Records and the Birth of Rock 'n' Roll*. New York: St Martin's Press.

Farrell, G. (1998) The Early Days of the Gramophone Industry in India: Historical, Social and Musical Perspectives, in A. Leyshon, D. Matless and G. Revill (eds) *The Place of Music*. New York and London: Guilford Press, pp. 57–82.

Frith, S. (1987) The Industrialisation of Music, in J. Lull (ed.) *Popular Music and Communication*. Newbury Park, CA, and London: Sage.

Gelatt, R. (1977) *The Fabulous Phonograph* (2nd revised edn). New York: Collier Books.

George, N. (1986) *Where Did Our Love Go?* New York: St Martin's Press.

Gillett, C. (1974) *Making Tracks: Atlantic Records and the Growth of a Multi-Billion Dollar Industry*. New York: Dutton.

Gillett, C. (1996 [1970]) *The Sound of the City: The Rise of Rock 'n' Roll* (3rd revised edn). London: Souvenir Press.

Gitelman, L. (1999) *Scripts, Grooves and Writing Machines: Representing Technology in the Edison Era*. Stanford, CA: Stanford University Press.

Gladwell, M. (2000) *The Tipping Point: How Little Things Can Make a Big Difference*. New York: Little, Brown.

Goldsmith, P.D. (1998) *Making People's Music: Moe Asch and Folkways Records*. Washington DC and London: Smithsonian Institution Press.

Goodman, F. (2010) *Fortune's Fool: Edgar Bronfman Jr., Warner Music and an Industry in Crisis*. New York and London: Simon & Schuster.

Graham, R. (1988) *Stern's Guide to Contemporary African Music*. London: Pluto.

Gronow, P. and Saupio, I. (1998 [1990]) *An International History of the Recording Industry*. London and New York: Cassell.

Gronow, P. and Englund, B. (2007) Inventing Recorded Music: The Recorded Repertoire in Scandinavia 1899–1925, *Popular Music*, 26 (2), May: 281–304.

Houghton, M. (2010) *Becoming Elektra: The True Story of Jac Holzman's Visionary Record Label*. London and San Francisco, CA: Jawbone.

Huygens M., Baden-Fuller, C. and Van Den Bosch, F. (2001) The Co-evolution of Firm Capabilities and Industry Competition: Investigating the Music Industry, 1877–1997, *Organization Studies*, 22 (6): 971–1011.

Johnson, J. and Orange, M. (2003) *The Man Who Tried to Buy the World: Jean-Marie Messier and Vivendi Universal*. New York and London: Viking Portfolio.

Jones, G. (1985) The Gramophone Company: An Anglo-American Multinational, 1898–1931, *Business History Review*, 59, Spring: 76–100.

Kenney, W.H. (1999) *Recorded Music in American Life: The Phonograph and Popular Memory, 1890–1945*. New York and London: Oxford University Press.

Kittler, F. (1999) *Gramophone, Film, Typewriter*. Stanford, CA: Stanford University Press.

Koenigsberg, A. (1990) *The Patent History of the Phonograph*. New York: APM Press.

Laing, D. (1998) Knockin' On China's Door, in T. Mitsui (ed.) *Popular Music: Intercultural Interpretations*. Kanazawa, Graduate Program in Music, Kanazawa University, pp. 337–42.

Laing, D. (2004) Copyright and the International Music Industry, in S. Frith and L. Marshall (eds) *Music and Copyright* (2nd revised edn). Edinburgh: Edinburgh University Press.

Laing, D. (2009) International Federation of the Phonographic Industry, in C. Tietje and A. Brouder (eds) *Handbook of Transnational Economic Governance Regimes*. Leiden and Boston, MA: Martinus Nijhoff Publishers, pp. 585–94.

Lebrecht, N. (1996) *When The Music Stops: Managers, Maestros and Corporate Murder of Classical Music*. London: Simon & Schuster.

Manuel, P. (1993) *Cassette Culture: Popular Music and Technology in North India*. Chicago, IL, and London: University of Chicago Press.

May, C. (2007) *The World Intellectual Property Organisation: Resurgence and the Development Agenda*. London and New York: Routledge.

Moore, J.N. (1999) *Sound Revolutions: A Biography of Fred Gaisberg, Founding Father of Commercial Sound Recording*. London: Sanctuary.

Nathan, J. (1999) *Sony: The Private Life*. London: HarperCollins Business.

Negus, K. (1999) *Music Genres and Corporate Cultures*. London and New York: Routledge.

Nolan, P., Zhang, L. and Liu, C. (2007) *The Global Business Revolution and the Cascade Effect*. Basingstoke, Hants.: Macmillan.

Olmstead, T. (2003). Folkways Records: Moses Asch and his Encyclopedia of Sound. New York: Routledge.

Pandit, S.A. (1996) *From Making to Music: The History of Thorn EMI*. London: Hodder & Stoughton.

Peterson, R. and Berger, D. (1975) Cycles in Symbol Production: The Case of Popular Music, *American Sociological Review*, 40: 158–73.

Pohlmann, K.C. (1989) *The Compact Disc: A Handbook of Theory and Use*. Cambridge: Cambridge University Press.

Ro, R. (1998) *Have Gun Will Travel: The Spectacular Rise and Violent Fall of Death Row Records*. New York: Doubleday.

Sanjek, R. (1988) *American Popular Music and Its Business: The First Four Hundred Years*, 3, 1900–84. New York and London: Oxford University Press.

Siefert, M. (1995) Aesthetics, Technology and the Capitalization of Culture: How the Talking Machine Became a Musical Instrument, *Science in Context*, 8: 417–49.

Southall, B. (2009) *The Rise and Fall of EMI Records*. London: Omnibus Press.

Stapleton, C. and May, C. (1987) *African All-Stars: The Pop Music of a Continent*. London: Quartet.

Sterne, J. (2003) *The Audible Past: Cultural Origins of Sound Reproduction*. Durham, NC, and London: Duke University Press.

Stewart, G. (1992) *Breakout: Profiles in African Rhythm*. Chicago, IL, and London: University of Chicago Press.

Stokes, M. (2004) Turkey, in J. Shepherd and D. Horn (eds) *Continuum Encyclopedia of Popular Music of the World, Vol. VI, Africa and the Middle East*. London: Continuum, pp. 233–40.

Wallis, R. and Malm, K. (1984) *Big Sounds from Small Peoples: The Music Industry in Small Countries*. London: Constable.

Walser, R. (1998) The Rock and Roll Era in D. Nicholls (ed.), *The Cambridge History of American Music*. Cambridge: Cambridge University Press, pp. 345–87.

Waterman, C. (1990) *Juju: A Social History and Ethnography of an African Popular Music*. Chicago: University of Chicago Press.

Weheliye, A.E. (2005) *Phonographie: Grooves in Sonic Afro-Modernity*. Durham, NC, and London: Duke University Press.

Welch, W.L. and Burt, L.B.S. (1994) *From Tinfoil to Stereo: 1877–1929*. Gainesville, FL: University Press of Florida.

Yetnikoff, W. with Ritz, D. (2004) *Howling at the Moon: Confessions of a Music Mogul*. New York: Broadway Books.

Young, R. (2006) *Rough Trade*. London: Black Dog.

Zolov, E. (1999) *Refried Elvis: The Rise of the Mexican Counterculture*. Berkeley and Los Angeles, CA: University of California Press.

4 The recording industry in the twenty-first century

Lee Marshall

Introduction

It is no secret that the twenty-first century has thus far not been kind to the recording industry. Declining sales, a series of public relations misjudgements (not least of which involved suing their own customers), superstar defections, shrinking retail space and the sorry tale of EMI have all contributed to the impression of an industry in serious difficulties and struggling to adapt to the pace of change in an online music environment. Indeed, some have argued that the twentieth-century model of the recording industry is no longer relevant as 'the commercial value of providing access to an individual track is infinitesimally close to zero' (Wikstrom 2009: 6). It is easy to find many pronouncements that the major labels in particular have entered a terminal decline (for example, Williamson and Cloonan in this volume).

So, the first decade of the new century has been one of turmoil, not unprecedented in the history of the recording industry (similar crises occurred in the first decade of the twentieth century, at the start of the 1930s and end of the 1970s), but certainly serious. The major labels have been caught out by the transformations prompted by digital audio, mobile phone use, online retail and the like, and they have remained rudderless for much of the decade. However, the recording industry in 2011 is not completely unrecognisable from the one of 1997 and, while we continue to hear predictions of the demise of the major labels, they remain some of the largest and most influential companies in the music industry. Perhaps the current turmoil is not so much a revolution as merely one of a series of evolutions in the history of the popular music industry. After all, it is always easier to make sense of the past rather than the present; the tensions and contradictions have already been smoothed out, the implications already known. In this chapter, I will tell the story of the global recording industry in the first decade of the twenty-first century, recognising the drama of some of the transformations that have been experienced while at the same time maintaining a broader historical perspective that does not exaggerate the implications. Finally, I shall briefly explain why an understanding of the global industry is necessary for understanding the local industries that are the subject of this book.

The bottom line

Like any good business analyst, we should start by looking at the bottom line. What has happened to revenue in the recording industry? According to the annual data published by the IFPI, the overall value of recorded music has declined by roughly 40 per cent since 1999 (Table 4.1).

Clearly, these figures seem to indicate a dramatic decline in the value of recorded music sold or licensed by record companies. However, while not intending to dismiss this trend, there are a number of reasons to adopt a critical stance to the data. First, it is important to note that these are official IFPI figures derived from data submitted by its member companies. While the IFPI does state that it extrapolates its raw data to make the final figure representative of 100 per cent of the national market in question, it is still unlikely to account for all of the revenue generated by smaller, independent labels who are not part of national recording associations such as the RIAA and BPI (this is a theme that will recur throughout the national case studies in this book). Furthermore, the figures are unlikely to include, for example, revenue generated by artists selling recordings

Table 4.1 Trade value[a] of recorded music (in billions of dollars) (adapted from IFPI 2011)

	'99	'00	'01	'02	'03	'04	'05	'06	'07	'08	'09	'10
Physical music sales[b]	27.3	26.9	26.5	24.7	22.9	22.3	20.8	18.8	16.4	13.9	12.2	10.4
Digital music sales[c]						0.4	1.2	2.2	3.1	4.0	4.4	4.6
Performance rights[d]				0.4	0.4	0.5	0.5	0.6	0.6	0.8	0.8	0.9
TOTAL	**27.3**	**26.9**	**26.5**	**25.1**	**23.3**	**23.2**	**22.5**	**21.6**	**20.1**	**18.7**	**17.4**	**15.9**
Annual decline in dollar terms		0.4	0.4	1.4	1.8	0.1	0.7	0.9	1.5	1.4	1.3	1.5
Annual percentage decline		1.5	1.5	5.3	7.2	0.0	3.0	4.0	6.9	7.0	7.0	8.6
Cumulative percentage decline		1.5	2.9	8.1	14.7	15.0	17.6	20.1	26.4	31.5	36.3	41.8

Notes:
a 'Trade value' refers to the price that record labels sell their items to retailers (sometimes referred to as 'wholesale price' or 'dealer price'). The alternative is 'retail value', which refers to the price that recordings are sold to consumers. Retail value is a less reliable indicator of income to manufacturers as it is subject to fluctuations in the price charged to customers (the price of CDs has fallen in the last ten years) although they are related, as explained later. Up until 2005, the IFPI's data referred to retail value. This is important to note because, although this table refers to trade value, when I later offer historical comparisons I will be referring to retail value as trade value data is unavailable.
b Includes formats such as CD, tape and music DVD.
c Includes income from subscription and streaming services.
d Income from the licensing of recorded music for use in TV, games, restaurants etc.

Source: adapted from IFPI 2011

at their gigs, or revenue generated by bands using online services such as Tunecore to sell their records. According to Tunecore founder Jeff Price, Tunecore 'released' 90,000 albums in 2009, selling over 42 million tracks (Price 2010), so these are not insignificant sums missing from the 'official statistics' (though they are, to a large extent, more significant culturally than economically; Price states that these sales generated revenue of $32 million, which is less than 1 per cent of the total US market). While the IFPI data provides a snapshot of mainstream industry trends, it is always likely to produce a partial picture.

A second reason to investigate this data relates to the kind of historical comparisons being made. One of the best years that the recording industry has experienced was actually 1999, with a retail value of $38.8 billion (IFPI 2006a: 113) and a trade value of $27.3 billion (IFPI 2011: 7). Making comparisons with this year may, therefore, exaggerate the downward trend experienced in the last 10 years. Rather than considering the current situation as a deviation from the highest point, it is perhaps advisable to consider the industry's best years as something of an anomaly. Between 1993 and 1994, the retail value of recorded music rose by almost $5 billion, from $31.2 billion to $36.2 billion. Value peaked in 1996 at $39.8 billion and remained relatively steady until 1999. Retail value dropped by roughly $2 billion between 1999 and 2000 (IFPI 2006a: 113). Considering the period 1994–99 as an anomaly and broadening our historical comparison thus provides a somewhat different picture. Comparing over a 20-year period (1990–2010) suggests that the retail value of recorded music rose by roughly 5 per cent, from $24.1 billion to $25.3 billion (though, allowing for inflation, this is actually a 9.3 per cent decrease in real terms). However, a 25-year comparison (from 1985 to 2010) reveals that, during this time, the retail value of recorded music slightly increased in real terms (by 1.6 per cent).[1]

This is not to suggest that the value of recorded music has not fallen over the last ten years – it clearly has. It is, however, possible to infer different trends from the available IFPI data, highlighting that the conclusions that you draw significantly depend upon your frame of reference. My comparison years of 1999, 1990 and 1985 are significant dates in relation to the history of the CD technology, which I shall discuss below.

A third reason to consider these figures critically actually reflects the *raison d'être* of this book – they are global figures that mask a variety of trends within different national markets.[2] The overall downturn in the recording industry undoubtedly affects the relationship between the global major labels and their national subsidiaries, and thus the global figures discussed here are certainly relevant. At the same time, however, it is necessary to consider the available data at a local level to begin to understand the nature of the data. Considering the data at a national level reveals some interesting trends. First, it is clear that the major markets are being hardest hit by the decline in sales: the IFPI records that the USA and Japan, the two largest music markets combining for roughly half of global sales between them, accounted for 57 per cent of the global decline in 2010 and 80 per cent of the global decline in 2009 (IFPI 2011: 7). The US in particular has been affected badly. Whereas it used to account for almost 40 per cent of the (much bigger) global market in 2001 (IFPI 2003: 8), it now accounts for just 26 per cent of the global market and is likely to be soon overtaken by Japan as the world's biggest music market (IFPI 2011: 95). This is significant because media reporting of the recording industry often considers just the US situation when it is not wholly representative. It is certainly worth considering how and why the decrease in sales is affecting the major markets more markedly (similarly, to understand how this data reflects different aspects of musical consumption, it is worth considering how the downturn affects genres differently), but not all of the major markets have been so badly affected: Germany in particular has so far survived quite well, declining just 11 per cent between 2006 and 2010, while Japan has declined 18 per cent. There are other examples of national markets that diverge from the global trend: Sweden, considered a haven for pirates, declined just 12 per cent between 2006 and 2010; the Netherlands just 6 per cent. The market in Poland actually increased 22 per cent during that period while the recorded music market in Greece, affected badly by the global financial crisis, fell by 40 per cent in 2010 alone. Looking beyond Europe, it is interesting to see that the market in some Asian countries has expanded considerably (India and South Korea 42 per cent, Malaysia 13 per cent). South America, too, has witnessed some considerable increases (Argentina 16 per cent, Uruguay 12 per cent, Venezuela 61 per cent and Peru 84 per cent). Of course, many of these are small markets that hardly register on the global data, but that is the point – if we want to consider the effects that the global downturn in recorded music is having at a local/international level, then we must investigate the local circumstances of each market as the global tallies reveal little.

When considering the available data on the downturn in the recording industry it is, therefore, important to maintain a critical perspective. It needs to be recognised that the data may not fully reflect all of the recorded music bought and sold, and that it is collected and presented by an industry organisation that will want to present it in a particular way. It is, therefore, necessary to consider alternative ways of analysing the data (by, for example, using different historical comparison points). Finally, it is always worth remembering that if we want to understand how a particular music market is being affected, then we must fully investigate popular music production and consumption in that locality.

Notwithstanding these points, it is clear that the value of recorded music *has* fallen quite considerably in the last ten years. In the next section, I will discuss how the major labels have responded to the downturn.

Piracy

The labels' response to the downturn in music sales followed a well-established historical pattern. In the 1930s, labels argued that piracy was a significant explanation for the decline in disc sales. After all, why would anyone purchase records when the radio was giving away their tunes for free? Similarly, in the late 1970s, the recording industry blamed piracy for the dramatic fall in record sales. Why would anyone buy records when they can use blank tapes to record from the radio or from their friends' collections? It was not entirely unpredictable, therefore, when, in the late 1990s, the labels insisted that the downturn in record sales could be explained by piracy.

The labels' initial concern was with the popularisation of recordable CD technology, which emerged as a consumer format around 1998. Whereas blank audio tapes had reduced audio fidelity in every generation of recording, recordable CDs were able to produce perfect clones of digital master recordings. Labels were thus quick to equate the rising number of blank CD sales with the declining number of official CD sales and argued in favour of, for example, a levy to be charged on recording equipment (including computers) and blank discs.

It was a different invention that propelled piracy into public discourse, however. The MP3 algorithm, which enabled the compression of reasonable-fidelity music into smaller data files was first patented by the Fraunhofer Institute in 1989. It soon began to be used on websites offering pirated music but its position as the *de facto* standard for digital music distribution depended on the emergence of a complementary technology – peer-to-peer distribution (P2P) – and, particularly, a piece of software called Napster. By connecting one computer with a network of peers, the Napster user was able to access other people's music collections while also making their own files available to other users.

Napster was developed by a college student seeking a way of sharing music files with his friends. However, it soon expanded beyond one small social circle to become an online phenomenon. Napster was launched in August 1999 and was sued by the RIAA in December that year, but the publicity generated by the lawsuit facilitated an increase in Napster usage. In February 2000, Napster had 524,000 users, which increased to 4.6 million in June that year (Kot 2009: 31–2). At its peak, users on Napster were sharing 330 million music files (King 2001). On Napster you could find everything from the latest chart hits to obscure blues singers from the 1930s. Napster became a very useful, and very cool, way of accessing music.

Understandably, the recording industry did not see it this way and, again, their response demonstrated historical consistency. As Simon Frith points out (2001: 197), the recording industry sees most business problems as legal problems. Thus, they sued. First, they sued Napster itself, bringing a suit in December 1999 that accused Napster of 'contributory and vicarious copyright infringement'. Then they threatened to sue university campuses, arguing that due to fast connection speeds, the majority of unauthorised sharing was occurring on their premises.[3] Finally, record industries in some countries, notably the US, turned their attention to individual consumers, either sending threatening letters to induce an out-of-court compensation payment or, if that was ineffective, suing them. The first, and by far the most active country involved in prosecuting individual users was the USA, with the RIAA sending notifications of legal action to 261 users in September 2003. By 2005 the total had reached 9,000. The majority of these individuals agreed to settle the claim for a compensatory payment of a few thousand dollars, but two cases made it to trial: in 2009, Joel Tenenbaum was fined $675,000 for sharing 31 songs online (this was subsequently reduced to $67,500 on appeal, although currently both parties are appealing the verdict); in 2010, Jammie Thomas was ultimately fined $54,000 for sharing 24 songs, having had damages range from $222,000 to $1.92 million in earlier trials.

Cases against individuals have also been brought in countries outside of the USA. The IFPI announced a first wave of prosecutions in March 2004, prosecuting 247 individuals in Denmark, Germany, Italy and Canada. A further tranche, this time including the UK and France, were announced in October. By October 2006, over 13,000 individuals had been sued, with 2,300 of them settling out of court for an average of €2,420 (IFPI 2006b).

October 2006 was the last time (so far) that the IFPI announced cases against individual users and, in late 2008, the RIAA announced that it would no longer be pursuing actions against individuals (McBride and Smith 2008). By this time, it had sued approximately 18,000 individuals (Anderson 2009), making the total number of individuals sued by the recording industry worldwide around 31,000. The industry then seemingly changed strategy and began focusing on Internet service providers (ISPs). Two cases were brought against ISPs in Ireland and Australia, accusing them of enabling illegal file sharing on their services but the more significant strategy has involved lobbying governments to introduce 'graduated response' approaches to file-sharing, often referred to as a 'three strikes' policy, whereby individuals' Internet connections are slowed or disconnected if they ignore repeated warnings about file-sharing. Such policies are beneficial for the recording industry because they make the telecommunications industry at least partly responsible for file-sharing. One of the earliest such policies was the HADOPI law in France, which will be discussed in Chapter 8. In July 2011, the RIAA announced that it had reached a voluntary agreement with major American ISPs to introduce a graduated response policy (Bruno 2011).

As well as pursuing legal redress, the labels also sought to develop digital rights management (DRM) systems that limited digital copying: in 1998, they established the Secure Digital Music Initiative (SDMI), a committee intended to develop ways of preventing the copying of digitally stored music but, riven with internal tensions, it produced little of practical benefit and it disbanded in 2002; the majors' first efforts at online music, Musicnet and PressPlay, released in 2002, featured highly restrictive DRM regimes that contributed to their unpopularity; in 2003, when the majors licensed their music to be sold on the iTunes store, they insisted that the files should incorporate a DRM system (known as Fairplay) that prevented unlimited copying; and, in 2005, Sony scored a spectacular own-goal by placing virus-like software on CDs which installed on to a user's computer without their permission.

In developing technological locks and aggressively pursuing rights claims in the courts, the major labels sought to delay, or even prevent, the emergence of online digital music. As Kretschmer *et al.*'s interviews with major label executives revealed, the labels did not want a new market to develop that cannibalised its existing market (2001: 426). It certainly seems that the labels were unprepared for the online music world and reluctant to enter it, or to let anyone else enter it (by, for example, refusing to license their back catalogue to new services. McCourt and Bukart argue that the legal case against Napster was in part an attempt to discourage venture capitalist investment in competing services (2003: 341)). They were also slow to realise the implications of the MP3 format and digital distribution. There was a sense that if they could 'stop Napster', then everything could go back to the way things were, the labels could continue to sell CDs and profits would continue to rise.

Things did not turn out this way, however. The labels were successful in stopping Napster: during a series of trials, Napster was ordered to close until it developed a filtering system that was 100 per cent effective (the judge was not satisfied when Napster achieved 99.4 per cent efficiency); Napster reached a settlement with music publishers in September 2001, paying them $26 million in damages. It did not reach an agreement with the record labels before it filed for bankruptcy in May 2002. At the time, some analysts suggested that the Napster victory would establish the major labels' control of online music. For example, McCourt and Bukart argued that 'the Napster decision formalize[d] the implementation of intellectual property controls on the Internet, and consolidate[d] the [then] Big Five's advantages in gatekeeping content and distributing products' and described the decision as achieving 'the lockup of the Internet' for the major labels (2003: 343). With hindsight, however, such an outcome has (so far) failed to materialise. Indeed, other commentators argued that Napster represented a last chance for the major labels to dictate the terms of the online music market (for example, Pareles, 2001; Shachtman, 2001; Knopper, 2009). Legally, Napster's weak point was the fact that details of songs being shared by its users passed through a central server and could thus be overseen by Napster. This means that, had the labels sought to use Napster themselves, they could have provided an online music environment which they controlled.[4] However, when Napster closed down, users switched to new P2P services such as Limewire and Gnutella, which did not utilise central servers and were thus much harder to control (and prosecute). In August 2001, the month after Napster closed down, 3.05 billion music files were downloaded on the three most popular P2P services, slightly more than Napster at its peak (Wired.com 2001). The invention of the more efficient (and even harder to prosecute) Bittorrent format in 2001 also made the P2P field harder for the recording industry to counter. The genie was out of the bottle and unauthorised downloading has continued throughout the decade. The recording industry still views this behaviour as the major explanation for declining sales.

What if piracy wasn't the problem?

However, two simple facts suggest that piracy cannot be the sole explanation for the decline in sales experienced by the recording industry. First, sales had already started to decline before CD burners and Napster emerged. Second, if piracy was the sole explanation for the decline in record sales then, given the number of files that have been downloaded, one would expect record sales to have dropped much further than they have. Just because Napster and declining industry revenue occur at the same time does not mean that the two are necessarily causally linked.

The various studies conducted on the effects of piracy have yielded ambiguous results. Unsurprisingly, the record industry has referred to a number of market research studies that, according to them, 'proves overwhelmingly that illegal file-sharing has contributed to the decline in global music sales' (IFPI 2004), suggesting that 'online music piracy is the single largest factor impacting lost music spend' (IFPI 2009). For example, a Forrester Research European study in 2004 stated that 36 per cent of illegal downloaders say they buy fewer CDs because of downloading, a Pollara survey in Canada in 2004 argued that 28 per cent of consumers who spent less on music in the previous twelve months attributed it to file-sharing, and an IFPI/Jupiter European survey in 2005 stated that 35 per cent of illegal file-sharers are buying fewer CDs.

The recording industry presents these arguments in a more black-and-white fashion than the data allows, however, and often presents logically dubious conclusions in their analysis.[5] When considering studies not endorsed by the recording industry, there has been more ambiguity. An infamous study, conducted by Oberholzer and Strumph (2004), suggested that the effect of file-sharing was 'statistically indistinguishable from zero'. This was heavily criticised by Lieberwitz (2011), who concluded that file-sharing could be held accountable for more than 100 per cent of the decline in sales (i.e. sales would have increased without file-sharing). Research by Zentner (2006) offers a similar conclusion, suggesting that file-sharing could be responsible for an 8 per cent decline in US record sales up to 2001 (which is 73 per cent of the 11 per cent drop in sales experienced up to that point). Later research has suggested different conclusions, however: a report for the Canadian government (Anderson and Frenz 2007) suggested that, for every twelve tracks downloaded, CD purchasing increases by 0.44; a Demos survey in 2009 suggested that illegal downloaders spent more money on music purchases than non-downloaders, which supports research conducted by a Norwegian management school, which suggests that people who use P2P sites buy ten times as much music as those who have never downloaded illegally (MusicAlly 2009).

Elsewhere, I have written in detail about the dangers of trying to quantify the effects of piracy (Marshall 2004a, 2004b). The fundamental problem with these surveys is that they treat a social activity as an economic one, reducing music listening to buying or not buying records (Frith 2002: 208). They also fail to explain the underlying causes of file sharing, adopting a simplistic economic approach that assumes people download merely because it is a cheaper alternative to paying for CDs. So, without wishing to suggest that downloading has played no part in the fall of record sales, let us assume for a moment that piracy is not the major reason for declining sales and consider alternative explanations.

The first possibility is that records now exist in a much more competitive entertainment marketplace than they did previously. The DVD was introduced in 1997/98 and had achieved sales worth $11.6 billion in the US alone by 2002 (DEG 2003), though this has subsequently declined. Digital games have also recorded increased growth during the decade and account for significant entertainment spending ($25.1 billion in the US in 2010 (ESA 2011)). Furthermore, the dramatic increase in mobile phone use, particularly among young people, offers further competition for records that did not exist in the past (sales worth $215 billion in 2009 (TIA 2010)). The emergence of these three new entertainment technologies alone offers ample explanation for a decrease of $11.4 billion in the US recording industry between 1999 and 2010.

A second explanation for the declining *retail* value of recorded music (which creates downward pressure on trade value) is the fact that the price of CDs has fallen during the last decade. While this downward pressure is partly driven by the emerging digital market and subsequent closure of many independent record stores, it was a trend that was already emerging beforehand. In particular, the emergence of 'non-traditional' retailers ('big-box' retailers such as Wal-Mart and Best Buy in the US and Tesco in the UK) pushed down the price of mainstream CDs, as they would often sell CDs at very low prices as a loss-leader to encourage customers into their stores. Ultimately, however, the non-traditional retailers began to dominate the record-selling business, with Wal-Mart becoming the biggest seller of music in the US until it was usurped by iTunes in 2008 (Bangeman 2008).

Concerned that the non-traditional retailers were 'devaluing music', and under pressure from independent record stores who were being forced out of business by the big-boxes' strategy, the labels introduced a 'minimum advertised price' programme (MAP) designed to ensure that CDs were not sold too cheaply. However, in 2000, the US Federal Trade Commission found the major labels guilty of price-fixing because of the MAP, forcing them to pay compensation to consumers (Fox 2005: 506). While on first glance this may seem a victory for consumers, the ramifications of this decision are more complex given that these stores have used their power in, for example, refusing to carry albums that were deemed as antithetical to 'family values' (Knopper 2009: 109–10). The rise of the big-box retailer has also resulted in declining competition within the retail sector and, for our present argument, a strong downward pressure on CD prices.

One explanation often put forward by fans and journalists, though less often by academics, is simply that the music being released by the major labels is not as good as it was (for example, Lefsetz 2011). While it is difficult to make judgements on the quality of music being released, or to make causal connections between quality and sales (some *really* bad records have sold a lot of copies), it is perhaps plausible to argue that music means less to (young) people than it did in the past, although there has been no research to investigate the thesis, and we should be wary of overly-nostalgic readings of the past. What we can say with some certainty is that the recording industry benefited from a teen-pop boom around the turn of the century (Knopper 2009: 81–2), which has since subsided.

Perhaps the most significant explanation for the decline in recording industry revenue is that the 1990s witnessed the end of the 'CD replacement cycle'. The emergence of the CD offers the most convincing explanation for the recording industry's successful 1990s and is the foundation of my earlier suggestion that we should consider the 1990s, rather than the 2000s, as an historical anomaly. The CD was publicly introduced in 1982 and made available in the US in March 1983. Early players and discs were expensive, however, and mainly utilised by audiophiles and classical music listeners. Worldwide CD sales totalled just 5.5 million in 1983, rising to 20 million the following year and 61 million in 1985 (IFPI 2004: 210). 1985 was something of a watershed year for the CD: Dire Straits' *Brothers in Arms* was released and would eventually be the first CD to sell a million copies. Global CD sales rose to 140 million in 1986 and continued to rise, passing one billion in 1992 and two billion in 1996 (ibid). It is easy to gloss over figures when reading so please look at them again to recognise this extraordinary growth. Starting at 5 million sales in 1983, global CD sales rose by 135 million (2,400 per cent) in 3 years, increased a further sevenfold in the next 6 years before doubling again within 4 years.

If we consider the sales trends within the recording industry in the first half of the 1980s we are able to ascertain the effect that the introduction of the CD had on record sales revenue. In 1981, global record sales reached a then-record $12.3 billion before falling 9 per cent to $11.2 billion the following year. They increased to $12 billion in 1983, remained flat in 1984 and increased slightly in 1985 to $12.25 billion. Record sales then began to accelerate rapidly: $14 billion, $17 billion and $20.3 billion in the following 3 years (IFPI 2007: 113). Even if we assume modest growth without the invention of the CD, a significant proportion of this growth can be explained by the emergence of the new format, in two respects.

First, a large proportion of CD sales came not from new albums such as *Brothers in Arms* but from people buying old albums on CD to replace their battered old vinyl copies. Since Soundscan was introduced as a means of measuring record sales in the US (1991), the biggest selling artist has been country star Garth Brooks. However, the second biggest selling artist has been The Beatles, a band who broke up twenty-one years before Soundscan was introduced (Nielsen/Billboard 2011). 'Catalogue sales' have thus always been a large, perhaps the largest, part of CD sales. Thus, when analysing record sales in the 1980s and 1990s, it is possible to see that the record industry reaped the benefit not only from the sales of new releases but also from the resale of old releases, in effect duplicating the sales of the 1960s and 1970s. As we have entered the 2000s, however, the benefit from catalogue sales has declined, as listeners no longer have vinyl to replace.[6] Furthermore, as listeners can easily convert their own CDs to digital files, the emergence of the new MP3 format has not forced listeners to replace their old-format recordings in the way that CD compelled the repurchasing of vinyl.

There is a second reason why the introduction of the CD had such a positive impact on record industry revenues, however, and that relates to retail price. Knopper argues that 'the CD was an opportunity to change consumers' expectations about what music should cost' (2009: 32). Because of their high-tech allure, CDs were expensive. When they were introduced in the US, the initial price of a CD was $16.95, in contrast to the well-established top price for a vinyl album of $8.98 (ibid.: 31). The price of a CD carried similar premiums in Europe and Japan. It is not hard to see how, if sales remain steady, doubling the price of your primary product will improve your revenue. For a variety of reasons, however (the elimination of the minimum recommended price, the decline of the album format, the pressures of the digital marketplace), the retail price of CDs has fallen steeply during the 2000s. Although not a complete explanation for the declining value of record sales (the volume of sales has decreased also), this downward pressure does contribute to the reduction of the industry's bottom line.

The changing music industry

Rather than merely being the result of piracy, therefore, there are a variety of alternative explanations for the fall in recording industry revenue during the 2000s. However, the decline in revenues cannot be entirely explained by recourse to the issues outlined in the previous section. We also need to consider how the emergence of digital music has changed the nature of the music industry more generally and what the implications of these changes may be. It is not merely a case of unauthorised MP3 files eating into legitimate music consumption, or of sales being displaced by competing products. Rather, some more fundamental changes are occurring, to both music production and music consumption. In this section, I will briefly outline the most significant changes.

In the 'old style' music industry, record labels made their money in three ways. First, they funded the recording of music. Recording an album is (or maybe was) an expensive task and beyond the reach of most musicians. Labels would provide the capital required for recording and marketing an album and, in return for putting up the money, owned the rights to the recordings and received the lion's share of any profits made. Second, they distributed records.[7] Getting roughly the right number of records from manufacturing plants to all of the stores selling records in a territory is (or maybe was) an immense task, requiring warehousing, shipping, a sales force, inventory management and so on. Only big companies could achieve the economies of scale required to do this efficiently and so, as well as distributing the records that their own label produced, the majors would also distribute records produced by smaller labels, charging a fee to do so. Finally, labels made money from exploiting intellectual property rights (IPRs). Since the 1980s, the exploitation of IPRs has become a much more significant part of the cultural industries generally and the music industry is no exception. Licensing recordings to things such as TV shows, films, advertisements and digital games has become a core part of record label business.

While the exploitation of IPRs continues to be an important source of revenue for the major labels, the emergence of a digital music market has affected the labels' roles in both the production and distribution of music. With regard to production, it has been suggested that the costs of recording an album have reduced considerably in recent years, putting the price of recording an album within the reach of many bands (Wikstrom 2009: 123). Perhaps more importantly, the emergence of social media, of the iTunes store and of sites such as Tunecore that perform many of the functions of record labels, has reduced the inherent promotion costs associated with releasing a record. Whereas in the past the record labels gained their strength from being the only players with sufficient capital to record and publicise an album, the Internet has created a somewhat viable alternative to options for artists seeking to release music.

It is important not to overstate this argument, however. Despite these changes to record production, the major labels have remained significant players in the production of new music, with the majority of successful records still being released by labels (van Buskirk 2010). Changes to music distribution may have a more serious long-term effect on the majors, however. The strong position of the major labels in the old industry arises more from their control of distribution than the records they produced, as the majors distributed not just their own releases but also those of many independent labels. This meant that not only did they make some money on virtually every record sold, they also had significant influence over the inventory listings of independent labels (Negus 1999: 58–9). The rise of online music has affected the retailing, and thus the distribution of music quite considerably. The decline in physical sales in major markets has decimated the number of independent record stores, reduced the number of record chain stores and reduced the shelf-space given to records by supermarket retailers such as Wal-Mart. For obvious reasons, distributing digital files is less capital intensive and alternative distributors such as Tunecore and Bandcamp, as well as independent record labels, can get their releases into the major online retail stores – most notably iTunes and Amazon –without the help of the major distributors. Distribution has ceased to be the cash cow it once was, and many of the major labels have now outsourced their distribution.

At the same time as these structural changes within popular music production, fascinating shifts are occurring within popular music consumption. For our present purposes, the most important factor is the decline of the album format and the re-emergence of the single. Invented in the late 1940s, the 45 rpm single became an important foundation in the history of popular music, providing a cheap and fairly disposable commodity that could be bought by teenagers chasing the latest pop trends. It is not unreasonable to suggest that rock and roll would not have developed in the 1950s without the invention of the single. However, as Keightley (2004) explains, it was the development of the long-playing album that proved fundamental to the sustainability of the popular music industry from the 1960s onwards. Not only were albums more expensive than singles, but the associated rock ideologies of the album – being a more sustained artistic work and career longevity depending on creating a body of work defined in albums – meant that labels could rely on catalogue album sales to cover the investment risks of developing new artists. The single remained important, though, in genre terms (put very crudely, pop is constructed around singles, rock around albums), in acting as promotion for albums (Fox and Kochanowski 2007) and, importantly for the current argument, in creating an accessible commodity to encourage children into the habit of buying music. However, because of the profit margins associated with CD albums, several commentators argue that the major labels consciously depressed the singles market in the 1990s to encourage young people to buy CDs instead (Fairchild 2008: 69; Knopper 2009: 106; Kot 2009: 45). The number of singles sold globally fell from 800 million in 1983 (first year of the CD) to 370 million in 2000 (at the height of the teen pop boom) to 233 million in 2003 (IFPI 2011: 87). By contrast, Britney Spears, The Backstreet Boys and N'Sync sold a combined 96 million CDs in the US at the height of the teen pop boom (Knopper 2009: 81).

One frequent criticism of the record industry during this period was that an individual had to buy an expensive full-length CD for one or two great tracks and lots of filler material (see Samuels 2011, for a rather late reiteration of the complaint). The emergence of digital music has significantly shifted this dynamic. Now that fans can select which tracks from an album to download, we are witnessing a dramatic increase in the number of individual tracks being downloaded and a decline in album sales. Since digital sales were included in IFPI numbers in 2004, singles sales have risen from 346 million to 1.636 billion in 2009 (IFPI 2011: 87). In the longer term, the re-emergence of the single as a cultural force may have a major impact on what kind of music gets released, with artistic careers becoming constructed around more frequent, but smaller, single or EP-style releases, rather than periodic album releases. What impact this has on the structure of the music industry is difficult to predict, but it will have significant economic implications for the major labels as singles are much less profitable (and less sustainable in catalogue terms) than albums.[8]

The shift in music consumption towards the single track neatly captures the paradox in which the labels find themselves. Recorded music today is actually extremely popular: there were almost three billion recorded music transactions in 2009, and this number excludes all of the unauthorised downloads and the use of streaming services that listeners also use. The problem for the labels is that people are choosing to consume music in smaller chunks, and thus most of the transactions are actually quite small and less profitable than CD purchases.

The major label merry-go-round

The emergence of online music has created a period of instability in the recording industry and this has resulted, among other things, in a period dominated by discussions of takeovers and mergers among the major labels. At the dawn of the new century there were six major labels, but then the Big Six became the Big Five, then the Big Four, and it is altogether possible that we shall see the Big Three in the not too distant future. In this section, I shall briefly outline the changing nature of the majors' oligopoly before considering the implications for the current Big Four.

What is now the largest of the four majors, Universal Music Group (UMG) first came into being in 1996 when, the year after Canadian drinks manufacturer Seagram bought an 80 per cent stake in MCA records, it rebranded MCA as UMG. At that point, UMG had a global market share of just 6 per cent (*Music & Copyright* 1997) but it became much more powerful in 1998 when it took over one of the other big six labels, PolyGram and merged operations to create UMG 2.0 (Wikstrom 2009:74). This gave UMG a position of market dominance entering the new century.

The first merger talks of the new century occurred in its first month. Following the announcement of the gigantic merger between AOL and Time Warner, there were discussions to merge EMI and WMG (Warner Music Group). Merging these two companies would have produced the largest major label with a market share of 27.7 per cent (compared to UMG's 21.1 per cent). However, the European Commission was reluctant to approve the deal, in particular raising concerns about the new organisation's monopolisation of music publishing, which would have exceeded a 50 per cent market share in some territories. The merger application was withdrawn in October 2000 (Southall 2009: 100–12). Immediately following the withdrawal, however, the German major label Bertelsmann began negotiating a merger with EMI; wary of the regulatory hurdles, however, discussions were abandoned in May 2001 (ibid.: 116–18).

Athough 2002 was a quiet year for merger talks, 2003 was the opposite. It began with further discussions between EMI and WMG, but by July WMG was negotiating with Bertelsmann. Then, in September, EMI offered $2.5 billion for WMG, in a deal that excluded Warner's publishing division so it was expected to overcome the regulatory issues. However, November 2003 turned out to be a bad month for EMI. First, Sony and Bertelsmann announced they were merging. The merger of these two major labels would create the second largest major, just behind UMG, and made it less likely that a merger between EMI and WMG would also be approved. Then, in the same month, the former CEO of Vivendi-Universal, Edgar Bronfman Jr. made an offer to buy WMG for $2.8 billion which, without the threat of regulatory scrutiny was more attractive to WMG's owners and accepted. EMI was left on the sidelines and became viewed as the weakest of the majors (ibid.: 155–61).

Sony's merger with BMG was approved in July 2004 (creating SonyBMG)[9] while, later that year, the new owners of WMG released a share issue to transform Warner into a public company. In 2006, however, EMI returned with a new bid for WMG, this time offering $4.23 billion. WMG rejected that offered and issued a counter-offer to buy EMI. EMI rejected and issued a second offer for Warner, who rejected it and, just for good measure, offered a second counter offer. In June, however, following an appeal by independent labels at the European Court of First Instance, the EU reopened its investigation into the merger of Sony and BMG, pouring cold water on further merger discussions (ibid.: 180–2).

Despite this, early in 2007, Warner approached EMI again but the offer was rejected. However, by this time, EMI was seen as very weak and susceptible to takeover, with rumours of offers and takeovers appearing almost daily throughout the summer. Finally, in August 2007, the venture capitalist firm Terra Firma, led by businessman Guy Hands, purchased EMI for £2.4 billion (ibid.: 204–7). You might expect that to be the end of the matter, but no: Hands' time in charge of EMI was little short of disastrous and it came to an end in early 2011. Having borrowed billions of dollars from investment bank Citigroup, it became apparent that Terra Firma was likely to default on its repayment terms, so Citi seized control of EMI and reduced its debt-load from $3.4 billion to $1.2 billion (Christman 2011). It has been speculated that Terra Firma's investment in EMI has resulted in the largest private equity loss in corporate history (Peoples 2011). In November 2011, Citi agreed to sell the recording division of EMI to UMG, although this remains subject to regulatory scrutiny in both the US and the EU. Given that the takeover would give UMG approximately 40 per cent of the global market, and more than 50 per cent in some territories, it is by no means certain that the deal will be approved.

Finally, seemingly to pre-empt the EMI sale, Edgar Bronfman Jr. sold WMG to Access Industries in May 2011 for $3.3 billion (Peoples and Christman 2011). WMG is once again a private rather than a public company and were one of the bidders for EMI.

As can be seen from the preceding discussion, EMI and Warner have been the central actors in the discourse about mergers and takeovers. In part, this reflects their position not only as the two smallest majors, but also as the two 'standalone' or 'independent' majors that are not, unlike Sony and Universal, divisions of bigger entertainment corporations that can insulate them against fluctuations in the industry.[10] Added to this, until 2011 the two standalone majors were also publicly listed companies with a legal duty to report financial data every three months. This regular publicising of the financial tribulations experienced at major labels has contributed to the public perception of these companies, and EMI in particular, being in serious difficulties.[11]

The difficult years have thus been experienced by all of the majors, but they have also been affected to different extents. Given that profits have been falling, market share has become the most important way for the majors to judge their company's success relative to its competitors. Considering global market share demonstrates the relative fortunes of the major labels.[12] The biggest winner has been Universal Music Group: following its merger with PolyGram in 1998, UMG had a market share of 22 per cent, which it had increased to 29.3 per cent by 2010. With its merger and subsequent buy-out of BMG, Sony Music Entertainment has consolidated its position as the second largest major, increasing its market share from 14.4 per cent in 2000 to 22.8 per cent in 2010. Warner Music Group started the century badly, its market share falling from 15 per cent in 1996 to 11.3 per cent in 2004. Since then it has strengthened, however, and had a 14.8 per cent market share in 2010, down slightly from a high of 15.3 per cent the previous year. Finally, EMI has been the worst performing of the majors: consistently reporting roughly 14 per cent of market share throughout the 1990s, its share steadily declined to 10 per cent in 2009, improving slightly to 10.6 per cent in 2010.

Major label strategies

So, how have the major labels sought to address the challenges they have faced in the twenty-first century? First, it is important to recognise that all of the majors are able to rely on more than merely record sales to make a profit as they are also attached to music publishing companies.[13] Publishing – exploiting the rights of *songs* rather than *records* – has declined a little in the last decade but not nearly as much as recorded music. Thus, short term at least, losses in the recorded music division can be countered by income from the publishing division. Labels are also able to exploit their extensive back catalogues, licensing to streaming services such as Spotify, to conventional radio and to other entertainment media such as TV shows. The exploitation of IPRs is currently perhaps more important to the majors than in the past, and the recording industry has also attempted to extend the duration of copyright in sound recordings in the EU from 50 years to 95 years (an extension to 70 years was agreed in September 2011).

Perhaps the most obvious response to the market difficulties has been the drastic job cuts that have affected the recording industry. There have been several announcements of major cuts over the last decade: EMI announced 1,800 job losses in 2002, a further 1,500 in 2004 and between 1,500 and 2,000 in 2008 (Southall 2009: 141,165, 239); Knopper (2009: 205) suggests that Sony's workforce was reduced by 2,400 between 2000 and 2003 (although this could include jobs lost as a result of the Bertelsmann merger); Warner cut 20 per cent of its workforce (1,000 jobs) following the Bronfman Jr. takeover (Goodman 2010: 189), with another 400 losses announced in 2007 (Southall 2009: 208). As well as these headline-grabbing losses, there have also been small, incremental, losses (Universal, for example, announced 60 losses in January 2011 and 50 losses in January 2010). Overall, 29 rounds of job cuts were announced by the majors between 2004 and 2008 (Barthel 2008). Wikstrom (2009: 65) suggests that the record industry has seen a 25 per cent reduction in its workforce since 2000.

Labels have also significantly reduced the number of artists that they have on their rosters: while cutting its workforce by 20 per cent in 2003, Warners also reduced its roster by 30 per cent (Goodman 2010: 189); EMI reduced its roster by 25 per cent (400 acts) in 2002 and a further 20 per cent in 2004 (Southall 2009: 142, 165). They have also reduced the number of records they release and been involved in extensive cost-cutting. For example, the amount of money spent on recording albums has been reduced (Leyshon (2009: 1326) suggests that it has fallen to as low as £20,000), as has the money spent on producing videos and doing promotional work. Knopper suggests that the average cost of a video for an MTV level artist at a major label has fallen from roughly $1 million to $100,000 and the cost of photo sessions 'drop from $25,000 to $5,000 in just two or three years' (2009: 208–9). The 2000s has witnessed a significant amount of belt-tightening in the record industry.

The major labels have also been seeking new ways of making money in the 'new music industry'. Perhaps the most widely known of these has been the '360 deal', in which the label receives income from a wide range of artist activities (such as touring and merchandising) and not just from the sale and licensing of recorded music. These deals have been controversial, with many artist managers arguing that they take money from the artist without justification (see Marshall 2012), but they are now established as the new standard contract for artists in the recording industry. As evidence of the new direction, most of the major labels have been involved in some kind of internal reorganisation, forming artist services divisions and developing, or buying in, artist management skills. It is clear that the major labels realise that they will not be able to rely solely on recorded music for their survival but, rather, will have to be involved in a wide range of music activities. In recognition of this, all of the majors have stopped referring

to themselves as 'record labels' or 'record companies', preferring to call themselves 'music companies'.

Conclusion

So, is it all over for the major labels? There are certainly commentators, both in
the music industry and on the sidelines, that believe it is. And, as outlined in this
chapter, there is much evidence to suggest that the majors are getting considerably
weaker. The recording industry itself is shrinking and, when presented alongside
the somewhat exaggerated live music boom, this makes the recording industry's
future, compared to that of both live music and music publishing, seem bleak.
Furthermore, the declining concentration of the recording industry makes the major
labels relatively weaker than they were a decade ago. The major labels are left
with a declining share of a declining industry.

It is, however, rather premature to be sounding the death knell of the major
labels. As the table compiled by John Williamson in Chapter 2 shows, the four
major labels still feature in the five biggest music companies by turnover. And,
while Apple is obviously a very significant player in the new music industry,
controlling at least two-thirds of online music sales in the US (Smith and Fowler
2010), Billboard estimated its income from the iTunes store amounts to only $570
million (Christman 2008).[14] The US recording industry may be declining, but it
was still worth $4.2 billion in 2010 and is showing signs of stabilising following
years of steep decline (early indications are that music sales actually increased in
2011). Being on a label also remains the most important characteristic of successful
artists (van Buskirk 2010) and being signed to a major remains the goal of three-
quarters of unsigned artists (Reverbnation 2010). While the music industry is
changing, forcing the labels to change with it, the labels have sufficient expertise,
capital and power to be able to weather the storm as they did in the 1930s and
early 1980s. They may not be as important as they were in the 1990s but they
will remain important players in the future music industry.

Maintaining a historical perspective can thus provide a more balanced view of
the difficulties currently being experienced by the major labels. Labels are clearly
not as dominant as they were in the 1990s but it is plausible that it is actually the
1990s that were the historical anomaly and that the 2000s have witnessed
something of a return to a historical equilibrium. It is rare to see a historical
perspective being taken within the recording industry. The air of crisis pervading
the recording industry is real, however, and the lack of direction exhibited by the
major labels illustrates that they have had to be dragged kicking and screaming
into the Internet age. Even though the crisis has been experienced most acutely
in the US, it has significant implications for the local recording industries all around
the world, including those presented in this volume. For example, there may be
increased pressure on local companies to prioritise international stars (on whom
the global company has invested significant money) in an attempt to counter
declining sales in major markets. Or there could be pressure to impose 360 style
contracts on local artists.[15] All of the major labels have a presence, and an

influence, in most of the territories discussed in the case studies and the pressure being experienced in the global centres of the recording industry will influence the strategies used by the majors' local branches and the instructions being sent from the global headquarters.

Notes

1 A retail value of $12.3 billion in 1985 (IFPI 2006a: 113) is equivalent to $24.9 billion in 2010.
2 This is not a criticism of the IFPI, as their Recording Industry in Numbers publication does provide data on a country-by-country basis.
3 To a certain extent this prefaces later attempts by the recording industry to make ISPs responsible for the actions of those using the ISP's services.
4 At least one major label did recognise the potential of Napster: while in the midst of its legal battles, Napster was offered a $60 million loan from Bertelsmann in exchange for a majority stake in Napster. This resulted in the bizarre situation where one of the plaintiffs in the Napster trial was the majority owner of the defendant. Unsurprisingly, the investment was unsuccessful: by September 2007, Bertelsmann had paid $400 million in damages to its major label competitors (Kot 2009: 37–8).
5 For example, referring to the Forrester 2004 survey, the IFPI claim that because 36 per cent of people say they buy fewer CDs because of file sharing and only 10 per cent buy more, then the negative impact of file-sharing outweighs any positive impact by three to one (IFPI 2004). It is impossible to deduce this without knowing the purchasing habits of the 36 per cent and the 10 per cent – if the 10 per cent buy 5 times as many records as before, and the 36 per cent only buy 0.75 as many records as before, then a net positive could accrue, especially if the 10 per cent were already heavy consumers of music.
6 The benefits of catalogue sales have not disappeared entirely, however, and catalogue sales form a large proportion of iTunes sales. Indeed, a report by accountants KPMG suggested that EMI had actually *lost* £750 million releasing new music between 2002 and 2007, and would have been considerably better off just selling their back catalogue (Southall 2009: 244). The major record labels have found ways of encouraging fans to rebuy their CDs through the promise of 'remastering' original recordings, or offering 'deluxe editions' of albums with bonus live performances or studio outtakes.
7 Technically, the four major distributors (EMI, Sony, Universal and WEA) are separate companies from the major record labels but, as their names suggest, the distributors are owned by the labels (or, more specifically, the labels and the distributors are owned by the same parent companies).
8 Indeed, the individual 'track' – which is what is actually being downloaded rather than a 'single' – is even less profitable than physical singles were. When calculating overall sales volume, the IFPI used to weight three singles as the equivalent of one album. Today, it weights ten tracks as equivalent.
9 Sony bought out BMG's share in 2008 and renamed the company as Sony Music Entertainment.
10 EMI demerged from Thorn in 1996; WMG split from Time Warner with Bronfman's purchase in 2003.
11 This is not to suggest that EMI has not been in serious difficulties, but the revenue and profit for all major labels will fluctuate on a quarterly basis due to release schedules and the potential for a star artist to be late delivering an album. Having to publicly announce these difficulties every few months has not helped generate investor or consumer confidence.

12 The IFPI collected global market share data from 1998 until 2005, when it stopped due to disagreements over how to calculate market share for digital tracks. Since 2006 the trade journal *Music & Copyright* has provided global market share data. All of the data used in this table comes from *Music & Copyright* reports, although they relied on IFPI data up to 2005.

13 Conventionally, the major labels are actually part of 'music groups' incorporating a recorded music division, a music publishing division and, increasingly, an artist management division.

14 Of course, Apple's overall profit is much bigger due to sales of the iPod, iPad and iPhone and it thus yields more power than the profit figure implies. However, it is a reasonable contrast, as Sony's figure of $6.29 billion solely relates to music and not Playstations, CD players etc.

15 For example, in 2010 the Finnish Musicians' Union brought a legal case arguing that 360 contracts were illegal under Finnish business law. See Decision of Market Court of Finland in Suomen Musiikkojen Liitto ry vs. Spin-Farm Oy, 265/09/M7 (22 December 2010) (available online at: www.oikeus.fi/markkinaoikeus/53337. htm).

Bibliography

Anderson, N. (2009) Has the RIAA Sued 18,000 people . . . or 35,000? *Arstechnica*. Available online at: http://arstechnica.com/tech-policy/news/2009/07/has-the-riaa-sued-18000-people-or-35000.ars (accessed 19 January 2012).

Anderson, B. and Frenz, M. (2007) The Impact of Music Downloads and P2P File-sharing on the Purchase of Music: A Study for Industry Canada. Department of Management, Birkbeck, University of London. Unpublished manuscript.

Bangeman, E. (2008) Apple Passes Wal-Mart, Now #1 Music Retailer in US, *Arstechnica.com*. Available online at: http://arstechnica.com/apple/news/2008/04/apple-passes-wal-mart-now-1-music-retailer-in-us.ars (accessed 19 January 2012).

Barthel, M. (2008) How Quickly is the Music Industry Shrinking? *Idolator. com*. Available at: http://idolator.com/5069414/how-quickly-is-the-music-industry-shrinking (accessed 21 December 2011).

Bruno, A. (2011) Labels Reach Deal with ISPs on Antipiracy Effort. *Billboard.biz*. Available online at: www.billboard.biz/bbbiz/industry/legal-and-management/labels-reach-deal-with-isps-on-antipiracy-1005267702.story (accessed 19 January 2012).

Christman, E. (2008) Dollars and Cents: iTunes Store, *Billboard.biz*. Available online at: www.billboard.biz/bbbiz/content_display/magazine/upfront/e3ia99a189e2d22c6c 7e6b9697d33f76984 (accessed 19 January 2012).

Christman, E. (2011) How Citigroup Outfoxed Guy Hands in its Takeover of EMI, *Billboard.biz*, 3 February. Available online at: www.billboard.biz/bbbiz/industry/record-labels/how-citigroup-outfoxed-guy-hands-in-its-1005020642.story (accessed 29 January 2012).

DEG (2003) DVD Software Sales Drive Video Industry to Record Breaking $20 Billion Year. Available online at: www.dvdinformation.com/news/press/010903.htm (accessed 19 January 2012).

ESA (2011) *Industry Facts*. Available online at: www.theesa.com/facts/index.asp (accessed 19 January 2012).

Fairchild, D. (2008) *Pop Idols and Pirates: Mechanisms of Consumption and the Global Circulation of Popular Music*, Aldershot, Hants.: Ashgate.

Fox, M. (2005) Market Power in Music Retailing: The Case of Wal-Mart, *Popular Music and Society*, 28(4): 501–19.

Fox, M.A. and Kochanowski, P. (2007) Multi-stage Markets in the Recording Industry, *Popular Music and Society*, 30(2): 173–95.

Frith, S. (2001) The Popular Music Industry, in S. Frith, W. Straw and J. Street (eds) *The Cambridge Companion to Popular Music*, Cambridge: Cambridge University Press, pp. 26–52.

Frith, S. (2002) Illegality and the Music Industry, in M. Talbot (ed.) *The Business of Music*, Liverpool: Liverpool University Press. pp. 195–216.

Goodman, F. (2010) *Fortune's Fool: Edgar Bronfman Jr., Warner Music, and an Industry in Crisis*. New York: Simon & Schuster.

IFPI (2003) *The Recording Industry in Numbers 2003*. London: IFPI.

IFPI (2004) *Record Industry Steps Up Action Against Illegal Music File-Sharing and Urges People to Buy Legally Online*. Available online at: www.ifpi.org/content/section_news/20041007.html (accessed 29 January 2012).

IFPI (2006a) *The Recording Industry in Numbers 2006*. London: IFPI.

IFPI (2006b) *Recording Industry Launches Fresh Wave of Actions Against Illegal File-Sharing*. 17 October. Available online at: www.ifpi.org/content/section_news/20061017.html (accessed 29 January 2012)

IFPI (2009) *IFPI Responds to New UK Music Downloading Study*. 4 November. Available online at: www.ifpi.org/content/section_news/20091104.html (accessed 29 January 2012).

IFPI (2011) *The Recording Industry in Numbers 2011*. London: IFPI.

Keightley, K. (2004) Long Play: Adult-oriented Popular Music and the Temporal Logics of the Post-War Sound Recording Industry in the USA, *Media Culture and Society*, 26(3): 375–91.

King, B. (2001) *Farewell Free Downloads*. Wired.com. Available online at: http://wired.com/news/print/0,1294,44412,00.html (accessed 19 January 2012).

Knopper, S (2009) *Appetite for Self-Destruction: The Spectacular Crash of the Record Industry in the Digital Age*. London, Simon & Schuster.

Kot, G. (2009) *Ripped: How the Wired Generation Revolutionised Music*. New York: Scribner.

Kretschmer, M., Klimis, G.M., Wallis, R. (2001) Music in Electronic Markets: An Empirical Study, *New Media and Society*, 3(4): 417–41.

Lefsetz, B. (2011) *Mediocrity*. Available online at: http://lefsetz.com/wordpress/index.php/archives/2011/05/23/mediocrity/ (accessed 19 January 2012).

Leyshon, A. (2009) The Software Slump? Digital Music, the Democratisation of Technology, and the Decline of the Recording Studio Sector within the Musical Economy. *Environment and Planning*, 41: 1309–31.

Lieberwitz, S. (2011) *Copyright Issues, Copying and MP3 File Sharing*. Available at: www.utdallas.edu/~liebowit (accessed 19 January 2012).

Leunig, S.M. (2000) A&M Records V Napster Inc: The Fate of Peer-to-peer File Sharing Technology, *Intellectual Property Law Bulletin* (Fall 2000).

McBride, S. and Smith, E. (2008) Music Industry to Abandon Mass Suits, *Wall Street Journal*, 19 December. Available online at: http://online.wsj.com/article/SB122966038836021137.html (accessed 19 January 2012).

McCourt, T. and Bukart, P. (2003) When Creators, Corporations and Consumers Collide: Napster and the Development of On-Line Music Distribution, *Media, Culture and Society*, 25(3): 333–50.

Marshall, L. (2004a) The Effects of Piracy upon the Music Industry: A Case Study of Bootlegging, *Media, Culture and Society*, 26(2): 163–81.

Marshall, L. (2004b) Infringers, in S. Frith and L. Marshall (eds) *Music and Copyright* (2nd edn), Edinburgh: Edinburgh University Press, pp. 189–207.

Marshall, L. (2012 forthcoming) 360 Deals and the 'New' Music Industry, *European Journal of Cultural Studies*.

Music & Copyright (1997) Universal: Dramatic US success and a Growing World Presence. *Music & Copyright*, 119 (27 August), 12–13, 7. London: *Financial Times*.

MusicAlly (2009) Report Claims P2P Users Buy More Music, Not Less. Available online at: http://musically.com/blog/2009/04/21/report-claims-p2p-users-buy-more-music-not-less (accessed 17 August 2011).

Negus, K. (1999) *Music Genres and Corporate Cultures*. London: Routledge.

Nielsen/Billboard (2011) 2010 Music Industry Report. Available online at: www.businesswire.com/news/home/20110106006565/en/Nielsen-Company-Billboard%E2%80%99s-2010-Music-Industry-Report (accessed 29 January 2102).

Oberholzer, F. and Strumpf, K. (2004) The Effect of File-sharing on Record Sales: An Empirical Analysis. University of North Carolina. Unpublished manuscript.

Pareles, J. (2001) Envisaging the Industry as the Loser on Napster, *New York Times*, 14 February.

Peoples, G. (2011) Is Terra Firma's Investment in EMI the Biggest-Ever Private Equity Loss? *Billboard.biz*. Available online at: www.billboard.biz/bbbiz/industry/record-labels/is-terra-firma-s-investment-in-emi-the-biggest-1005024732.story (accessed 19 January 2012).

Peoples, G. and Christman, E. (2011) It's official: Access Industries to Acquire Warner Music Group for $3.3bn, *Billobard.biz*, 6 May. Available online at: www.billboard.biz/bbbiz/industry/record-labels/access-industries-to-aquire-warner-music-1005172972.story (accessed 29 January 2012).

Price, J. (2010) How People Use Nielson to Hurt Musicians, *Tunecore blog*. Available online at: http://blog.tunecore.com/2010/01/how-people-use-nielsen-to-hurt-musicians.html (accessed 18 June 2011).

Reverbnation (2011) Survey Results: 75% of Indie Artists Seek a Label Deal – Sony Top Label of Choice. Available online at: http://blog.reverbnation.com/2011/03/29/survey-results-75-of-indie-artists-seek-a-label-deal-sony-top-label-of-choice (accessed 15 June 2011).

Sameuls, J. (2011) *Spotify's US Launch Highlights the Good, the Bad, and the Promise of Subscription Based Services*. EFF.com. Available online at: www.eff.org/deeplinks/2011/07/spotifys-u-s-launch-highlights-good-bad-and (accessed 19 January 2012).

Shachtman, N. (2001) What if Napster Was the Answer? *Wired*.com. Available online at: www.wired.com/news/print/0,45234,00.html (accessed 19 January 2012).

Smith E. and Fowler, G (2010) Amazon Can't Dent iTunes, *Wall Street Journal*, 16 December. Available online at: http://online.wsj.com/article/SB10001424052748704073804576023913889536374.html (accessed 19 January 2012).

Southall, B. (2009) *The Rise and Fall of EMI Records*. London: Omnibus.

TIA (2010) *2010 ICT Market Review & Forecast*. Available online at: www.tiaonline.org/market_intelligence/mrf2010/index_MRF_page_1.cfm (accessed 17 August 2011).

Van Buskirk, E. (2010) What's Wrong with Music Biz, Per Ultimate Insider. *Wired.com*. www.wired.com/epicenter/2010/07/tom-silverman-proposes-radically-transparent-music-business (accessed 12 January 2011).

Wikstrom, P. (2009) *The Music Industry*. Cambridge: Polity.
Wired.com (2001) Napster Eclipsed by Newcomers. Available online at: www.wired.com/techbiz/media/news/2001/09/46596 (accessed 19 January 2012).
Zentner, A. (2006) Measuring the Effect of File Sharing on Music Purchases, *Journal of Law and Economics*, April: 63–90.

Part II

The international recording industries

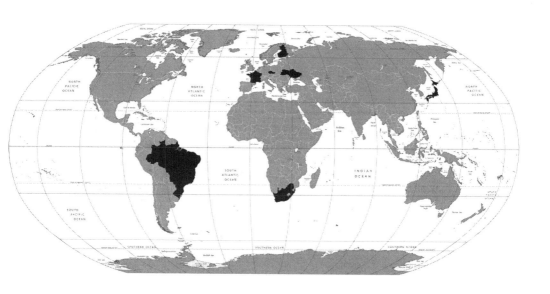

Brazil

Population:	203.4 million (5th)
Languages:	Portuguese
Capital:	Brasilia (pop 3.8 million)
Currency:	Real (BRL). $1 = 1.77BRL
GDP:	$2.09 tn (7th)
GDP (PPP)/capita:	$11,127 (75th)
Median age:	29.3

GDP data from World Bank

Population data from CIA world factbook

Exchange rate used by IFPI (2011) (source: Oanda)

2010 Recorded music market

Overall income:	$228.5m (R$404.5m)	
World ranking:	10th	
	Income	**World ranking**
Physical sales	$172.5m	10th
Digital sales	$38.1m	12th
Performance rights	$18.0m	12th

Historical recorded music market ($m, at IFPI's 2010 exchange rate)

	1999	2000	2001	2002	2003	2004	2005	2006	2007	2008	2009
Trade Value			398.4	427.9	353.7	415.6	364.4	284.9	212.8	230.2	231.3
Retail Value	749.3	685.3	597.5	641.9	530.5	619.4	541.1				

Proportion of domestic repertoire (market value, physical sales only)

1991*	1995*	2000	2005	2010
61%	63%	75%	70%	59%

*based on units sold, not market value

Album certification levels

	2010	**1999**
Gold	Domestic – 40,000	Domestic – 100,000
	International – 20,000	International – 100,000
Platinum	Domestic – 80,000	Domestic – 250,000
	International – 40,000	International – 250,000

5 Brazil

Sam Howard-Spink

Brazil, the perennial 'once and future country' that, despite its vast size and abundant natural resources, has for so long sat on the sidelines of international affairs, is poised at last to fulfil its potential in the twenty-first century. It has one of the fastest growing economies on the planet, with ample room for expansion; it is one of the four recognised giants of the developing world, the B in BRIC;[1] thanks to domestic ethanol production, it benefits from unparalleled energy independence and, as keeper of the Amazon, environmental policy is taken seriously. Above all else, however, Brazil's future lies in its human capital, with a rapidly expanding middle class of networked, entrepreneurial and creative citizens. Extraordinary inequalities of wealth are still the norm but, today, the trend is towards more progressive redistribution and, for the first time in recent history, expat Brazilians are returning home in more numbers than are leaving.

The country's recent economic acceleration notwithstanding, Brazil has long occupied a unique space in the global imagination thanks to its distinctive melange of creative forms and forces. Ask any outsider what they know about the country and the likely answers will be samba and soccer, not its status as the powerhouse behind a newly energised South-American bloc. Music is arguably the country's the most potent symbol in this regard, 'more successful than any other area of Brazilian culture in generating syntheses that are simultaneously local and cosmopolitan, popular and experimental, pleasurable and political . . . the least colonised and the most Africanised branch of Brazilian popular culture, as well as the most successful in disseminating itself not only within Brazil but also around the world' (Robert Stam, quoted in Dunn 2001).

More than this, however, the songs, genres and dances that are the product and raw material of centuries of cultural hybridisation are essential to how Brazilians perceive themselves as a people in relation to the rest of the world. Brazil has an extraordinarily rich musical culture, with a deep history and endless vivacity. Brazilians take their music seriously (there were street protests over the introduction of electric guitars to samba in the 1960s) and they are proud of their capacity to generate new cultural forms through processes of hybridisation, a discourse with its own localised critical theory of *antropófagia* or 'cultural cannibalism' (Andrade 1928; Dunn 2001) and Lusotropicalism (Almeida 2008). Such accounts are deeply woven into contemporary Brazilian perspectives on their own country, which has seen centuries of colonisation and its attendant slave trade, the oppression of indigenous peoples, and a repressive military dictatorship that lasted from 1964 to 1985, as well as the tradition of carnival (which for a few days a year throws a rope across the chasm between the haves and have-nots), the law-unto-themselves *favelas* (hillside shantytowns), even its national soccer team – all of this and more is documented, argued over and celebrated in a multitude of Brazilian musical genres and standards.

At the same time, music divides Brazilians along lines of geography, race and, especially, class, the deepest fault line of all in a country with one of the widest disparities in wealth in the world. Brazil's recorded music industry in the late twentieth century reflected and even contributed to these schisms. By the end of the 1990s there existed a clear bifurcation between Brazil's two music industries: at the centre was the major label CD business, catering to Brazil's small middle and upper classes. On the periphery, however, there has long been a swirling mix of semi-formal, informal, and unregulated black (now also called 'grey') markets made up of myriad music-based enterprises, collectives, entrepreneurs and musicians catering to the much larger population living in or near poverty. Over the past decade this cleavage has remained in place, but each side has undergone enormous structural change in line with the rise of digitisation, networked computers, and mobile phones.

Given its polarised nature and the dramatic changes experienced in the last decade, this chapter can only offer a glimpse of the dynamics of the recording industry in Brazil. In later sections the fortunes of the major labels and the innovative new business models developed in the independent sector are discussed. To begin, however, the most conspicuous trope in discussions of Brazil's record industry – piracy – should be addressed.

Pirate nation

Piracy, or the unlicensed reproduction and distribution of musical recordings, has remained the chief frame for the discussion of music economies in Brazil since at least the 1990s. Intellectual property (IP) generally has become an increasingly controversial issue in Brazil's recent history, especially with regard to international relations with the United States, Brazil's largest trading partner until 2010 (it's now China). From the 1970s to the 1990s, numerous disputes arose concerning pharmaceutical patents, which were illegal in Brazil until 1996, and technology importation which, to foster local industrial innovation, is highly taxed. Copyrights on music and film recordings did not begin to dominate IP trade debates until the late 1990s, when unlicensed CD reproduction, distribution and sales became more widespread in Brazil. Home CD burning took time to become a major antagonism because the hardware was expensive, but industrial level disc piracy grew with the ease due to lowered costs of mass CD replication. More recently, Internet peer-to-peer (P2P) file-sharing has been the focus of attention – the decline in the value of CDs generally has made disc-based piracy less attractive to organised criminals – with the prospect of mobile-based piracy now considered a more serious threat.

With the Office of the US Trade Representative (USTR) bolstered by victories over pharmaceutical patents in the 1990s, entertainment content industry bodies such as the Recording Industry Association of America (RIAA), International Federation of the Phonographic Industry (IFPI) and the International Intellectual Property Alliance (IIPA) began to lobby the USTR to force Brazil to address its 'inadequate' IP laws. Since that time, the US has put intense diplomatic pressure on the Brazilian government over its approach to copyright enforcement through the USTR's 'Special 301 Process'. Special 301 is a list of nations deemed to have inadequate IP protection and enforcement policies. The list is compiled on the basis of data provided by a private trade association (the IIPA), which is accepted without further investigation by the USTR (Karaganis 2011). Brazilian cooperation with the US on pharmaceutical and other patents during the 1990s led the USTR to 'demote' Brazil to its 'Watch List' of the less serious of the countries under scrutiny in 1996. However, pressure from the multinational content industries over CD and DVD replication, as well as the explosion in P2P MP3 file-sharing, saw Brazil returned to 'Priority Watch Status' in 2002. Five years later, in recognition of the government's anti-piracy efforts, Brazil was returned to the lower 'Watch List'.

The power of the USTR is that its remit is not limited to IP or cultural products but extends to all aspects of overseas trade. Thus, in 2002, under the threat of trade sanctions from a major trading partner, the Brazilian government made a sharp turn towards enforcement and education, and implemented the most comprehensive set of legal and institutional changes to a domestic copyright regime anywhere in the world over the past decade. In 2004, the Ministry of Justice formed the National Council on Combating Piracy and Intellectual Property Crimes (CNCP), a body comprised of private industry actors and various government departments, to develop and implement a national plan to combat piracy. A host of new policy initiatives were declared and enacted, including raids on CD/DVD vendors in street markets and a huge increase in the numbers of arrests (though with no corresponding increase in prosecutions or imprisonments). A mass 'downloading music is a crime' advertising campaign was launched, course materials on copyright crime were distributed in schools and universities, and special prosecutors, police and lawyers were trained in copyright enforcement.[2]

As a result of these policies, Brazil has become subject to a double narrative; it is at once a 'pirate nation' of widespread illegal activity, while simultaneously a model of 'piracy fighter' on the domestic front. As far the major labels and the IIPA were concerned, the effect of this state-led intervention was immediate and substantial: in its 2005/6 market report, the trade association of the majors in Brazil, ABPD (Brazilian Record Producers Association) cited an increase in seized counterfeit DVDs from 144,000 units in 2004 to 6.7 million units in 2005, with 1,200 arrests made in the year compared 39 arrests in 2004. In 2005 ABPD's estimate of the country's piracy rate fell to 40 per cent of the market – back to the level it had peaked at in the previous decade – from 52 per cent in 2004.

Despite the impressive numbers (which are not subject to independent verification), much of what took place is better described as 'enforcement theatre':

abundant press converage of teams of police raiding markets and the trashing of thousands of counterfeit discs, but not properly reflective of a wider impact. This is partly because the Brazilian authorities lack the resources necessary to police copyright offences. Given the incredible stress on Brazilian courts and the country's dangerously overcrowded prisons, it is a practical impossibility to meet the enforcement demands of the USTR and IIPA, and media piracy does not rank highly when competing for priority with murder, rape and robbery. The prosecution of non-commercial infringements are even more rare, since under Brazilian law they must be brought by the owner under a private action. It is also clear that the new copyright policies have grown further removed from the experiences of media consumers, users and sharers in Brazil. This has not gone unnoticed by the IIPA, which in every Special 301 report since 2007 has first acknowledged the efforts of the Brazilian government, before stating bluntly that not enough is being done.[3]

While the cooperation of the Brazilian government eased some of the pressure from the USTR, the rising threat of digital and mobile piracy has seen continued pressure brought to bear on Brazil. This led to the drafting of a new set of Internet and information access and sharing laws that are, on paper at least, among the most rigid in the world,[4] but they are being resisted by the country's population. A 2005 Internet bill proposing stiff penalties for unlicensed downloading of media – in a country where Apple did not set up a dedicated iTunes Music Store until December 2011 – provoked such a public and civil sector outcry that it had to be sidelined. An alternative proposal in 2006 offered a more balanced approach to consumer rights, but was strongly opposed by ABPD (under pressure from IFPI and IIPA). By 2011, the recording industry and its lobbyists had largely given up on CD piracy and turned their attention to Internet file-sharing and unlicensed music downloading to mobile devices. Efforts to adopt a graduated-response mechanism, such as HADOPI in France, have floundered on public antagonism towards such measures.

Overall, despite the decade-long efforts of the Brazilian government to meet the demands of the USTR and multinational content companies, the 'impact on the overall availability of pirated goods has been minimal' (Karaganis 2011: 293). To be sure, this is far from exclusively Brazilian problem, but Brazil is unique in that for ten years its government, in concert with international private industry, made every practical effort it could to meet the demands of the USTR and IIPA with the exception of the mass imprisonment of alleged copyright infringers. Despite this, expanded enforcement has proven to have little to no discernible impact on music sales or consumption, legitimate or otherwise. Given the myriad cultural, technological, and economic influences on music use, to isolate a 'piracy effect' independent of other variables is highly unrealistic.

Market structure

High piracy rates – or, to phrase it differently, participation in an informal local economy – are actually a reflection of Brazil's market structure. In particular, the pricing strategies of the international multinationals in Brazil creates a situation in which a culture of piracy is the only way in which citizens can engage with music.

It has been argued that Brazil's positioning as a 'pirate nation' is a direct result of a long-term pricing strategy by the major record companies that maintains retail prices for legitimate CDs at levels comparative to the US. This put most CDs, even those of popular domestics acts released and distributed by major labels, well beyond the reach of the vast majority of Brazilian buyers – in 2010, the Brazilian GDP per capita was $10,800 compared to $47,200 in the US. A recent collection of empirical studies, *Media Piracy in Emerging Markets* (*MPEE*) (Karaganis 2011) offers the most comprehensive study of piracy in BRIC and other developing countries to date. It firmly identifies pricing as the baseline explanation for unlicensed distribution of media goods. Researchers gathered price comparisons of pirated and legitimate goods and translated those numbers into a 'comparative purchasing power' (CCP) price that reflects what an American buyer would pay at an equivalent percentage of GDP per capita. The findings were stark. A legitimate CD of Coldplay's *Viva La Vida* (2008) retailed for $17 in the US and $14 in Brazil. When comparative income levels were factored in, however, the CCP price for an American consumer – what an equivalent Brazilian would be expected to pay – was $80. Clearly, if a single CD album cost $80 in the US, UK or Japan, piracy in those countries would likely be considerably higher. Legal recordings are unobtainable for the vast majority of Brazilians, leaving a huge gap in the market that can only be filled by unlicensed copying and distribution. Piracy is thus the only way for most Brazilians to access many of their own musical icons, as well as the albums of global megastars.

The *MPEE* study was published in 2011, but *The New York Times* had noted the pricing issue in an article ten years earlier (Rohter 2001). In an article headlined 'In a Land of Sun and Music, CD Pirates Play Robin Hood', Marcio Goncalves, the director-general of the Brazilian Association of Reprographic Rights (ABDR), was asked why such obviously prohibitive prices were maintained. He replied that otherwise 'artists would cancel their contracts and move to another label'. Two other reasons can be proposed, however. First, that higher prices mitigate against parallel import markets – wherein a non-counterfeit product is imported from another country without the permission of IP owner, often to exploit price differentials.[5] Second, and far less discussed given that it undermines the majors' arguments for continually expanded copyright enforcement, is that the pricing strategy is actually profit maximising. Lowering disc prices to the point where they could be competitive with local informal markets would generate such low levels of revenue that it is ultimately more profitable to keep them high for the smaller number of consumers able and willing to pay the premium.

The existence of a 'predatory pricing policy' has proven infuriating to many Brazilians. A former Sony and BMG executive quoted in the 2001 *New York Times* article stated that 'it is the avarice, the unyielding rapaciousness of the record companies that foments the violation of recording copyrights in Brazil'. The blame is placed squarely on demands from global corporate headquarters for their Brazilian arms to toe the company line. Notably, many Brazilians view this pricing strategy as a continuation or reframing of colonial exploitation, whereby Northern and Western powers take valuable raw materials, from Amazonian plants to musical innovations, and sell them at home as expensive finished products such as pharmaceuticals and exotic rhythms. It is especially galling to see these newly patented or copyrighted goods reimported into Brazil at prices beyond the reach of locals, who can find themselves in breach of alien IP regulations when finding alternative means of accessing them.

The major industry

The implications of colonialism demand that an analysis of the recording industry in Brazil takes into account the broader power dynamics of globalisation and, in particular, the tensions between local music cultures and the global priorities of the multinational entertainment companies. Today's majors have deep roots in Brazil, given the near century-long history of steady consolidation of the global recording business. Sony, as the parent company of RCA Records, traces its origins in Brazil to 1929 when RCA Victor entered the market. EMI released recordings under its Odeon subsidiary (a German label acquired via the 1931 merger of Electrola and HMV that created EMI) from the 1930s until the mid-1980s, after which it operated as EMI Brazil. Universal's account of its history begins in 1945 and the founding of the Sociedade Interamericana de Representações (Sinter) which, in 1955, established the Companhia Brasileira de Discos (CBD) to begin manufacturing 12-inch records and, in 1957, introduced Brazil's first stereo recordings. Dutch electronics company Philips, which had founded Philips do Brasil in 1924 to produce radios and light bulbs, bought CBD in 1958 as part of its expansion into the recording business. Rechristened CBD-Phonogram in 1973, the company was absorbed into the Polygram empire in 1978 (first as Polygram Discos and then as Polygram do Brasil from 1985), then by Seagram in 1997, becoming Universal Music Brazil. Warner Music Group has only existed under its current incarnation since 2004, but the labels associated with its past and present – including Warner Bros, Elektra and Atlantic (WEA), Nonesuch, Reprise, Rhino, EastWest, and others – have all had histories in Brazil. Nonesuch released Brazilian music in the 1960s under its Explorer Series, and signed Caetano Veloso as its first non-classical artist; Frank Sinatra's *Reprise* was a driver of the popularity of bossa nova internationally, and Elektra released a handful of Sergio Mendes albums in the 1970s.

By the 1990s and continuing today, the same oligopoly has existed in Brazil as elsewhere. Roughly 80–85 per cent of all direct music sales in Brazil (i.e. those sales captured by an official scan or recorded paid download) is divided between the four multinational major recording companies. This unusually high concentration reflects the majors' long presence in the country, during which time they have built relationships with all the important post-war Brazilian artists – in 2010 domestic artists made up 65 per cent of the total market – while also dominating sales of albums by international superstars such as Michael Jackson, Madonna, U2 and Metallica and, more recently, Beyoncé and Justin Bieber.

Reconstructing data from a variety of sources, the market share of the major labels in 2010 was, roughly: Universal Music Group (30 per cent), Sony Music Entertainment International (27 per cent), Warner Music Group (13 per cent) and EMI Music Group (11 per cent), although these figures need to be recognised as an estimate. Large 'independents' such as Som Livre (the in-house recording label and publisher of Brazilian media giant Globo), Walt Disney Records and a small handful of other Latin America-wide publishers and labels make up a further 17 per cent of the Brazilian market (Som Livre, which is bigger than both WMG and EMI, makes up the majority of this total). These six multinationals and four relatively established local independents make up the entire membership of ABPD, the IFPI affiliate in the country and its chief lobbying force.

The multinational majors themselves have strikingly similar artist rosters. At least one or more of the types of the following acts can be found at a major: a samba or bossa nova star of the old guard; an established MPB (*Música Popular Brasileira*), *axe* or *pagode* superstar; a *sertanjo* duo, almost always two 'brothers'; an 'alternative' rock band with a following developed in the 1990s or earlier; a teen and/or tween pop star; a hip hop or other 'urban' act from Rio or São Paulo; and a representative of the more popular regional genres, likely from Bahia or Porto Alegre.

For a number of years now, the very best-selling recording stars in Brazil have been Catholic priests. In 2008 the top two albums were Padre Fabio de Melo's *Vida* (Som Livre) and Padre Marcelo Rossi's *Paz Sim, Violencia Não Volume 1* (Sony) respectively. *Volume 2* by the latter was at number six. In 2010, three similar releases were in the year-end top ten, all on Som Livre and helping to push the company to nearly a full 15 per cent market share that year. Padre Rossi holds televised masses in stadia with an elaborate live show featuring choirs and aerobic dance performances.

While the big international acts are marketed in ways familiar to music fans in other mature markets, the nature of pop stardom among the domestic stars is more distinctive, with close ties to other media. They are promoted vigorously across all forms of broadcast media, with TV and radio remaining the key publicity drivers, as well as print media, outdoor advertising and, more recently, on the most popular Internet and mobile portals. Many often also do double-duty as actors or TV presenters and are as likely to have started their careers in TV rather than as singers as such. This TV stardom can also contribute to a certain degree of international success, primarily in South America or Portugal, and sometimes in Spain or continental European markets. On very rare occasions a Brazilian act singing in English will appear on North American or British cultural radars, and hence sales charts. Examples include heavy metal veterans Sepultura and electropop band CSS.

Despite the limited success in Anglophone markets, the Brazilian record industry has remained strong. According to the IFPI, in 2005 Brazil moved up to tenth spot in the global rankings of national music markets ordered by size. By 2009 it had risen to sixth largest in the world. One reason for this was the explosive popularity of the DVD format in the middle of the decade – in 2004 DVD sales made up 26 per cent of the majors' income (IFPI 2005). The bigger surprise came in 2008, when the national market grew 8.1 per cent on the year to R408.2 milllion ($221.8 million), making it the first of the world's large music markets to do so in several years. Digital format sales had doubled from the year before, with nearly 80 per cent of those to mobile devices. There was even a small growth of 1.2 per cent in physical sales, which by then was quite an anomaly.

So why the reversal? Anecdotal evidence and discussions with Brazilian music businesspeople point to the likelihood that online downloading and both on- and offline sharing, regardless of legality, has been encouraging various forms of offline spending on music, performances and music-associated goods. A further factor appears to be eagerness among Brazilians of all classes to use mobile phones for various digital services as the country's 3G network improves (reliable Internet connections via desktop computers are relatively scarce and notoriously expensive to maintain). Brazilians are well informed of technological advances in the North; since they have limited access to PCs, the Internet-enabled mobile phone becomes the average Brazilian's personal entry point to the wider network.

Co-marketing and branding deals with a wide variety of corporate clients, from telecommunications and mobile phone companies to supermarket chains and sports teams are driving music licensing revenues, as well as contributing to a halo effect of direct music sales. Promotional mobile phones pre-loaded with pre-album-release singles and other artist-specific inducements (ringtones, wallpapers, merchandise discounts etc.) have driven sales of those devices into the hundreds of thousands. A good example of this type of post-label strategy is folk-rock singer Magalhães, who recorded her debut album in English and released it online to social networks in 2008. It was picked up by Agencia de Musica, a hybrid music and branding/advertising company, who placed her first single in a television campaign for telco Vivo. Her album was then included on preloaded Vivo-networked Motorola phones and went on to sell over 20,000 physical copies by the middle of the year, with Vivo building the singer a media-rich website and sponsoring concert performances.

IFPI figures for 2010 show 76 per cent of recorded music trade revenue were on physical formats, with 17 per cent digital and 7 per cent from performing rights (IFPI 2011: 76). The growth in performance rights income from commercial use of recordings over the decade is partially a result of Brazil's unique model of collective rights management, which is centralized under the Central Office for the Collection and Distribution of Rights, or ECAD (Page et al 2010), formed in 1998 to address fragmentation in the rights market. ECAD is the single body for the collection and distribution of both authors' and neighboring rights royalties from uses on radio, television, cinema, live performance, digital web/simulcasting, and general uses (in hotels, restaurants, bars etc.). This highly unusual system – normally there are two or more such bodies in any given national market operating as local monopolies over specific rights sectors – turns the competition for domestic rights holder members over to ten royalty distribution societies: six full members and four associate members. Rights users are licensed directly by ECAD, which collects the money and distributes it to its member societies, who pass it on to their author members and publishers.

ECAD's financial performance has outpaced the recording sector over the past decade, with collections up 47 per cent between 2005 and 2009 – compared to a 40 per cent decline in recorded music revenues over the same period – and double-digit growth anticipated for next few years at least (View 2010). This has been achieved through increased productivity, new technologies that speed up licensing requests (Mobile ECAD Tec) and automate identification of musical works (ECAD Tec Sound), and increasing the number of 'general' licensees such as stores and restaurants.

The non-major industry

There is a discrepancy between the proportion of the mainstream music industry dominated by the majors and their role in the development of musical cultures outside of the main urban areas of Brazil. As in many national and regional markets around the world, the true dynamism in music business is in the so-called independent sector, where survival often depends on flexibility and adaptation. There are estimated 400–500 medium and small independent labels spread around the country – many working exclusively in highly localised, regional or urban subgenres – and innumerable entrepreneurs and self-employed performers. The overwhelming market share of the international majors in Brazil is partially a function of the historic gatekeeping roles of Rio de Janiero and São Paulo, under which an act or genre could only reach national prominence if approved of by the dominant cultural elites. And, while it remains a long shot for independent musicians to gain any significant level of national fame, the opportunities to develop sustainable revenue opportunities have expanded considerably.

It is only very recently that the most organised and established companies in the independent sector have emerged as a coherent, identifiable group. In 2002 a small number formed the Brazilian Association for Independent Music (ABMI). By 2008 this organisation represented over 120 labels and distributors, with an average of six new companies joining them every month. As of 2011, the association has some 150 small and medium-sized member companies, some of whom put out between five and thirty albums a year. Members include labels such as Trama, Biscoito Fino, Deck Disc, ST2, Abril, Atração, Azul, Velas, Dabliú, USA, Eldorado, Visom, Dubas, Nikita and Jam, distributors Distribuidora Independente and Tratore, online retailer iMusica and export company HPI. Trama in particular blazed a trail through the decade, setting up a MySpace-like site called Trama-virtual for domestic acts to upload and share their music on before there was an actual MySpace. Electropop group CSS are a product of Tramavirtual, their popularity on the site leading to a recording deal with Trama and, later, success in Europe and the US.

The companies joining ABMI are rarely pure record labels in the traditional sense of the term. In order to survive, many diversify across various product offerings and services, including live concert and festival bookings, promotion, local and international marketing, private and public cultural tourism projects, book publishing, website design, and so on. Retaining song publishing and performance rights has also become much more important to these enterprises, as the commercial and public performance use of their songs and recordings remain potentially lucrative for small companies. It has also become more common for artists to self-release albums themselves online and physically via street-level distribution, particularly in the wake of the widespread shuttering of specialty music retailers following the shift of CD retailing to big-box retailers and convenience stores.

Domestic music companies receive support from the Brazilian Music Export Office, part of Brasilia Music e Artes (BM&A), which has emerged as a key hub within the indie community. BM&A's work is partially sponsored by APEX-Brasil, a government agency launched in 1997 as a special department of SEBRAE, or Brazilian Support Service to Micro and Small Enterprises, which was created to grow the diversity and scope of Brazil's exports by helping small companies penetrate and open markets overseas. SEBRAEs, local associations and BM&A organise training courses and conferences on issues such as digital distribution, international copyright and tax incentives for cultural projects. The Música do Brasil project, a partnership between ABMI, BM&A and the ABGI (Brazilian Association of Independent Labels) and supported by APEX-Brazil, SEBRAE and the Ministry of Culture, has been developed in recent years to expand export opportunities for Brazilian music. Musica do Brasil also promotes and logistically supports Brazilian companies wishing to participate in the larger music industry conferences around the world.

The first important study of Brazil's independent music markets was published in 2008 by SEBRAE. Prepared by the School of Advertising and Marketing (ESPM) in Rio, the study examined the indie market's overall structure, value chains and digital trends. It found a wide range of professionals involved in numerous stages of pre- and post-production, distribution and marketing, indicating a potential for nationwide coordination between cooperative business sectors. Online sales growth also drove exports of local Brazilian music to buyers in countries worldwide. The study quoted ABMI's finding that 80 per cent of domestic recorded music production was by independent labels and music companies – the vast majority by about 400 small and micro-businesses dotted around the country – representing 25 per cent of all domestic product sold in Brazil.

ABMI has identified several problems faced by small music companies and artists in Brazil, including limited access to radio and television given the close ties between the majors and Som Livre/Globo and the most mainstream, popular and national media channels. In particular, the expense of payola for radio play as a cost of doing business is prohibitive for small firms, meaning ABMI members are ill-positioned to benefit from the nationwide structures in place to promote major label and Som Livre product. The lack of a 'culture of cooperation' among indies, low bargaining power with suppliers, the relative quality of recordings and the lack of access to major retailers are also all significant hurdles.

One solution proposed in the report is for firms to focus on niche markets, defined according to region, style or audience. Another bright spot is the growth in music festivals around the country, giving smaller artists greater exposure to more people in more places than ever before. The independent sector is also significant for the alternative business models and practices it has developed. The most unorthodox examples centre around the *Fora do Eixo* Collectives (FEC) of cultural producers, which are now present in 26 out of the 27 Brazilian states. The development of 'solidarity economies' (Poljokan *et al.* 2011) in Brazil's music and cultural sectors beyond Rio and São Paulo began with the Cubo Card, a 'creative currency, credit and exchange system' developed from 2005 to 2006 by a loose group of music creators and entrepreneurs in Cuiabá, in Mata Grosso state, looking to enhance and sustain economic opportunities around local music and festivals.[6]

The Cubo Card system provides participants discounted access to quality recording services and studios, bringing together independent working musicians and professional producers. As the programme has expanded, added benefits included access to photographers, video makers, journalists and graphic designers, and even discounts at participating hotels and restaurants in order to mitigate some of the costs of travel between relatively remote places. As well as improving the quality of the demos and albums produced by local bands, the collaborations facilitated more, and better organised, live concerts and events. Seeing the benefits the scheme brought to Mata Grosso, versions in other regions were initiated under the network label of FECs, which now includes a *Fora do Eixo* bank and National Fund to coordinate cooperative and sustainable growth.

The goal of the FECs is to balance competition with collaboration to allow many new and different types of musicians, collectives, event promoters and tangential enterprises to expand in regions where the lack of a physical or organisational infrastructure had previously made this impossible. It hopes to do this via minimising fluctuations in cash flow through the development of a cultural market based on service exchanges and trust networks. The effect that this collective support has had on direct physical music sales countrywide is impossible to quantify. However, in the Brazilian edition of American music magazine *Rolling Stone*'s selection of the top albums of 2009, the number one spot went to an independent instrumentalist rock trio called Macaco Bong that had benefited directly from the Cubo Card system.

Brazil has been a fertile site for the emergence of 'open business models' that challenge the way popular music has been traditionally industrialised and regulated. The key characteristics of these systems or strategies differentiate them clearly from the industrial model developed by the major international music companies. Briefly, their shared features are as follows:

- They are not based on copyright exploitation, and in some cases are explicitly dubbed as 'post-copyright'.
- Physical recordings, in the form of CDs or DVDs, are not profit sources per se, but part of the marketing alongside local radio and advertising for more lucrative live performances.
- Artists and producers rely on informal street level distribution networks to reproduce, package and disseminate their recordings at the distributors' own

expense, and build audiences either at street markets where the discs are sold alongside pirated Western content, or via individuals known as *camelos* (literally, camels) selling discs from shoulder bags in bars or other public gathering places.

• The musics made to be marketed and sold this way reflect the economic and social realities of their fans and consumers, and are not designed for mass mainstream consumption.

• The music is not designed to be acquired and collected on CDs (except perhaps as a souvenir from a particularly special event), but to be experienced live, at parties, or listened to on local radio stations.

The emergence of these models reminds us that, in countries such as Brazil, the vast majority of popular music culture and consumption occurs on (and beyond) the periphery of IP regimes. To Western content industries these are invariably 'pirate' operations that result in lost jobs and revenue, but this ignores the reality that many media distribution systems in the developing world began as competing rogue commercial operations (including those of the US when it was a developing country (Vaidhyanathan 2001; Litman 2001)). But as the MPEE study demonstrates, informal and/or 'black' or 'grey' markets are the spaces within which ground-level media piracy is challenged by local competitors selling at locally affordable prices. An increasing number of creators and entrepreneurs building and benefiting from these emergent hybrid business models, as well as their fans and willing buyers, tend to resent demands for greater enforcement by Western copyright owners and the US government, principally because disruption to informal distribution networks is bad for their interests. These open business models are, in fact, how music creators outside the major label system build reputations and a supportive local fan base. In Brazil, as elsewhere, obscurity is a far more serious problem for working musicians than the threat of a few potential lost sales.

Many local scenes are geographically bounded, and some are more structured than others. For example, the *favela* or *carioca baile funk* scene in urban shanty towns at the edges of Brazilian cities are too embedded in those areas' criminal subcultures to be safely studied (Bellos 2004). *Carioca* (meaning 'of Rio') *baile* ('ball' as in party) *funk* is the best known genre of 'underground' dance music in Brazil, and has a reputation for rapid adaptation to changes in music tastes and technologies which has, in turn, allowed it to find its way on to the dance floors of clubs around the world. Much of today's *baile funk*, at least in its most popular and non-sanitised form, is illegal under Brazilian law, which prohibits the performance or sale of songs that promote or glorify gang violence (known at street stalls as *proibidao*). In recent years, the musical tropes of *baile* have been appropriated with enthusiasm by American and European DJs. Diplo and M.I.A. created the first mainstream use of *baile* rhythms on M.I.A.'s first album *Arular* and the hit single 'Bucky Done Gun'.

The 2008 publication of a survey of the *tecnobrega* scene in Belém do Pára (population 1.4 million) in northern Brazil, conducted by researchers from

Fundação Getulio Vargas University in Rio and Yale's Center for Technology and Society, marked the first fully quantitative and qualitative research study of a particular informal music market in the country (Mikukami and Lemos 2007). *Tecnobrega* is a locally created spin-off of the older *brega* genre. The word *brega* itself translates roughly as 'tacky', 'kitschy' or 'cheesy' and, as a genre, has traditionally been associated with the working poor of northern Brazil. From the 1980s until around 2000, traditional *brega* was released and marketed at local levels (i.e. non-national) according to local conventions: songwriters and performers signed with publishers and recording labels that produced tapes and discs, and promoted new songs through local radio and television, and sold via normal retail channels. However, as the 1990s progressed and media businesses became more consolidated, it became harder for the majority of *brega* bands and singers to find their way on to radio playlists. Around 2001, Belém party DJs began mixing *brega* styles and songs with electronic music and samples from Western popular music, from metal to rap and pop, as well as lines of dialogue from Hollywood films and other found material (Amaral 2006). This was facilitated by the lowered costs digital technologies which allowed for a rapid growth in the number and sophistication of in-home studios, and encouraged experimentation with sampling and mashing traditional and electronic elements. Dubbed *tecnobrega*, the scene grew into a fully fledged ecosystem made up of a host of mutually supportive, yet internally competitive, participants. These included *brega* bands and singers, live DJs (in a matter of just a few years DJs went from playing vinyl to CDs, to MDs, to MP3s), studio operators/DJs that produce compilations of the latest hot *tecnobrega* tracks; disc replicators from home burners to large-scale industrial operations, street-level vendors operating from stalls at markets or other shopping areas, *camelos* selling cheap compilations and mixes out of shoulder bags, *tecnobrega* party promoters, and the operators of mobile sound systems known as *aparelhagens*, combining walls of amps with computer-controlled sound, video projection and elaborate lighting systems.

According to the study, in 2008–09 *aparelhagem* parties attracted crowds of 3,000–5,000 people and sometimes as many as 8,000 for special events. Over 4,000 *tecnobrega* parties took place in and around Belém each month. Solo performers and bands who built strong reputations among the *tecnobrega* network's taste-makers (the studio and performance DJs) and its eager audience made approximately R$2,200 (approximately $1,200) per concert, not including sales of recordings at the shows themselves, which averaged 77 CDs and 53 DVDs per show. These were sold for higher prices than the street vendors, about R$7.50 for a CD and R$10 for a DVD, compared to street prices of $3.45 and $4.20, respectively. An especially important strategy at *tecnobrega* parties was to interweave local references and 'shout-outs' to neighbourhoods in the performances, which were recorded live and then burned to CD for sale as attendees left the venue. These made the event itself unique and were a huge attraction for those present, who bought the freshly minted CD by the thousands as souvenirs. Meanwhile, the replicators/distributors/vendors bore the cost of reproduction and packaging, and were the primary marketers of new product. Cumulative sales at scores of street-market vendors averaged 286,208 CDs and 178,708 DVDs each month in Belém alone.

Since the scene's beginnings, it has spawned a variety of off-shoot genres, including *cybertécnica* in which guitars are removed altogether, and a more melodic or *romantico* variant for couples to dance to. The most notable success of contemporary *brega* is Banda Calypso, arguably the most successful domestic act in Brazil of the past decade, a position they have achieved without a record deal (Vianna, 2007). The husband and wife team of guitarist/producer Chimbinha and singer/dancer Joelma formed Calypso in the late 1990s as part of the then burgeoning *tecnobrega* scene. The band produce their own CDs (15 by 2010, not including bootlegs of live shows) and are estimated to have sold well over 10 million copies, almost entirely through direct sales at their massive concerts or via street market distributors. The band makes little to no money from these sales, nor does it expect to, given that the reproduction and distribution costs of the CDs are met by the vendors themselves; revenues are generated almost entirely though live performances and some proportion of DVD sales.

The example of *tecnobraga* shows that, like rest of recorded music business worldwide, Brazil's industry is dominated by the majors, but there are whole other cultural economies that never show up in official statistics, and yet arguably are more attuned to the variety of Brazilians' musical preferences. With a global network at their disposal, new markets for Brazilian music have opened up around the world as well as at home. Hybrid models are flourishing and offer clues to the medium to long-term future of music businesses not just in the ascendant parts of the developing world, but also in the declining areas of the (over)developed world.

Notes

1   BRIC is an acronym for the four major developing countries – Brazil, Russia, India and China – coined by Goldman Sachs chief economist Jim O'Neill in 2001.
2   The creation and actions of the CNCP are covered in detail in the Brazil chapter of Karaganis (2011) by Pedro N. Mizukami, Oona Castro, Luiz Moncau and Ronaldo Lemos. This also provides the most thoroughly researched and comprehensive dissertation on media piracy in Brazil to date.
3   This example is from the Executive Summary of the IIPA's 2008 Special 301 Report: 'Notwithstanding greatly enhanced government efforts and a continuing high level of cooperation between the government and rights holders, piracy for copyrighted materials remains very serious. This can be attributed to the problems of unsuccessful prosecution and the difficulty of concluding criminal copyright infringement cases. While the IIPA and its members can report that Brazilian authorities have conducted a significant number of raids with accompanying seizures of pirated products, there has not been a corresponding drop in the availability of pirated goods in the Brazilian market'.
4   See Mizukami *et al.* (note 2 above).
5   Given the ubiquity of music on the Internet, the parallel imports argument has lost most of its traction over the past decade.
6   Thanks to David McLoughlin at BM&A for details on the Cubo Card.

Bibliography

ABPD (2000–09) *Mercado Brasileiro de Musica*. Associação Brasileira dos Produtores de Discos. Available online at: www.abpd.org.br/estatisticas_mercado_brasil.asp (accessed on 13 June 2012).

de Almeida, M. (2008) Portugal's Colonial Complex: From Colonial Lusotropicalism to Postcolonial Lusophony. Queen's Postcolonial Research Forum, Queen's University, Belfast. Unpublished paper.

do Amaral, P. M. G. (2006) Estigma e Cosmopolitismo Local: Considerações Sobre uma Estética Legitimadora do Tecnobrega em Belém do Pará. Available online at: http://www.bregapop.com/home/index.php?option=com_content&task=view&id=4951&Itemid=835 (accessed on 13 June 2012).

de Andrade, O. (1928) *Manifesto Antropófago*. English trans. Bary, E. (1991). Cannibalist Manifesto, *Latin American Literary Review*, 19(38): 35–7.

Armstrong, P. (2000) The Brazilianist's Brazil: Interdisciplinary Portraits of Brazilian Culture and Society, *Latin American Research Review*, 35(1): 227–42.

Bellos, A. (2004) Samba? That's So Last Year, *The Guardian*, 11 March. Available online at: www.guardian.co.uk/brazil/story/0,12462,1166938,00.html (accessed on 13 June 2012).

Ben-Yehuda, A. (2009) Billboard Brazil Launches Monthly Magazine With Local Charts, *Billboard Magazine*, 22 October.

Brazil–US Business Council (2004) *Counterfeiting and Piracy in Brazil: The Economic Impact*. US Chamber of Commerce, Washington, DC.

Cravo Albin, R. *Dicionário Cravo Albin da Música Popular Brasileira*. Instituto Cultural Cravo Albin. Available online at: www.dicionariompb.com.br/default.asp (accessed 22 April 2007).

Dunn, D. (2001) *Brutality Garden: Tropicalia and the Emergence of a Brazilian Counterculture*. Chapel Hill, NC: University of North Carolina Press.

Howard-Spink, S. (2006) Brazil's Two Music Industries, *OpenDemocracy*, 5 December. Available online at: www.opendemocracy.net/media-copyrightlaw/brazil_music_3880.jsp (accessed on 13 June 2012).

Howard-Spink, S. (2007) Combinação Brasileira: Tropicália, OMPI e o Surgimento do Mix de Cultura e Política em Nível Global (Brazilian Blends: Tropicalia, WIPO and the Emerging Global Mix of Culture and Politics) (Carboni, G. trans.), in E.B. Rodrigues and F. Polido (eds) *Propriedade Intelectual: Novos Paradigmas Internacionais, Conflitos e Desafios*. São Paulo: Campus Jurídico.

IFPI (2005) *The Recording Industry in Numbers*. London: International Federation of the Phonographic Industry.

IFPI (2011) *The Recording Industry in Numbers*. London: International Federation of the Phonographic Industry.

Karaganis, J. (ed.) (2011) *Media Piracy in Emerging Economies*. New York: Social Science Research Council.

Lemos, R. (2007) From Legal Commons to Social Commons: Brazil and the Cultural Industry in the 21st Century. Working Paper Number CBS-80–70. Centre for Brazilian Study. University of Oxford.

Lemos, R. and Mizukami, P.N. (2007) O Tecnobrega Paraense e o Modelo de Negócio Aberto. *Open Business Models Latin America*. International Development Research Centre (IDRC).

Litman, J. (2001) *Digital Copyright: Protecting Intellectual Property on the Internet*. Amherst, NJ: Prometheus Books.

Page, W., Gabdelman, M. and Dickinson, B. (2010) ECADonomics: Understanding Brazil's Unique Model of Collective Rights Management, *Economic Insight*, 21. London: PRS for Music.

Poljokan, B., Lenza, L., Tendolini e Silva, C.E., Farias, L. and Andrade, D. (2011) Fora do Eixo Card: The Brazilian System for the Solidarity Culture. Conference Paper. Presented at International Conference on Community and Complementary Currencies. Available online at: http://conferences.ish-lyon.cnrs.fr/index.php/cc-conf/2011/paper/view/76 (accessed on 13 June 2012).

Rohter, L. (2001) In a Land of Sun and Music, CD Pirates Play Robin Hood, *The New York Times*, 20 May.

SEBRAE (2008) Estudos de Mercado Musica Independente. Serviço Brasileiro de Apoio às Micro e Pequenas Empresas. Available online at: www.biblioteca.sebrae.com.br (accessed on 13 June 2012).

Shaver, L. (ed.) (2008) Access to Knowledge in Brazil: New Research on Intellectual Property, Innovation and Development. Information Society Project. Yale Law School, New Haven, NJ.

Vaidhyanathan, S. (2001) *Copyrights and Copywrongs: The Rise of Intellectual Property and How it Threatens Creativity*. New York: NYU Press.

Veloso, C. (2002) (trans. De Sena, I.) *Tropical Truth: A Story of Music & Revolution in Brazil*. New York: Da Capo Press.

Vianna, H. (2007) This is Calypso, 17 July. Available online at: www.overmundo.com.br/overblog/isso-e-calypso-ou-a-lua-nao-me-traiu (accessed on 13 June 2012).

View (2010) ECAD Update. Available online at: http://www.theviewfromtheboundary.com/default.aspx?ArticleID=419 (June 13, 2012).

Czech Republic

Population: 10.2 million (82nd)

Languages: Czech (95%), Slovak (2%).

Capital: Prague (pop 1.2 million)

Currency: Koruna (CZK).
$1 = 19.12 CZK

GDP: $192.0 bn (45th)

GDP (PPP)/capita: $25,299 (37th)

Median age: 40.8

GDP data from World Bank

Population data from CIA world factbook

Exchange rate used by IFPI (2011) (source: Oanda)

2010 Recorded music market

Overall income: $27.6m (CZK525.5)

World ranking: 37th

	Income	World ranking
Physical sales	$19.3m	34th
Digital sales	$1.4m	42nd
Performance rights	$6.9m	22nd

Historical recorded music market ($m, at IFPI's 2010 exchange rate)

	1999	2000	2001	2002	2003	2004	2005	2006	2007	2008	2009
Trade Value		50.2	40.2	39.2	39.8	31.1	33.1	32.8	37.2	34.3	
Retail Value	92.4	81.9	76.5	61.4	59.8	59.2	52.6				

Proportion of domestic repertoire (market value, physical sales only)

1991	1995	2000	2005	2010
61%	29%	43%	49%	51%

Album certification levels

	2010	1999
Gold	Domestic – 6,000	Domestic – 25,000
	International – 3,000	International – 15,000
Platinum	Domestic – 12,000	Domestic – 50,000
	International – 6,000	International – 30,000

6 Czech Republic

C. Michael Elavsky

To understand the structure and dynamics of the contemporary Czech recording industry is to grasp how its evolution and development are directly connected to the country's dramatic cultural experience of communism, which for forty years largely sequestered it from the broader flows, trends and advances within global music culture. Since the Velvet Revolution of 1989, the Czech music market has been dramatically transformed into a commercial enterprise and integrated into the broader flows of global finance and industrial practices associated with the operations of the Big Four record labels in advanced capitalist markets. Yet, the proclivities of its music culture remain distinctly haunted by the country's history and driven by its small size and distinctive ethnic constitution. While post-communism's promise to provide greater opportunities for musical expression and the wider dissemination of Czech musical articulations have been ostensibly delivered, the ideological underpinnings and infrastructure within the processes of globalisation in fact constrain Czech music culture in ways that paradoxically mirror those of their communist forebears. Sometimes the more things change, the more they stay the same.

The transition over the last two decades has been anything but easy or predictable. Despite catering to a small and distinct global demographic (11 million people – 95 per cent of the population is ethnically and linguistically Czech, 3 per cent are Slovak, and the remaining 2 per cent a mix of Roma (Gypsy), Vietnamese, Germans, Poles and Hungarians) – the Czech music industry nonetheless retains attributes that link it to the industries and music cultures beyond its borders, including the important corporate cultural signifiers and many of the transnational policies and practices which mark it as a 'developed' territory in the international music realm. Most of the majors maintain a formal subsidiary presence in the country, and the local TV, radio and film industries (often partnered with foreign investment) are central components within the Czech music industry. Having become an official member in 2004, Czech music laws and policies are also closely linked to those of the European Union, although adherence and enforcement remain somewhat uneven. Like most record markets today, its retail sector is undergoing considerable reconfiguration, impacting music production and consumption practices and patterns in ways particular to the Czech context. And while it is yet a territory that is officially integrated, mapped and surveilled within the purview of the International Federation of Phonograph Industry (IFPI), its tenets, aesthetic undercurrents and, most importantly, its tensions related to global cultural production cannot be ascertained solely through the data produced by this organisation.

Czech popular music culture before 1989

The nation-state of Czechoslovakia emerged formally in the aftermath of the First World War (1918), the lands having previously been part of numerous European empires across history. As such, its music culture shares distinct affinities with the European cousins which surround it. However, despite being a nation with deep Slavic roots, the Czechs have always been ambivalent about their designation in popular consciousness as an 'Eastern' European nation, perceiving their national identity instead as a confluence of Eastern and Western influences. The country's central geographic position, at the crossroads of Europe, coupled with its history of cultural transition and occupation have been central in forging the character, logics and dynamics of the contemporary Czech music culture/industry.

Like most European populations, the Czechs have produced a rich and deep legacy in the realms of traditional/folk (polka, Moravian cimbalom, and so on) and classical music (for example, Dvořák, Smetana and Martinů). Being a central component in the forging of the Czech nation in the 1800s up until 1918 (Locke 2006; Holy 1995; Kimball 1964), this music continues to provide a foundation for the country's identity as well as tremendous cultural pride.

During the 1920s and 1930s, jazz found its way across Europe and took root in the local music culture such that Czechoslovaks readily identified with and were integrated within the dominant musical styles and trends traversing the continent prior to the Second World War. However, the outcomes of that war, namely the eventual formation of the People's Republic of Czechoslovakia as a communist state in 1948 (in alignment with the Soviet Bloc) would radically isolate and transfigure the maturation of Czech music culture/industry for the next forty years.

Timothy Ryback (1990) has ably documented the significant distinctions that existed between the popular music cultures of the Soviet Bloc countries. As such, their popular music industries also differed by degree in practices and policies. Like most communist nations, Czechoslovakia initially had one record label through which it monopolistically produced and distributed the country's musical recordings. This label – Supraphon – emerged from the remnants of Ultraphon and Esta, Czechoslovakia's private recording firms that were merged during the deprivatisation of Czechoslovak assets in 1949–50 (Kotek 1998). In 1958, Panton was established as a sheet-music publishing house within the state structure and, through the establishment of a proper record label (in 1967), was eventually designated as the primary outlet for product servicing the burgeoning youth music market. In a strictly productive sense, it thus became Supraphon's competitor. Although Panton was primarily responsible for releasing records by smaller acts, a sense of rivalry nonetheless formed between the workers of these two Prague-based labels (Elavsky 2003). A third label, Opus, was eventually established in

Bratislava in 1971 with the primary focus of releasing Slovak artists. However, as Czech and Slovak are close linguistically and were mutually comprehensible by the respective populations, the popular musics in each language travelled easily across the country such that Opus was also soon viewed as another 'competitor' to Supraphon and Panton (ibid.).

During the 1950s, jazz and musical theatre dominated Czechoslovak popular music culture and maintained a tenuous relationship with the authorities actively regulating cultural production. Similar to Western countries at the time, the emergence of 'subversive,' primitive' or 'scandalous' sounds/motifs across this decade caused state officials no shortage of duress. However, these were most often effectively regulated through the operations of official review boards and policies (as well as occasional police actions) which neutralised their broader sociocultural impact. Music production was centrally planned and permits were required to be a qualified performing musician, a fact which also served to delimit those who could officially release records, play concerts, be on the radio and work professionally in the state music industry. Only one retail chain outlet was officially sanctioned by the state (also called Supraphon, with approximately 360 very small stores around the country). As production ran according to state quotas and subsidies, there were few concerns about commercial viability in structuring output. Yet, even with all these constraints, Czechoslovak music culture operated nonetheless as an engaging and serene pastime for most of the population.

While still fairly authoritarian overall, Czechoslovak music culture eventually witnessed a loosening of governmental oversight during the 1960s, coinciding with the powerful impact of Westernised counterculture ideas on the local music scene, all of which seeped in through foreign broadcasts and clandestine dissemination. Moreover, bigbít (the robust Czech manifestation of early rock and roll culture) emerged and flourished, providing an exciting alternative to the immediate tenets of the state (high) culture. While bigbít might initially appear derivative to Western eyes and ears, its texts, melodies and connotations are deceptively complex and innovative in their symbolic relationship to the Czech communist context (Opekar 1994). Czech music industry policies under the Dubček regime (1968–69) began to tacitly support these initiatives by incorporating bigbít releases into their annual plans and opening up the *kulturaky* (regional cultural centres) to concerts, dances and youth group activities.

Unfortunately, these developments (along with the broader sociopolitical changes occurring in Czechoslovakia at the time) were viewed more conservatively by the Kremlin. As such, the possibilities for greater cultural freedom and expression associated with the Prague Spring of 1968 came to an end in August of that year with the invasion, occupation and subsequent crackdown by Warsaw Pact forces, which brought on 'normalisation' and perhaps the most repressive sanctions any music culture experienced in the history of the Eastern Bloc. This gave Western popular music and its iconography a deep symbolic importance as a c/overt means to express dissent and resistance to official state ideology, especially in light of new state policies which banned most Western popular music outright.

The 1970s were subsequently a time of oppressive sanctions. Music clubs and theatres were highly regulated and/or closed, stipulations were placed on the images, sounds and repertoires musical artists could employ, and specifications were put in place regarding the conditions for performance and recorded music production/distribution overall. This crackdown also affected media broadcasting, whose emphasis returned to more 'traditional' Czech musics (brass band, classical, folk, and, somewhat ironically, jazz). Yet, while these policies served to strengthen the divisions between Czechoslovakia and the 'West,' and although Western music was for the most part officially banned, seepage occurred through many avenues. The private dissemination of *samizdat* recordings (illegal copies) were one way in which state sanctions were circumvented. These original recordings, most often obtained through Western contact (e.g. family and friends who emigrated after 1968, or tellingly, communist party member elites and their family members who could travel abroad) were perhaps not widely shared but their impact was enhanced through their reinterpretation in local performances by Czech artists. An underground music counterculture began to materialise, engaging in creative and more coordinated methods for domestically circulating original as well as Western music/music products not officially condoned by the state (e.g. unofficial concerts in rural areas, listening parties, production/dissemination of bootleg tapes of Western and amateur (unlicensed) local artists). Another avenue was through radio, either through unjammed broadcasts from western 'propaganda' stations (e.g. Radio Free Europe, Radio Liberty) or adjacent states (e.g. Poland, Hungary) with looser broadcasting restrictions regarding Western content. Interestingly enough, a small percentage of Western releases were actually distributed in Czechslovakia by their being brought in officially through industry channels as designated 'imports' from other Bloc countries with looser international restrictions (for example, certain records by the UK rock group Queen entered Czechoslovakia officially as 'Hungarian' rock music imports, in turn delineating them officially as a 'communist' product).

Consequently, the terrain of popular music became (somewhat inadvertently) an important site of struggle for Czech cultural identity. The sanctions generated creative avenues for localised dissent in that some Czech musicians began to employ compositional tactics and rhetorical word-play to communicate explicitly with their audiences 'in-between' the musical tropes of official compliance and overt resistance. Despite this, direct Czech engagement with Western popular music culture developments generally diminished for the population and industry alike throughout the seventies. The state labels found it profitable to release localised cover versions of Western popular songs with Czech and Slovak lyrics (often unbeknown to unmindful government officials as well as the general public), largely ignoring global copyright laws while simultaneously embedding these songs in Czech popular conscious as local culture (since the population was not aware of the original versions, most assumed they were Czech).

These transformations obstructed the flow of global popular music culture flow in and out of Czechoslovakia. One consequence of this relative isolation was to stifle the broader development of Czech popular music scenes and their aesthetics by discouraging the regular emergence and turnover of new styles and trends (hence, for example, the lasting impact of progressive rock in Eastern Europe) and the evolution of music technology (the audio cassette and compact disc formats did not arrive in the Czechoslovakia until almost a decade after they were introduced to Western markets). Normalisation meant that Czechoslovakia was even more cut off from the West than its Bloc cousins. Yet, through Czech tenacity – including the operation of black markets or the 'second economy' by which Czechs were able to obtain goods and services the state inadequately provided – a certain segment of the musically inclined population was able to stay abreast of Western musical developments. By contrast, almost nothing was known about Czech popular music culture beyond its borders.

Czech popular music culture did for one moment achieve international acclaim in the late 1970s when dissident Vaclav Havel publicly defended the band *Plastic People of the Universe* (PPoU) and their right to free artistic expression through their music. However, while this moment eventually led to the formation of Charter 77 and a broader movement for more political freedom in Czechoslovakia, it is atypical of Czechoslovak popular culture and more the result of broader cold war dynamics. While the 1970s witnessed their fair share of local musical innovation in the subcultures that sprang up in response to normalisation (of which PPoU were a part), the Czech general public remained largely oblivious to these developments, embracing instead the light pop/rock love songs of romance and heartbreak that the state labels produced in ever-greater quantities.

Czechoslovakia's rapidly deteriorating economic situation during the 1980s produced cultural fissures such that the state found it necessary to be less aggressive in enforcing state policies as a means to pacify the general public's emerging social discontent. The state industries continued to cultivate a stable of popular music performers whose apolitical and rather vapid (Eurodisco) styles were nonetheless immensely popular across generations (e.g. Michal David, Elan, Karel Gott, Helena Vondrockova; Western comparisons/cultural equivalents, although certainly inexact, might be Rick Springfield, Survivor, Neil Diamond and Cher respectively). The Czech underground culture progeny, however, were increasingly tolerated and incorporated into the Czech music industry mainstream (e.g. Prazky Vyber, whose sound might be described as something like a mix of seventies progressive/fusion rock, Frank Zappa's sardonic wit and distinctly Eastern European performative/lyrical tropes). Correspondingly, the flow of Western music culture/products was also formally increased as a means to stave off mass discontent. This opened the door for more official contact between the Czechoslovak music industry and its Western counterparts, an upsurge in Western releases and tours in the Czech landscape, and the maturation of an emergent indigenous punk subculture which provided an outlet for the growing frustration of Czech youth. However, while these changes enabled new opportunities within Czech music culture, substantial restrictions regarding artistic and personal expression remained in effect such that official control could be utilised when necessary (though it apparently rarely was). The fact that pop/rock shows (including those by established Western artists) began to be held in the National

Theatre by the late 1980s certainly suggests that, in the eyes of Czech state officials, rock music had lost some of its adversarial potential.

This brief history suggests that, contrary to Wicke (1992), Mitchell, (1992) and Ryback (1990), Jolanta Peckacz's (1994) argument against idealized notions of popular music's role in dismantling communism in the Soviet bloc is quite compelling. Peckacz argues that real existing socialism was incongruent with Western totalitarian visions of it, that the collapse of communism was neither as sudden, unexpected, or singularly resultant from pressure below as is often celebrated in western narratives of these events and that, in fact, rock culture, real socialism, and the politics of the communist regimes were, by the late 1980s, actually much more compatible than usually theorized. Her argument finds support in the Czech context for, by the late 1980s, Czech music culture and the industry servicing it had settled into a rather politically banal symbiotic existence whereby the state machinery ably provided local products both for those wishing to rage against it (punk music) as well as for it (pop music). To be clear, while the symbolic meaning of western music in Czechoslovakia between 1968 and 1989 cannot be denied, its impact and implication in relation to stimulating the Velvet Revolution should not be overstated. In turn, the Czechoslovak music industry and culture were perhaps positioned somewhat more favourably for post-communist transitional developments than their communist neighbours in that the relationships between its political and music cultures were by 1989 neither as overtly antagonistic, repressive nor as underdeveloped as those in its Bloc counterparts.

The 'post-communist' Czech music industry

When the Velvet Revolution unfolded across roughly eleven days in 1989, it surprised the Czech population every bit as much as the Western world beyond. The promise of transition to a democratic state and the free market initially made the general population euphoric. However, the demise of communism also had a profound impact on the local contours of meaning and organisational praxis throughout the country's entire socioeconomic infrastructure, and the Czechoslovak music culture and industries were no exception. In very real terms, the old ways of doing business and seeing things no longer applied (at least in theory). The dissolution of state subsidies to the media industries and its former employees produced immediate and far-reaching considerations for their professional and financial futures, as well as their legal and sociopolitical standing, for anyone and anything formerly associated with the communist system was now perceived (at least nominally) with great suspicion, if not contempt.

However, a similar sense of dislocation applied almost universally to the careers and symbolic meaning of all Czech musicians. Those officially sanctioned pop performers who were formally scions of the state now represented the past and, as such, their identity carried the baggage of a time and experience most wanted to immediately leave behind. Likewise, those artists (especially in the underground folk scene) whose careers and music had done so much to covertly and overtly resist the mental oppression of the communist government across the years had now, in an ironic twist of fate, lost their meaning with the erasure of their real and symbolic nemeses.

As such, the post-communist Czech music landscape was open both figuratively and literally for dramatic structural and psycho-social reconfiguration. The dominant global music corporations and their concomitant logics of production would help to facilitate these changes in the post-communist Czech music culture, although there were many initial hurdles that needed to be resolved. Within months of the Velvet Revolution, international advisers and investors were on the ground helping the locals to re-establish the Czech music market in commercial terms. Unsurprisingly, many of the local private labels that emerged after the revolution (and there were over a hundred) were directed and staffed by former communist party members, associates and/or employees of the state's former labels. Of course, this also meant that many shady deals went down in the cracks of the emergent market as it began to settle into its new organisational/juridical form. The state's physical assets (production plants, distribution infrastructure and retail sector, including Supraphon's individual retail stores) were privatised and sold off to budding (though not necessarily competent or ethical) local entrepreneurs. Newly privatised radio stations hired international consultants to design their formats, advertising began to proliferate in broadcasts, and such signs of commercial enterprise in media production were popularly perceived as a mark of cultural progress.

Despite these developments, the Czech music market, like its former-Bloc counterparts, was popularly characterised in Western investment circles as 'the wild East' in the early 1990s, a seemingly apt description of its chaotic character as it struggled to reform itself and shed the tenets of its communist past. Establishing a civil society where the social etiquette of customer relations as well as laws related to intellectual property rights were effectively implemented and respected by the population was a significant challenge not only for the new state but also for establishing a healthy commercial sector. Copyright and intellectual property rights were largely foreign concepts, without merit, to most Czechs, and black markets initially thrived openly in the new economy. Consequently, music piracy (tapes, CDs, VHS tapes) exploded to meet new consumer demand for Western music products with its practitioners favourably perceived (at least locally) as legitimate entrepreneurs meeting the needs of a new and active consumer base.

Consequently, foreign investment and official business relations in the Czech music industry developed cautiously. Nonetheless, Western government representatives, industry advisers and corporate investors remained confident that the Czech music market would eventually settle into a more stable entity, and thus remained committed to assisting the Czech government and local businesses in establishing local policies and practices that would align the Czech market more closely with the ideals and parameters of its Western European neighbours.

Arguably the most important factor for sustaining the fledgling operations of any local music label in the early 1990s was licensing and distribution deals with foreign record corporations. Such agreements offered to the local labels not only products with exotic appeal and less financial risk (as the parent corporation covered the initial artist development costs), but also more secure profit potentials, as foreign releases – despite rampant piracy – still sold significant numbers and provided substantial financial returns (sales increased from CZK858 million ($30 million) in 1991 to CZK1,307,600 ($44 million) by 1993 (IFPI 1999)). By 1994, the market had settled such that a smaller coterie of local labels had emerged as the dominant players in the Czech industry (the market was still growing with registered sales of CZK2,061,100 ($50.6 million) that year). By 1995, all of the global majors had established formal links to, or offices within, the Czech market: EMI formed a joint venture with Monitor (1994), Sony with Bonton in 1998 (having licensed its catalog to Bonton from 1990); BMG, Polygram and Warner established formal subsidiaries in the market in 1991, 1994 and 1995 respectively after initially licensing their catalogs to a variety of local labels (BMG also acted as the local licensee for MCA, the last of the big six global music corporations at the time, which chose not to link up with a local partner). As such, the Czech market had largely 'matured' into an oligopoly by 1996, the majors/joint ventures accounting for 66 per cent of market share sales (Monitor-EMI (26 per cent), Polygram (16 per cent), Warner (13 per cent) and BMG (11 per cent), with 24 other record labels accounting for the other 34 per cent) (*Music & Copyright* 1997). These ventures were hardly 'imperialist' affairs, however, for while these subsidiaries maintained formal ties with the broader organisation and culture of their global parent corporations, the local organisational cultures and praxes of these subsidiaries were anything but similar to their Western counterparts. As described by former employees, working in these entities in the early mid 1990s was an exhilarating and chaotic affair, as organisational protocol emerged in an ad hoc fashion and building market share operated as the overarching goal, rather than producing specific sales figures. As one former BMG employee stated:

> All of the [major label] offices were small, maybe 20 people, with a mix of young and old thinking and very little clear-cut organizational hierarchy. We all had to do everything, so there was no official A&R or marketing department – we all did each other's jobs because we had to. We didn't really have an organizational plan because you couldn't make it work. The market was so random and backwards [in relation to western standards]. It was more about releasing whatever you wanted to while feeling no pressure to succeed, as money was flowing in from all around and nobody was checking up on you [from the home offices]. To be honest, we were making it up as we went along because there were no established rules of how things work. Nothing worked as it did in western markets, though. I remember trying to talk to the retail folks about how to sell records – they had no clue on how to do it. They kept the new releases hidden behind the counter so they wouldn't get stolen! Of course, nobody knew they were also available either! Ingrained communist thinking that was hard to change or reason with from [a western] perspective.
>
> (Elavsky 2005a)

By 1997, the Czech music market was more or less structured into a set of dominant industry players/arbiters: the aforementioned record label subsidiaries (besides the Indies record company, based in Brno, few independent labels could effectively compete in the market, although a large number remained active releasing a smaller number of products annually which served niche music genres); the major commercial (the networks of Evropa 2, Hitradio, Kiss Radio etc.) and public (Cesky Rozhlas) radio stations/networks; several television networks (ESO, Noc s Andelem); and print (reflex, rock and pop, etc.) media outlets which produced music programming/segments/content nominally. The local retail sector, however, never fully developed into any mature organisational schema (the closest being the development of the Bonton retail chain; it is worth noting that no significant foreign investment was ever secured in this realm). As such, music retail remained patchy in form and unpredictable in nature throughout the 1990s, ranging from random street kiosks to smaller organised shops to the Bonton Superstores (comparable to a medium-sized record retailer in the West) found in a few major cities.

The fragmented retail market may well have been one factor in the continuing cultures of unauthorised consumption in the Czech Republic. Despite the IFPI opening a local subsidiary, in 1989, to encourage anti-piracy enforcement, piracy rates remained high. In fact, one might argue that the IFPI actually contributed to the problem by encouraging the artificial inflation of prices for all music products in efforts to stave off the possibility of undermining 'Western' markets (the global music industry didn't want Germans or Austrians buying their products cheaper next door). As such, prices, especially in light of the weakened Czech koruna, were exorbitant for the locals. The average cost of a foreign CD (e.g. R.E.M's 1996 *New Adventures in Hi-Fi*) was roughly $23 – even higher than in Western markets and roughly 8 per cent of Czech monthly household income at the time. By contrast, CDs by local Czech artists at the time sold for approximately $12. Such pricing scales consequently stimulated and sustained significant local interest in the illegal market while fuelling innate perceptions in Czech consumers of a global cultural prejudice against them (McNeil 1998; CZSO).

While Western music imports largely dominated Czech music culture across the 1990s, the majors were nonetheless initially committed to investing in local artists, especially if they delivered strong local returns and were presumed to possess export potential beyond the Czech border (at the time, no region was considered off-limits to Czech exports, although the belief in the potential to successfully export any Czech music (except classical) would largely dissipate by 1998). Several artists such as Mňága a Žd'orp, Druha Trava, Lucie, Buty, Kabat, Vlasta Redl, and J.A.R. quickly achieved considerable success and cultural significance in the post-communist era.[1] However, despite several attempts, no Czech music artist was ever able to translate that into international acclaim. This was in part attributable to the fact that English was largely a new language to the region after 1989 (the study of Russian was mandatory under communism) and, thus, *few* Czech artists could speak English, much less sing in it (a necessity for transnational investment/distribution). Moreover, those who tried initially after 1989 were largely castigated for their 'pretentiousness', a process subtly codified by Czech media gate-keepers (especially radio) whose programming choices routinely if not explicitly kept any song in English sung by a Czech from getting broader exposure through the Czech media.

Moving into the twenty-first century

The turning point in the Czech recording industry occurred in 1998, when ithe largest sales figures ever were recorded that year (CSK2,503.6 million; $77.5 million; IFPI 1998*)*. The market had matured and become fully integrated into the global logics and circuits of commercial music production (international tour networks, coordinated release campaign partnerships, advanced commercial radio programming techniques, harmonisation of copyright laws, policies and (on paper at least) protective mechanisms). Most in the local industry felt that it was just a matter of time before the Czech market distinguished itself from its Eastern cousins in the eyes of its parent corporations, becoming accepted as an advanced and stable music market. This would prove to be a premature hope, however.

First, and rather unpredictably, the Czech Republic experienced a notable and rather unexpected resurgence of interest in Czech language music, which was initially manifested on radio. Emerging as something of an unspecific reaction to the dominance of English/Western influence on Czech culture (music in particular) after 1989, several radio stations began programming primarily Czech music (old and new) as a marketing strategy and found great success in doing so. As the older generations primarily drove this trend (the demographic of these stations was generally 40 and above), one might initially explain this phenomenon as a reaction from those challenged by the dynamics of post-communist Czech society. Indeed, a certain nostalgia for communist times actually emerged at this time, such that many of the music stars from the old system achieved renewed cultural prestige through this moment of cultural/media revisionism. However, while all of these developments initiated a renewed interest in the media over the questions of Czech identity and history, this nostalgia made little lasting impact on the younger generations who were growing up with a waning impression of the communist experience, decreasingly demarcated boundaries and cultural tensions between Czech and global culture, and a growing penchant for the consistent turnover of commercial music trends (including new Czech artists). To the point, this younger generation held Western culture in less awe, as their engagement with foreign ideas/languages was a part of their secondary education and daily life. In turn, for this generation, for example, the stigma surrounding the use of English as a form of pretentiousness had simply dissipated as more of this generation learned it. This did not mean, however, that their cultural practices and perspectives were no longer influenced by the residue of communist cultural logics.

Second, cultures of piracy remained prevalent. In light of continued policies for artificially inflating foreign music product prices domestically, consumers were quick to recognise the potential and economic merits of digital piracy. CD burning became such a burgeoning trend such that, by 2002, it was estimated that every second CD in the Czech Republic was a copy, many produced by the curious local phenomena of *Vypalovny* ('Burn shops' – namely, clubs that would operate like a library and allow members unlimited copying privileges for a $5 membership and $1 per CD; the biggest club in Prague had over 15,000 CDs and thousands of members (Andress and Kozakova 2002)). In turn, when P2P networks began to proliferate around the same time, Czechs embraced them readily, with local hard piracy networks stepping up their international production efforts through the auspices of these portals. When exploited in conjunction with the lax oversight of product runs at domestic pressing plants, individuals, domestic counterfeiting rings and international organised crime syndicates (e.g. the Russian and Vietnamese mafia, specifically) could successfully exploit these loopholes to profit handsomely from the circumstances surrounding locally inflated prices and domestic demand. The Czech Republic was ultimately put on the US Special 301 watchlist in 2008 for being both a formidable global supplier of hard pirate content and for lacking effective enforcement measures against local manufacturers and markets along the German border.

Such practices have impacted on the landscape of music retail in the Czech Republic. Many music retail outlets closed, while the rise of hypermarkets (big-box retail chains similar to Walmart in the US) had, by 2003, virtually monopolised the sale of hard music products, where they were utilised as loss-leaders but given ever-diminishing rack space. Coupled with the fact that no significant online option for developing emergent digital sales had emerged (the Czech market lagged significantly in this realm due to delays in technology transfer, shallower domestic Internet penetration and complications related to marketing), this development largely signalled the impending demise of retail sales as a site of revenue, as hard sales steadily decreased by 38 per cent (from $40 million to $24.8 million) between 2000 and 2007 (IFPI 2007, 2008).

Consequently, the first decade of the twenty-first century was marked by several significant changes in the Czech recording industry and its dynamics. When the downturn in the global industry occurred, the major labels began to reconfigure their global perspectives, including re-evaluating the structural organisation and operations of their subsidiary networks. Greater pressure was subsequently placed on the local Czech majors to 'make the quarterly numbers' (i.e. to achieve profit targets rather than merely a market share). Subsidiaries were also instructed to prioritise the marketing of global priority artists in local markets in order to benefit from economies of scale. Investment in local artists, both financial and in terms of time, was curtailed. This ultimately bred notable anger towards their corporate parents from Czech subsidiary employees, as the policies were considered insensitive to the proclivities and work constraints of the Czech market. Indeed, the change in global priorities produced significant tension across all Czech subsidiaries as the parent corporations looked for ways to streamline their international investments and cut their losses in underperforming markets, inducing fears in the Czech subsidiaries that they might be closed at any time. Ultimately, BMG Czech Republic was absorbed into Sony Czech Republic in 2004 (the latter, having the stronger presence in the Czech market) in light of the global merger of the two firms and Warner Music scaled back its operations largely to secondary distribution (through Supraphon) in 2009.

The Czech music industry today

What does all this mean for those working in the Czech music industry in 2011? Twenty-two years after the fall of communism, the Czech Republic has become fully integrated into the broader stream of global cultural flows and economic activity. Its music/media production cultures are strongly influenced by content and practices emanating from the German, US and UK markets, the main players in the local industry having established themselves as partners in pan-European/global corporate networks/flows of operations. Nonetheless, its population retains a distinct pride and personal investment in their local music culture, especially in relation to live music performance, even as their musical tastes are simultaneously aligned (willingly or not) with the broader proclivities of global music culture trends and pan-European flows of radio programming.

What follows below is a summary of considerations regarding the status of the market and contemporary dynamics which those working in Czech music culture (industry reps and musicians) face today. This is followed by an assessment of the continuing tensions surrounding developments related to the global-local nexus of the 'music industry' and culture as they play out in this particular context.

Record labels

It is impossible to avoid underscoring the power by which the Big Four continue to influence and delimit the dominant activity that often constitutes the 'global music industry' for casual listeners, and by turn, the Czech music industry and music consumers therein. While the global digital piracy crisis continues to impact activity within the corporate majors in every music market, combined with the proliferation of social media it has also produced fissures for increased local independent music production. However, in the Czech Republic, this often remains regional and underground in its impact, minimally filtering into the broader mainstream of Czech music media/industry culture developments. The activity of the global majors' subsidiaries (and those associated with them) largely proscribe contemporary Czech music culture/industry activity, just as Supraphon, Panton and Opus once did under communism.

Pressure from global parents on these subsidiaries to maintain profitability remains high, however, and their work environments are consequently stressful. In turn, as in other larger markets, Czech labels (majors and independents) are taking on less risk and minimising their investments. Instead, they are focusing on rights management (the selling of music use to telecommunication companies (e.g. ringtones), for example, where profits, as in most markets, are booming) and rarely fronting money to develop artists as they once did, utilising 360° contract deals instead (which have become the norm after first appearing roughly in 2008) to more effectively safeguard their outlays.

Music retail, as elsewhere in the Western hemisphere, is a dying entity despite continued nominal label investment in it. Most of the big-box stores in the Czech Republic have eliminated retail music sales, leaving kiosks and a small contingent of independent merchants (Bontonland, being the most prominent) to provide life support to Czech hard retail sales. The number of sales associated with gold and platinum status is indicative of how dire the situation is: whereas 10 years ago it took sales of 50,000 and 100,000 units to respectively register gold and platinum sales status, today the numbers are 6,000 and 12,000 for international repertoire, and just 3,000 and 6,000 for local artists. In certain weeks, selling less than 100 copies has been enough to put an artist in the top 50 chart. The labels remain nevertheless committed to this sector, quite frankly because promising alternative options for music commerce remain limited, given that local digital sales realm is simply anaemic. Digital sales have been erratic (digital sales fluctuated between $1.8 million in 2007 (5 per cent of the market) and $1.4 million (7 per cent of the market) in 2010, despite the expansion of local online retail options (such as eMusic, O2 Active, Ovi Music, Stream, t-music; Apple finally launched iTunes in the Czech Republic in September of 2011, which may change this trend) (IFPI 2011). Individual consumers have proven reluctant to embrace legal online retail, but they are not helped by cross-border retailer practices, namely that almost a third of all attempted online purchases by Czechs from foreign territories (using such online outlets as Amazon.de in Germany or iTunes in the UK) are declined because international vendors are wary of Czech consumers' ability to pay (*Technet.cz.* 2011).

In addition, since the use of digital rights management and formal prosecution procedures have largely been abandoned, illegal sharing activity and sites (especially bittorrent) have proliferated, expanding illegal digital traffic exponentially. And while *Vypalovany* have been legally eliminated (the IFPI recently recommending that the Czech Republic be removed from the 301 list for its work in addressing music piracy), Czech authorities remain weak with regard to enforcing the broader laws related to piracy, including addressing problems related to poor border trafficking enforcement, delays in criminal proceedings and lingering loopholes in Czech copyright law. With a majority of Czechs (including those in law enforcement) viewing copyright infringement cases as victimless crimes, it appears that after two decades of free-market enterprise, the validity/protection of intellectual property rights continue to be perceived (beyond the business community) as not a serious concern.

Despite these problems, local labels remain committed to producing physical content (CDs, DVDs) as a promotional product/revenue stream. However, in order to increase the profit margins in the retail realm, the Czech majors have begun to release two versions of their international products, namely an imported 'premium' version, offering the same sleeve and booklet to be found in Western markets and costing on average CZK379 (approximately $19) and a locally produced 'standard' version (often referred to as budget in Western markets), with perhaps a one-page booklet and cheaper locally produced packaging, with an average cost of CZK237 (roughly $12). Despite the lower retail price, the local subsidiaries make more money from the standard versions as they are cheaper to produce (given that there are no artist development costs and few design and packaging costs), and, as they are affordable to the majority of Czechs, they sell many more copies than the premium versions (for example, Nelly Furtado's *Loose* sold 2,000 premium versions and 23,000 standard versions). Similarly, special editions (digipacks) have begun to stimulate consumer interest, albeit in small numbers (selling perhaps

108   C. Michael Elavsky

500 copies; the Czech independent labels have been most proactive and successful in this realm). Around twenty local independent labels remain active (primarily in Prague) but, lacking financial capital, serve primarily as service providers/ distributors for artists who wish to self-produce their own work (i.e. few offer traditional label services such as management and marketing). Occasionally, however, they produce a breakout hit or artist (such as Xindl X on Good Day Records and Radusza on Indies) whose commercial success continues to stimulate independent production efforts. The former state label Supraphon has re-emerged as a significant player in the Czech market which, despite being 'independent', sustains itself by licensing Warner products locally. Similarly, Popron lives on by attending to niche local interests. However, all Czech record companies – be they major or independent – struggle to remain solvent.

Musicians

The downturn has obviously had an impact on the many local professional musicians who struggle to build and sustain their careers. With fewer local contracts being offered from the majors – and most of those being offered to established artists – 'development deals' have become the norm for breaking new acts, whereby independent producers assume the risk by securing outside investment (normally from the private sector with strings of some sort attached), positioning the artist to develop/finance their own identity/brand (with the producer) until a certain modicum of success is achieved whereby a major label might step in. It is important to note that local artists remain vital investments for the majors (in light of interest in local music) and, therefore, professional contact with the majors remains important for any artist's overall professional develop-ment. On the other hand, the majors are increasingly perceived as being too bureaucratic and inefficient in developing local music projects/new artist careers. Simply put, most well-paying professional opportunities for Czech musical performers generally go to the same established and long-standing names (artists/performers) that have been in the industry for years, if not decades. While older, established, Czech music stars may benefit from the majors' traditional operating methods (releasing an album annually, undertaking media campaigns, taking advantage of the few TV/print media opportunities available: maximising income through various related revenue streams such as live appearances, publishing royalties, advertising); selling 10,000 records or so and earning perhaps CZK2 million annually ($120,000), most Czech musicians will never attain this level, with one informant suggesting that 'earning CZK120,000 ($7,000) in one year [through musical enterprise] is like a major success' (Elavsky 2011).

For most Czech musicians, therefore, records provide no or minimal income. They remain important, however, as promotional and publicity devices, especially singles, which are essential and instrumental for achieving any form of success in the Czech market. After a single is released, a few television and print media opportunities may be exploited for promotion, but there are only a few such outlets/opportunities. Videos remain an important vehicle for promotion (though many of these are independently produced on shoe-string budgets) and they are most often posted to popular social media sites or shown during commercial breaks on the popular morning/news shows. However, while Očko remains an important local music media outlet (and video rotation here never hurts), it is through Czech radio that one's career is ultimately made and sustained. Czech commercial radio is largely programmed (at least the bigger stations/networks) to cater to a wide demographic in light of the smaller Czech market size. Evropa 2 and the Kiss Radio Network are the two most important players for breaking new music. Ceska Radio (public radio) effectively serves underrepresented musical niches and remains a revered institution, if not a commercial influence, for most artists.

As radio is so important for success, commercialism (i.e. 'selling out') is not viewed as disparagingly as one might find in other larger markets. Martin Ledvina, a producer with multiple Anděl's (the equivalent to America's Grammy) to his credit summed it up tellingly:

> From 1989 to 2004, no one cared about making money because they didn't have to. Today, one needs to be a businessman [*sic*] and think commercially. If that means I have to change a mix to get it played on the radio, I will. I will work with the radio programmers because they know what will be a hit. And besides, a commercial hit means ordinary people like it, no? That's not a bad thing is it?
>
> (Elavsky 2011)

While singles, videos and promotional appearances provide media exposure to artists, however, remuneration for them remains negligible. Instead, it is through live performance that acts make most of their income. Generally (and once again), established artists sustain and dominate the Czech concert circuit. Touring (or individual appearances which, regardless of their popularity, most acts must do almost without pause) generally consists of at least one specified string of dates annually across two to five weeks, coupled with single performances across the following months for the rest of the year, all of which occur within a varying range of venues, attendance capacities and locations. As one informant stated: 'you can't just play the halls in the larger towns, you have to play the spring beer festival or any other occasion in *every* village as well!' (Elavsky 2007). Such live appearances often include Slovakia and parts of Poland in light of the informal cross-border flows of content (people sharing music, language similarities, domestic radio broadcast interpenetration etc.). Playing 14 shows of 400 capacity constitutes success, and one tries to do this 'circle around the country' (in variation) two or three times a year and, especially, after every single is released. In fact, few performers can afford not to play regularly year round (ibid.). During the summer, the expanding festival circuit provides further opportunity for income, though not usually for emergent artists. In between, the more popular artists increasingly play private parties or corporate functions to augment their earnings quickly and significantly. Then, it is time to do the circuit again, and again.

Surprisingly, few Czech artists make any money by having their songs used in local advertising, not because they don't want to but rather because there is little interest by local companies to license local album tracks (the use of

Debbi Kahlova's single *Touch the Sun* in a Metaxa advertisement is a recent and successful exception). Similarly, while the use of music in advertising and film constitutes one of the most important growth sectors in the global music industry today, this has only been partially manifested in the Czech market. Rather, most local rights exploitation employs the same foreign songs used in other markets and is most often negotiated at the international corporate headquarters in relation to the development of global corporate product campaigns. Ironically, Czech musicians are often hired to perform these songs as a means to 'glocalise' these campaigns (using the local language), garnering only one-off performance fees for themselves in return.

On another commercial front, artist product endorsements are only just now emerging, such that an artist's ability to brand themselves across a spectrum of commercial possibilities remains much more circumscribed than in other larger markets. Ewa Farna stands out as a local innovator in terms of this, presenting broader branded/price-tiered packages for her fans (e.g. offering CDs, T-shirts, purses, pencil boxes, VIP tickets, meet and greets, etc. for different prices as part of these packages), but the success of these endeavours is not widely known or acknowledged.

Conclusion: local and global musical flows

Up-and-coming contemporary Czech musical performers face a radically different landscape from the previous generation. Ostensibly, they have more opportunities than their forebears in that they have greater freedom of expression and greater access to global culture and music production capabilities. Although distinctive alternative scenes or experimental production cultures have a minimal presence, Czech music has become a mix of musical roots, which is understandable given that the musical sensibilities of Czech youth are more cosmopolitan than in the past, growing up in a culture directly connected to the global flows of culture. It also means that many view Anglo-American and pan-European sources as part of their roots, including singing in English. Singing in English is no longer a controversial issue in the Czech Republic. The surprising success of Support Lesbiens, the first local act to achieve significant domestic acclaim singing in English (in 2002 with *Tune Da Radio*), was a watershed moment for the Czech music industry in this regard. Moreover, the profound popularity and growing impact of the localised 'Idol' franchise (*Česko hledá SuperStar* (Czechs are looking for a Superstar) now in its eighth year and rebranded as *Česko Slovenská Superstar* (Czech and Slovak Superstar) to expand its reach), where singing in English is regularly employed, has only further embedded this tendency. Furthermore, the 2004 Song of the Year Czech Anděl went to Dan Barta for *On My Head*, the first English language song to receive this prize (it has since happened again in 2005 and 2010).

In fact, for many artists, singing pop music in Czech is actually harder as there are 'fewer good influences or inspirations' (Elavsky 2011), and the language itself, full of consonants, is hardly mellifluous (though the best practitioners can make it sound as such). This does not mean, however, that the Czechs are as proficient as, for example, Scandinavians in mastering English delivery; Czechs singing in English remains a trend in need of further time to develop as many lack the feel for the language, having had less engagement with it than other European nations. However, this is changing rapidly, especially in light of the continued and overwhelming success of the *Česko Slovenská Superstar* franchise, which has proven that 'anyone' can emerge to achieve significant domestic commercial success, with or without a contract with the Czech majors. In contrast to communism and its restrictions on freedom of choice, it can easily be argued that real progress has been achieved since 1989.

And yet the Czech music culture and its associated industry remains largely marked as 'backwards' both by those on the inside who lament the rogue tendencies of their local market and their fellow citizens' lack of respect for intellectual property rights, and those beyond its borders, evident in the policies of the corporate majors and Western consumer opinion. Its music culture is now strongly influenced by global music trends, but these generally flow in one direction, from West to East, usually taking root several months, or even years, after they have lost their cutting edge in the West. Czechs now have the ability and technology to experiment with any sound or idea, yet many of them remain beholden to the idea of Western superiority with regard to music culture and production values. New artists continue to emerge, but Czech music consumers remain enthralled with the past, such that 'beer rock' guitar war horses such as Kabat and Tři Sestry, as well as lyrically intellectual folk poets such as Čechomor and Jaromir Nohavica (and reformed communist pop icons from the Czechoslovak 1980s such as Michal David and Elan) continue to define the Czech musical aesthetic twenty years on.

Czech artists write songs – increasingly in English – ostensibly to move beyond the local market but their quality as judged by Western arbiters (consumers, industry folks etc.) remains largely viewed as derivative, consequently diminishing their ability to compete on any level with Western artists. No Czech performer appears poised for significantly broader international distribution or success, a fact attributable to the Czech language, general conditions of the global music economy, the difficulties in every market to achieve local sales, and the growing fragmentation of global music culture and consumer attention. As one local representative summed it up:

> each market's [corporate] subsidiaries are concentrating on selling their own local music and don't have time to push a foreign act unless the parent home offices gets behind it. These [Global priority] acts are still largely Anglo-American. . . . Nobody is going to be looking for Czech pop music on their own.
>
> (Elavsky 2005b)

For those working in the power-centres that still largely define the operations of the 'global music industry', market activity and musical innovation in its Czech tributary remains a largely insignificant 'post-communist' phenomena. Although capitalism has come to the 'Eastern Europe', its populations (lumped together as they often are) have yet to define themselves in 'Western' eyes. While now securely linked into the networks of global culture, Czech music culture remains in many ways as isolated and misunderstood as it was under communism.

As a small, advanced, post-communist market firmly assimilated within the global commercial music industry networks, the Czech music industry continues nonetheless to negotiate asymmetrical power dynamics as it always has. The global music crisis that has radically affected the operations of the Big Four since 2005 has produced a reassessment of fiscal priorities, industry protocol and risky ventures in the Czech music industry. Those working for the local branches of the major labels, ostensibly participating in the development of global music culture as part of the global music industry are, in fact, delimited and isolated from participating in the real decisions and infrastructure of its power.

Yet, Czech music culture remains resilient – if somewhat prosaic – in its particular evolution. For while many of the same Czech music groups continue to occupy the prominent radio and festival slots (with old and new hits), and many of the same people continue to hold the primary industry jobs, the local industry nonetheless continues to nurture new trends and faces which inject new impulses into the identity of Czech popular music. The extent to whether they are innovative or distinctly Czech remains a question few seem concerned with today as the Czech music landscape has become infused with global music culture that neither dominates, nor is subservient to local cultural proclivities, a fact borne out by the recent introduction of MTV into the Czech landscape. Despite its global brand and economic power, it has been unable to usurp market share from its main rival, Očko, a local (relatively low-budget) music channel which began in 1999. While the latter continues to broadcast interviews, music videos and music-themed programming which caters to local interests, MTV Czech Republic imports the majority of its programming from MTV USA and UK – a point in fact (and taste) lost on (or largely ignored by) the locals.

Note

1   It is impossible to produce authoritative sales figures on which to base this assertion because of the structure of the local industry. Rather than computerised sales scans, retail music sales data in the Czech Republic circa 1994–98 relied on handwritten reports by record stores to the labels. Nothing like Soundscan was present in the Czech Republic until the early 2000s and even then it was only utilised effectively in the bigger retail outlets (i.e. hypermarkets/big box stores). As such, the assertion that these artists were particularly successful is based on personal conversations with the artists themselves about their financial success, affirmed by interviews with personnel in the local industry, as well as these stars' general ubiquity in Czech media/concert realms (i.e. filling the biggest halls, radio rotation, presence in the popular press etc.) during these years.

Bibliography

Andress, M. and Kozakova, P. (2002) Czech Music Industry Unites Against CD-Burning Outlets, *Billboard*, 19 October, p. 57.

Czech Statistical Office (CZSO). Average Gross Wage Czech Republic: 1985–2008. Available online at: www.czso.cz/csu/dyngrafy.nsf/graf/eng_mzdy_1985_ (accessed 4 April 2012).

Elavsky, C.M. (2003) Interview with Petr Belohlavek. Prague.
Elavsky, C.M. (2005a) Interview with Greg Jarvis.
Elavsky, C.M. (2005b) Interview with Romana Paškova.
Elavsky, C.M. (2007) Interview with Lenka Dusilova.
Elavsky, C.M. (2011) Interview with Martin Ledvina.
Holy, Ladislav (1996) *The Little Czech and the Great Czech Nation*. Cambridge: Cambridge University Press.
IFPI (1998) *The Recording Industry in Numbers 1998*. London.
IFPI (1999) *The Recording Industry in Numbers 1999*. London.
IFPI (2006) *The Recording Industry in Numbers 2006*. London.
IFPI (2007) *The Recording Industry in Numbers 2007*. London.
IFPI (2008) *The Recording Industry in Numbers 2008*. London.
IFPI (2011) *The Recording Industry in Numbers 2011*. London.
Kimball, S. (1964) Czech Nationalism: A Study of the National Theatre Movement, 1845–83. Urbana, IL: University of Illinois Press.
Kotek, J. (1994) *Dejiny České Populární Hudby a Zpevu* (History of Czech Popular Music and Singers). Prague: Academia.
Leff. C. (1996) *The Czech and Slovak Republics: Nation Versus State*. Boulder, CO: Westview Press.
Locke, B. (2006) *Opera and Ideology in Prague: Polemics and Practice at the National Theater, 1900–1938*. Rochester, NY: University of Rochester Press.
McNeil, J. (1998) Changes in Median Household Income: 1969 to 1996. U.S. Department of Commerce, Economics and Statistics Administration. Bureau of the Census. Current Population Reports Special Studies, 23–196. Available online at: www.census.gov/prod/3/98pubs/p23–196.pdf (accessed 12 May 2012).
Mitchell, T. (1996) *Popular Music and Local Identity: Rock, Pop, and Rap in Europe and Oceania*. Leicester: Leicester University Press.
Music & Copyright (1997) Czech Soundcarrier Market Rises 20%, Slovakian Market Doubles in 1996, 26 March, p. 8.
Opekar, A. (1994) Towards the History of Czech Rock Music: Turtle – the First LP by a Czech Rock Group, in *Central European Popular Music*, Prague, pp. 66–72.
Pekacz, J. (1994) Did Rock Smash the Wall? The Role of Rock in Political Transition, *Popular Music*, 13(1): 41–9.
Ryback, T.W. (1990) *Rock Around the Bloc: A History of Rock Music in Eastern Europe and the Soviet Union*. New York: Oxford University Press.
Technet.cz. (2011) Amazon i iTunes diskriminují Čechy a odmítají je. To by ted'mělo skončit, 18 April. Available online at: http://technet.idnes.cz/amazon-i-itunes-diskriminuji-cechy-a-odmitaji-je-to-by-ted-melo-skoncit-1z4-/sw_internet.asp?c=A110414_172747_sw_internet_pka (accessed 22 April 2011).
The Velvet Violin: Steep Fall in Czech Album Sales as Digital Market Remains Small.
The Prague Post Music Blog, 21 March 2011. Available online at: http://blogs.praguepost.com/music/2011/03/21/steep-fall-in-czech-album-sales-as-digital-market-remains-small (accessed 22 April 2011).
Wicke, P. (1992) The Times They Are A-Changin: Rock Music and Political Change in East Germany, in R. Garofalo (ed.) *Rockin' the Boat: Mass Music and Mass Movements*, Boston, MA: South End Press, pp. 81–92.

Finland

Population:	5.3 million (114th)
Languages:	Finnish (91%),
	Swedish (5.5%)
Capital:	Helsinki (pop 1.1 million)
Currency:	Euro (€). $1 = €0.75
GDP:	$238.7 bn (35th)
GDP (PPP)/capita:	$36,660 (19th)
Median age:	42.5

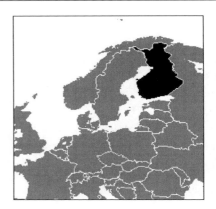

GDP data from World Bank

Population data from CIA world factbook

Exchange rate used by IFPI (2011) (source: Oanda)

2010 Recorded music market

Overall income:	$70.3m	
World ranking:	24th	
	Income	World ranking
Physical sales	$49.4m	26th
Digital sales	$11.0m	27th
Performance rights	$9.9m	18th

Historical recorded music market ($m, at IFPI's 2010 exchange rate)

	1999	2000	2001	2002	2003	2004	2005	2006	2007	2008	2009
Trade Value			107.7	100.8	103.7	89.7	87.7	92.5	87.2	87.0	73.3
Retail Value	151.5	157.7	216.8	202.9	208.7	180.5	176.5				

Proportion of domestic repertoire (market value, physical sales only)

1991	1995	2000	2005	2010
45%	37%	38%	52%	51%

Album certification levels

	2010	1999
Gold	Domestic – 10,000	Domestic – 20,000
	International – 10,000	International – 20,000
Platinum	Domestic – 20,000	Domestic – 40,000
	International – 20,000	International – 40,000

7 Finland

Pekka Gronow

Introduction

Finland, with a population of 5.3 million, is in many ways typical of the smaller European record markets. It is smaller than neighbouring Sweden, which has long functioned as a regional hub, but roughly the same as Norway and Denmark. The Finnish record market is also approximately the same size as Portugal and Greece, although the latter two have much larger populations. The four major multinationals all have branch offices in Finland, and their combined market share is about three-quarters of the total.

However, whether it is due to the language (Finnish is not an Indo-European language like English, French or Russian and has no close relatives except Estonian) or size of the country, the Finnish record market has been more insular than many Western European countries. The multinationals arrived relatively late in Finland, and the market share of domestic music remains high. Approximately half of all records sold in Finland are international repertoire.[1] Finland has never been culturally or politically isolated, and all major trends in popular music from the tango to punk have found their way into Finland, but sooner or later they have given birth to a local variant in the Finnish language. Nonetheless, a consideration of the Finnish recording industry gives us a chance to study in detail the way the multinationals have moved into and expanded their activities in ways that will be similar to their position in other smaller nations. It will also give us an opportunity to consider how the major record labels have maintained profitability and their strong position even during the current crisis in the recording industry.

The old record industry in Finland

The first Finnish records were made in 1901 by the Gramophone Company, the predecessor of today's EMI. But although most Finnish recordings for the next half century appeared on international labels such as HMV, Columbia and Odeon, the multinationals were satisfied to operate in Finland through licensing deals with local agents. The Finnish market was small so, whereas the Swedish and Danish branches of Gramophone were established in 1903, EMI Finland did not appear until 1968.

The local agent had the exclusive right to distribute in Finland the products of the multinational. The best-selling records were usually pressed in Finland from imported masters, and the agent paid a licence fee for each record sold; slower sellers were imported pressings. The agent was also obliged to issue a certain number of domestic recordings on the multinational company's labels and pay a fee for the use of the trademark. In order to keep the costs down, the agents also had their own labels for part of their repertoire. This way the multinationals did not have to make any investments in Finland, but received a steady income from the agents.

The case of Fazer Musiikki (until 1960, Fazerin Musiikkikauppa Oy) exemplifies the traditional music business in Finland. Established in Helsinki in 1898, it grew from a small music shop into the largest company in the Finnish music business. At its peak, from the 1960s to the 1980s, the concern was involved in retail sales, mail order, music publishing, instrument manufacturing and sales and record production. It also had an artist agency. The publishing catalogue included the songs of Finland's most famous classical composer, Jean Sibelius. Fazer Musiikki originally obtained the agency of Gramophone in 1910. In the 1950s and 1960s, it represented Decca in Finland, and also published its own productions on the Rytmi label. The company's managing director Roger Lindberg (1915–2003), a member of the owning family, was active in many areas of Finnish musical life and a well-known figure in the international recording industry. He was President of IFPI from 1968 to 1973.

In 1966, Fazer Musiikki and international company Philip-Polygram jointly established Finnlevy Oy, a production and distribution company. It operated on the premises of Fazer and in 1975 Fazer bought out the foreign partner. In 1972, when sales were expanding rapidly, Fazer Musiikki bought Scandia, their strongest competitor. In the deal they also acquired the agency for Warner. It has been estimated that in the best years of the 1970s the company had a 70 per cent share of the Finnish market. It was so profitable that it was able to buy most independent Finnish companies, and in 1990 it was listed on the Helsinki stock exchange (Aunola 2009).

Fazer-Musiikki had been one of the six companies that constituted the entire Finnish record industry until the early 1970s. Until 1970, the country's annual record sales were only about one million units, lower than many other countries of similar size. In that year, 3 million units were sold in Norway and 4 million in Denmark. In Sweden, with twice the population of Finland, 10 million records were sold (for more comparative historical data, see Gronow 1983). Record production was a relatively straightforward process. Record companies produced Finnish popular songs and Finnish-language cover versions of international hits and acted as agents for international record companies. Most were standard popular songs in dance tempo (known as *iskelmä*). The songs were normally published by a music publishing company affiliated with the record company. Often the publishing company also obtained sub-publishing rights for international hits that were translated into Finnish. 'Featured artists', performers whose names were on the labels, usually had a contract and were paid a percentage of the sales. Some were just paid a lump sum. Many artists were semi-professionals who had day jobs and performed on weekends. The accompanying musicians were professionals who were paid union scales on the basis of hours spent in the studio, but no royalties on sales. If a record received a lot of radio play, the accompanying musicians were entitled to a share of the performing royalties. (For more detailed studies of this period, see Gronow 1995; Muikku 2001).

The introduction of cheap cassette players in the 1970s proved a blessing to the Finnish industry. Until then, the ownership of record players had been limited to about a third of the population. In the 1970s, the market for pre-recorded music expanded rapidly. Previously, records had only been sold in traditional music stores, but cassettes could now be purchased at petrol stations, department stores and supermarkets. Established record companies now issued all of their albums in both LP and cassette formats, but the boom also gave rise to a number of smaller companies specialising in cassettes. Often they were just cover versions of current hits, but there was also a large cassette production of old-time dance music and religious songs. Amateur rock groups preferred vinyl singles (Gronow 1984).

Prompted by the introduction of the audio cassette and the emerging rock culture, the Finnish record industry expanded rapidly, with record sales increasing 280 per cent between 1970 and 1980. The first new company to enter the field was Love Records, founded in 1966. Love was a pioneer in producing Finnish rock records and helped to introduce many new artists. At first, the company benefited from increasing record sales in the 1970s, but went bankrupt in 1979 as a result of overproduction and a change in public tastes. In the 1970s, several other companies entered the field. Most proved short-lived, but some were actively involved in the breakthrough of new idioms such a punk rock and rockabilly. At this point, it seems appropriate to consider what kind of music is popular in Finland.

Musical trends at home and abroad

More than a thousand new CDs are published every year in Finland. The multinationals also market a part of their international repertoire, and there are smaller distributors and specialist record shops which also import records. There are no figures on how the record market is divided between various musical genres. Below the Top Ten, there is a huge 'long tail' of special-interest music. However, a study of the best-selling records at least gives us an idea of the most popular genres in Finland. Musiikkituottajat ry, the Finnish branch of IFPI, publishes detailed sales figures of best-selling discs.

Over the years, Finnish record buyers have been remarkably faithful to domestic music. The best-selling record of the 2000s was *Nummela* by singer-songwriter Anssi Kela, a nostalgic recollection of small-town youth with a catchy refrain (BMG 2001). The CD has sold a total of 157,199 copies, according to IFPI Finland. The most successful artist of the decade was the heavy metal band Nightwish, which had three CDs selling over 100,000 copies each on the independent Spinefarm label. The two other artists selling over 100,000 CDs were the rapper Pikku G (Warner) and singer Jenni Vartiainen (Warner).

Table 7.1 The year's number one best-selling records in Finland, 2000–10

Domestic

	Artist	Album	Label	Sales[a]	Genre
2000	Smurffit	Tanssihitit Vol. 3	EMI	91,410	Comedy dance hits
2001	Anssi Kela	Nummela	BMG	157,199	Singer-songwriter
2002	Gimmel	Lentoon	BMG	98,077	Girl trio
2003	Pikku G	Räjähdysvaara	Warner	121,204	Rap
2004	Nightwish	Once	Spinefarm	107,288	Metal
2005	Nightwish	High Hopes	Spinefarm	103,950	Metal
2006	Lordi	Arockalypse	SonyBMG	97,149	Eurovision winner
2007	Nightwish	Passion Play	Spinefarm	126,084	Metal
2008	Anna Abreu	Now	Sony	50,695	English-language pop
2009	Lauri Tähkä	Tänään Ei Huomista Murehdita	Universal	66,377	Singer-songwriter
2010	Jenni Vartiainen	Seili	Warner	124,893	Finnish pop

International

	Artist	Album	Label	Sales[a]
2000	Alexia	Fan Club	Sony	83,980
2001	Linkin Park	Hybrid Theory	Warner	62,629
2002	Shakira	Laundry Service	BMG	90,140
2003	Metallica	St. Anger	Universal	35,725
2004	Robbie Williams	Greatest Hits	EMI	40,367
2005	Robbie Williams	Intensive Care	EMI	62,524
2006	Juanes	Mi Sangre	Universal	51,811
2007	Amy Winehouse	Back to black	Universal	22,133
2008	Metallica	Death Magnetic	Universal	79,415
2009	Baseballs	Strike!	Warner	89,172
2010	AC/DC	Iron Man 2	Sony	25,022

a As at October 2010, except 2010 albums, which are as at September 2011.

The ten best-selling domestic records of the decade were a rather predictable mix of Finnish trends. They include singer-songwriters, rappers, heavy metal, a Eurovision winner and a comedy dance record (Smurffit). Half of them were in Finnish, the rest have English lyrics. All were produced by the four (originally five) majors, with the exception of Spinefarm, which was eventually also bought by one of the majors (see Table 7.1).

If we only consider the music, *Nummela*, the best-selling record of the decade, could have been produced almost anywhere in Europe or North America. It was the inventive Finnish lyrics which made it such a success. The hits of the 2000s prove that ever since the birth of Finnish-language rock in the 1970s, local artists have quickly adopted all major international trends into the Finnish language. Rap, for instance, was rapidly naturalised, and there have even been rappers performing in minority languages such as Sami and sign language. But there also was a growing number of Finnish artists writing successfully songs in the English language and, in some cases, this has led to international success, as in the case of Nightwish.

At the lower end of the top ten, we find several artists representing the Finnish *iskelmä*, a more traditional form of popular song. The all-time best-selling record in Finland has been Jari Sillanpää's *Jari Sillanpää* (273,000 copies, Edel 1996), by the artist who won the 'Tango King' award at the Seinäjoki tango festival in 1995. His latest compilation hit album from 2005 sold 25,000 copies. The Seinäjoki festival continues to be a major gateway to stardom in Finland. Every year hopeful men and women compete for the titles of 'Tango King and Queen' by singing well-known Finnish tango melodies at a concert, which is also one of the year's most-watched television shows. The Tango King receives a contract from the Auraviihde agency, which is today owned by Sony Music. After the competition, the winners switch to more modern material, but tangos continue to be an essential part of the Finnish dance hall repertoire.

Among other top artists in the traditional vein, Kari Tapio (Edel Records) has had twenty gold records since 1984. His best-selling CD *Myrskyn jälkeen* (1995) has sold over 115,000 copies. Although his sales have declined during the past few years, he was the most popular performer in the country's dance halls until his death in 2010. Paula Koivuniemi has had eleven gold records since 1981. The latest, *Yöperhonen* (Edel 2006) sold 21,890 copies. She is also one of the most popular performers in the country and a favourite subject of drag artists. Olavi Virta (1915–72), the tango idol of the 1950s, still continues to sell records and recently received a posthumous platinum disc for the compilation album Mestari in 2009.

The list of best-selling international records is also rather predictable: Shakira, Metallica, Robbie Williams, Amy Winehouse. International top CDs typically sold fewer copies in Finland than domestic products: none sold over a 100,000 copies. Actually, the best-selling foreign artist of the decade was good old Elvis Presley, whose collection *30 #1 Hits* sold 90,779 copies, a few hundred more than Shakira's 2002 hit *Laundry Service*. No independent labels are to be found among the top sellers, but it is interesting to note that it was not totally dominated by Anglo-American repertoire: Spanish and Italian artists also sell well in Finland.

On the lower ranks of IFPI-credited hits selling more than 10,000 copies, the repertoire is broader, and there is room for independents. Best-selling imports in this category included *Masters of Gregorian Chant* (Edel 2001) and *Helmut Lotti Goes Classic* (2002).

Of course, top hits constitute only one sector of the record marker. This is indicated by the existence of small record shops specialising in genres such as classical, hip hop or world music. The share of classical records is estimated at 4–5 per cent. Many specialised shops also import directly small amounts of records which do not show up in any statistics.

While Finnish musicians have remained popular at home, they have traditionally been less successful abroad. English has long been the international language of popular music. French, German and Spanish are also widely spoken beyond their national borders and this has given a natural advantage to artists performing in these languages. Finnish artists have no ready audience abroad and, until recently, Finland's music exports have been insignificant. The country's most successful music export is still the composer Jean Sibelius, whose music accounts for almost 10 per cent of the Finnish collecting society's foreign income. Beyond Sibelius, there have only been occasional sparks, like novelty dance fad Letkis in the 1960s (based on the music of Finnish composer Rauno Lehtinen) and the success of Finnish beat music in Japan. Finnish heavy metal is also currently enjoying some international success.

The majors move in and the industry changes

Between 1970 and 1990, the Finnish record industry enjoyed two decades of growth. This encouraged the multinationals to enter Finland. The first was EMI in 1968, but its early arrival can be explained by its dissatisfaction with the poor performance of the local agent rather than expectations of immediate growth. CBS (which became Sony) followed in 1978. Warner arrived in 1989, BMG the next year, Polygram in 1992.

The winds were now changing. When EMI and CBS established branches in Finland, their immediate motive was probably to secure more effective distribution for their international product. Although both also built a domestic catalogue, their investment in Finland was limited. When Warner opened a local branch in Finland in 1989, at first they just took over the agency from Fazer-Musiikki. However, in 1993 Warner purchased the shares of Fazer Musiikki. The willingness of the owners to sell the company may have in part been due to the recession and (temporary) decline in record sales in 1992–93. The concern was quickly stripped down. Warner absorbed the record business; the music publishing side was organised as the Finnish branch of Warner Chappell. The record stores were sold to the Free Record Shop chain and musical instruments taken over by former management. As a memento of the company's glorious past, Roger Lindberg personally took over the concert agency. As a result of this investment, Warner now owns a huge back catalogue of old Finnish recordings which were originally produced by a dozen different companies.

During this period, the music industry has undergone several major changes. The vinyl disc started to disappear in the early 1990s after the introduction of the CD. In 1992, more than a million LPs had still been sold in Finland; by 2000 this was down to practically nil. Perhaps even more important was the disappearance of the compact cassette, which had previously represented about half of the recorded music market in Finland. In 1998, over one million cassettes were still being sold, but in three years cassettes and cassette players had disappeared from the market.

In 1992, sales started to decline as a result of the global economic crisis but by the late 1990s, the sales improved again. In 2000 and 2001, IFPI member companies in Finland sold a total of 9.5 million records (about 2 records annually per capita), corresponding to a trade value of €68 million. The first decade of the millennium was a disappointment for the industry: sales declined to €41.7 million by 2009. The major labels have put this down to widespread file-sharing. There are no systematic studies on the uses of Internet music in Finland, but IFPI Finland claims that 90 per cent of all downloads are illegal, in spite of tightening legislation and stiffer sentences.[2] Recent court decisions have removed any question of the legality of this practice, but it continues to flourish and is difficult to regulate. So far the government has declined to introduce French-style legislation which would require telecommunications operators to discontinue broadband services to alleged offenders.

However, other developments in copyright have been more favourable to the industry, and the net result of these changes has been that record sales may have stagnated but the economic significance of secondary uses of recorded music, such as broadcasting and private copying, has considerably increased. Indeed, it could even be said that the Finnish government has used copyright law quite effectively to promote local record production. When neighbouring rights were first introduced into Finnish copyright law in 1961, the royalty that broadcasters had to pay for the airing of recordings was limited to domestic recordings. When Finland ratified the Rome convention in 1983, protection was extended to recordings made in all signatory countries, but there was an agreement between the government and the industry that all income from the broadcasting of foreign records would be kept in Finland and used to support local production. This gained even more significance when the radio sector started to expand in 1985 after the introduction of commercial radio, and the public performance right was extended in 1991 to all uses of recorded music, including discotheques, juke boxes and even background music in shopping malls.[3] The compensation for the broadcasting of recorded music is paid on the basis of detailed playlists collected from radio stations, and the money is divided between rights owners (producers and performers) in proportion with the number of times a record has been aired. Since the 1990s, music programming on Finnish radio has become more and more dependent on the rotation of current hits and this has tended to favour the majors. A recent study showed that, in 2004, 91 per cent of the records on the playlists of the 30 most listened radio channels were by the four majors (Vilkko 2010: 292). Smaller record companies argue that it has become increasingly difficult to get their music played on the radio.

Another important new form of compensation was been the so-called 'tape levy', which buyers of empty cassettes had to pay for the privilege of making private copies of protected music. With the advent of new technology, this was gradually extended to blank CD-Rs and other devices that can be used to make private copies.

Although there is little doubt that private copying is widespread, we do not know what exactly is being copied. The 'tape levy' is based on the unverifiable use of unidentified works and, as a consequence, the money collected is largely used to support new productions and other musical activities. The levy is administered by collecting societies representing artists, authors and media industries. The body responsible for recorded music is Gramex, which represents both record companies and performers. In 2010, the total amount of grants was €2 million. The grants are administered by ESEK (Esittävän säveltaiteen edistämiskeskus, Center for the Advancement of the Performing Arts, founded in 1981 and legally a part of Gramex).

In 2009, Gramex collected a total of €18.3 million. Of this amount, €7.3 million came from public performance, €6.4 million from 'electronic media' (mainly radio and television broadcasting) and the rest from the compensation for private copying and other sources. We can see how this income for the 'secondary uses' of recorded music has gained significant proportions in comparison to the industry's total annual sales of €41.7 million. At least to some extent consumers are already paying for their unauthorised downloads when they store them on a permanent medium.

As well as secondary income from recordings, there has been a remarkable growth in music exports during the last decade. In April 2011, Music Expo Finland, the industry's export association, estimated Finland's music exports in 2010 as €32.1 million, a considerable increase over €23.3 million in the previous year. The main target countries were the Nordic countries and Germany. The figures obviously reflect the international success of Finnish groups such as Nightwish, HIM, Apocalyptica, Sunrise Avenue, and others. However, these figures do not refer to records only, but all music-related exports of goods, services and copyright royalties from T-shirts to the performance rights of Sibelius's music. (Music Expo Finland was not able to give a more detailed breakdown of the sudden increase. They claimed that the information was confidential, but suggested that 'music technology played an important role'. Whatever the explanation is, it seems that the increase was not primarily due to the popularity of Finnish groups, but other music-related exports such as music for computer games, or simply just a change in the way the data was collected.)

Overall, the development of the music market in Finland suggests that, although record sales may have fallen, the major labels can remain profitable through secondary rights income and through income from things such as T-shirt royalties. Their recent strategies demonstrate some of the ways in which the major labels have pursued this kind of income. In the following section, I will outline the majors in Finland.

The four majors

In 2010, IFPI Finland (Musiikkituottajat ry, the national association of record companies) had 23 members, but more than three-quarters of the country's total record sales derived from the four majors, EMI, Sony, Universal and Warner. The first three have a joint Scandinavian distribution company, ENS (Entertainment Network Scandinavia) based in Borås, near Gothenburg, Sweden.

Over the past decade, the majors have increased their market share from 69 to 82 per cent, mainly by acquiring the most successful local independent companies. Although their turnover has fluctuated with the larger cycles of the industry, three of them have maintained impressive profit rates through the decade. The exception is EMI, which had several years with heavy losses.

From the viewpoint of the performers and the consumers, the arrival of the majors has not meant any immediate changes. In the case of Warner, for instance, the old Fazer staff stayed on for many years. The majors have both kept established stars and broken new acts. All also distribute a selection of the parent company's international repertoire in Finland. Today, each of the majors has about 20–30 employees in Finland. Their tasks vary somewhat, depending on how much each company is involved in related fields such as music publishing and artist agencies, but all have specialists for A&R, marketing, promotion and sales, as well as an economy department. Some have in-house graphic designers, and all have new posts with titles such as 'digital director' or 'digital key account manager'.

Over a longer period of time, however, the activities of the majors have changed, although some of these changes would no doubt have occurred even if the industry had remained completely domestic. One of the first decisions of Warner Music Finland was to discontinue their flagship classical label, Finlandia. The number of new productions seems to have declined. Typically, the majors now produce about twenty new Finnish albums a year. Sony calculates with a break-even point of 4,000–7,000 copies, and the others seem to follow a similar policy. Some prefer in-house producers, others also license finished masters from outside producers. However, all realise that in order to succeed in Finland, they need strong domestic catalogues.

The four majors are presented in more detail below.

Sony Music (Sony Music Entertainment Finland Oy) has gone through several incarnations in Finland. The first was CBS, which opened in Finland in 1976. After the purchase of CBS Records by Sony, CBS Finland became Sony Music Entertainment Finland. From 2004, after the merger of international Sony Music and BMG, the name was Sony BMG Music Entertainment, until the previous name was reinstalled in 2008.

The BMG side of the pedigree started in Finland in 1990. In the early 2000s, Sony and BMG were approximately of equal size. In 2003, BMG's market share of the Finnish market was 12.3 per cent and Sony's 11.2 per cent. Before the merger, BMG had been stronger in domestic repertoire, while Sony's international artists had been selling well. BMG brought to Sony several top artists such as Anssi Kela, Darude, HIM and Gimmel. BMG had also acquired the catalogue of Bluebird, a company founded in 1979 by a former producer from Fazer Musiikki. In the 1980s, Bluebird's market share had at times approached 10 per cent.

During the past few years, Sony has continued to attract and develop talent such as PMMP, Rajaton, Samuli Edelmann, Anna Abreu, Anna Puu and the Eurovision song contest winner Lordi. The company is not actively involved in music publishing.

After the merger in 2005, the market share of Sony BMG was 24.8 per cent. It has since remained above 20 per cent and was 21.2 per cent in 2010. The company's annual turnover stayed above €15 million in 2005–07, with profits ranging from 10 to 15 per cent. In 2008, record sales began to decline and the company's turnover dropped to €10.7 million in 2009 (fiscal year ending 2010/03). Profits sank to 0.7 per cent. However, the company considers 2009 an untypical year. In 2010, Sony decided to invest heavily in live music. In January it bought Auraviihde Oy, one of the biggest artist agencies in Finland. Over the past five years, Auraviihde has had a steady annual turnover of over €10 million. Sony also owns three other agencies – Popgee, Oktaavi Oy and Artistitalo Poket Oy. This activity is not limited to live music; it also gives Sony an interest in several successful television formats such as the annual Tangomarkkinat show and the Idols competition.

After the reorganisation, Sony expects that its annual turnover will rise to about €30 million, of which only 34 per cent will derive from recorded music. It expects to profit from the synergy of record production and live music.

EMI (EMI Finland Oy) was the first multinational to open an office in Finland in 1968. At first, operations were directed from the Stockholm office, but a local company was established in 1972. The start was difficult because of management problems and, at one stage in the late 1970s, local production was practically discontinued. In the 1980s, however, EMI established itself strongly on the Finnish market with several successful artists, including the rock singer Topi Sorsakoski.

In 2001, EMI Finland purchased Poko Rekords, an independent company founded by Epe Helenius in 1977. Poko had played a major role in developing Finnish punk and rockabilly music and issued more than 500 albums, of which the most successful was the compilation *Repullinen Riimejä* by the group Eppu Normaali, with total sales of 244,000 copies. In 2009, Poko was merged with EMI (for a history of Poko, see Aunola 2009).

Since 2001, the market share of EMI has dropped from 19 to 12.8 per cent (2010). The annual turnover has declined from €11.0 mi (2006) to €7.5 mi (year ending 3/2010). During the past 5-year period, the company's only profitable year was 2009, when it made a profit of 1.9 per cent. The worst was 2008, with a 19.2 per cent loss.

EMI has not been successful in developing a roster of top artists since 2000. The company's best sellers have been comedy and children's records, and the rock groups Neljä Ruusua, INDX and Yö.

Universal Music (Universal Music Oy) has also been successful in Finland in the 2000s. The Finnish branch first opened in 1998 and was merged next year with the older PolyGram Finland, which had been established in 1992. As a result of several acquisitions, its market share has increased from 14.7 per cent (2000) to 19.8 per cent (2010). Typically, the majors sell domestic and international repertoire in equal proportions, but Universal's strength has been its international catalogue. In 2007, for instance, it had a share of 32 per cent of international records sold in Finland, but only 16 per cent of domestic repertoire. (Since 2010, IFPI Finland has not published separate market shares for domestic and international repertoire.)

In 2002, Universal acquired Spin-Farm, a company that had had an international success with several Finnish heavy metal bands. In 2010, it purchased Siboney and Love Kustannus, two companies with an important back catalogue going all the way to the 1960s. The company's annual turnover has grown from €9.7 million (2004) to €13.1 million (2008), with profits constantly over 10 per cent. In 2009, the turnover sank to €10.3 million and the company showed a slight net loss.

Universal's recent top artists have been Tiktak, Kwan and the enormously successful Lauri Tähkä.

Warner Music (Warner Music Finland Oy) started operations in Finland in 1989, but the decisive moment was the purchase of Fazer Musiikki in 1993. Warner and Fazer continued to exist separately until 1998, when all operations were combined under the Warner flag. In the 1990s the combined companies had a third of the Finnish record market. As a result of the purchase, Warner now owns an overwhelming part of the Finnish catalogue from before 1990. Since 2005, Warner's turnover has slightly declined along with the total market. In 2005 the turnover was €11.3 million; in 2009 it was down to €9.0 million, but the profit rate was still a respectable 17.5 per cent (fiscal years ending September). In 2010, Warner claimed that it had become Finland's largest record company. Its market share was 28.4 per cent.

Warner's best-selling artists since 2000 have included Mamba, Pikku G, Maija Vilkkumaa, Vesa-Matti Loiri, Jenni Vartiainen, Juha Tapio and Chisu. In 2007 Warner purchased the independent production company HMC (Helsinki Music Company), which brought Warner several top groups including HIM. With the deal, Niko Nordström, co-founder of HMC, became managing director of Warner Music Finland. In the same connection Warner also acquired Popgram Oy and became the first major record company in Finland with its own artist agency. It has since been reorganised as Warner Music Live, with six full-time employees.

Warner's publishing activities are organised into Warner/Chappell Music Finland Oy, which 'inherited' the old Fazer catalogue. The latest published fiscal report from 2002 shows a turnover of €1.4 million and a profit of 58.8 per cent.

Regional majors

A distinct feature of the record market has been an increasing polarisation. The share of the major multinational companies has increased from 68.6 per cent (2000) to 82.2 per cent (2010). This does not leave much room to the other nineteen IFPI member companies. However, several Swedish and German companies have successfully competed for near-major status. At times, they have produced successful records in a variety of genres, but only one of them, Edel, has been able to create a clear profile.

Through the 2000s, Edel Music Finland has constantly had market shares approaching 10 per cent. Edel Gmbh was a successful Hamburg-based German company which expanded its activities into several European countries in the 1990s. It gained a strong foothold in Finland by purchasing Audiovox Records (AXR) in 1999, a local independent company (no relationship with the US company with the same name). AXR had a large catalogue of successful Finnish artists mainly in the traditional *iskelmä* vein, and the repertoire was developed in the 2000s by the company's A&R director Ilkka Vainio. The company's most successful Finnish artists was Kari Tapio, and in 2000 its market share was 11.9 per cent. Edel also had an interest in Playground Music Scandinavia AB (PMG), a Malmö-based production and distribution company which owns the Swedish Diesel label since 2006. PMG's best-selling artists had been the Finnish rock group Rasmus, which sold more than 2.5 million records worldwide. In 2010, Playground Music's turnover in Finland had declined to €2.4 million. Another Swedish company with considerable success in Finland was the Bonnier Amigo Music Group (BAM), which had several successful Finnish artists in the early 2000s. It had an annual market share in Finland ranging from 3 to 7 per cent over the decade. The principal owner of the company was the Swedish media conglomerate Bonnier. In 2009 Bonnier announced its decision to leave the record business, which resulted in a management buy-out and partnership with PMG. The new company is now called Cosmos Music Group. The company discontinued its own distribution and handed this side of activities to ENS, which already distributed the products of three majors.

In February 2010 Edel decided to discontinue its Finnish operations. Edel Music Finland was merged with Playground Music BAM Finland OY. The domestic back catalogue and artist contracts were bought by Ilkka Vainio, who will continue production under the AXR banner.

The minors

Small independent record companies have played an important role in developing new musical idioms throughout the world and most of the successful ones have eventually been bought by the majors. This trend has been obvious in Finland in the 2000s, and several IFPI member companies do not really exist as independent units today. Spin Farm, which developed the international careers of several heavy metal bands such as Nightwish, had a peak share of 8.6 per cent of all domestic records sold in 2004. The company has been fully owned by Universal since 2002 and today exists just as a division of Universal, as are two other companies, Siboney and Johanna Kustannus. The latter two held rights to the old Love Records catalogue and also introduced many important new artists in the 2000s. The remaining independents now have a combined market share of about 10 per cent.

Classical records are a special sector within the record industry with their own faithful audience. In Finland, the market share of classical records is estimated at about 4–5 per cent. The four majors all have an international classical repertoire but do not produce classical records in Finland. Warner dropped Fazer's classical flagship label, Finlandia, after the merger. Ondine, the leading Finnish classical label, is now fully owned by Naxos. The company's annual turnover is about €0.7 million. Its best-selling artist is the soprano Karita Mattila. The Finnish branch of the parent company, Fg-Naxos has declined from €1.5 million (2005) to €1.0 million (2009).

Of the remaining IFPI member companies, the most successful seem to be those that have carved a special niche for their own products. KSF Karaoke Stores has increased its turnover from €0.5 million (2004) to €1.2 million (2009). As the name reveals, it specialises in karaoke music. VL-Musiikki Oy specialises in budget records which are sold at supermarkets and discount stores; the turnover has grown from €1.2 million (2004) to €2.9 million (2010). Topi Sorsakoski Productions Oy is a single-artist company which produced and managed one of the country's older top rock artists, who died in 2011. Their turnover is about €0.5 million. Valitut Palat Oy is the Finnish branch of the international Readers' Digest company. It is the most successful producer of mail-order reissue compilations in Finland. The turnover of the business has not been published, but about three-quarters is domestic material licensed from other Finnish companies and one quarter the products of the parent firm.

More than a thousand new records are produced every year in Finland, which means that most are published by small companies that are not IFPI members. Many of these titles sell very little or not at all. Many are only issued to promote new artists. IndieCo, the organisation of independent record companies, has about fifty members, of which only half a dozen are also IFPI members. IndieCo members range from amateurs to successful professionals. Several have web pages that no longer function; one shares an address with a major multinational company. Only a few are exclusively involved in record production. The majority are also artist agencies and music publishers. Some operate studios or retail stores, sell merchandise, produce radio advertisements or distribute the products of other domestic and foreign independent companies. In general, however, several independents play an important role in certain areas of music, such as jazz, electronic music, and many types of rock which are ignored by the majors.

Sakara is currently one of the most successful independents. The company has so far issued 32 albums, which represent various types of metal music. The best-selling album so far has been *Uudet kymmenen käskyä*, by Stam1na, which has sold about 17,000 copies. The company expects a turnover of about half a million euros in 2010. About 20 per cent is expected to come from merchandising. The company also has several international representatives. Shadow World Records, on the the other hand, is an example of the smaller independents. It has so far issued a total of ten discs. In addition, it is involved in music publishing, merchandising and non-music related activities. The output in 2009 was only two records, with a turnover of a few thousand euros. Yet the company claims that its records are distributed in fifteen countries, including the Baltic countries, Germany, Austria, UK, Russia, Belarus and Kazakhstan. The company's best known act internationally is the heavy rock group Discardin Carrion. The example shows how even very small record companies are able to network widely.

It is very difficult to estimate the economic significance of the independent sector. A typical distributor specialising in domestic and international independent labels, Töölön Musiikkitukku Oy, reports an annual turnover of about half a million euros, which would correspond to about 50,000 CDs wholesale. Commercial success on a large scale is rare; since 2000 very few new labels have had hits in Finland. However, two independent labels had records in the Finnish charts in 2010 and show the potential of following the example of Love, Poko, Johanna and Spin Farm – successful minors that will eventually be bought out by one of the majors. Others operate consciously in the fringes of the music business, like the more extreme varieties of heavy metal or folk music.

Conclusions

Until 1968, when EMI opened an office in Helsinki, all Finnish records had been produced by domestic companies. The small size of the market and the strong preference for domestic music did not attract the multinationals. They did not become heavily involved in Finland until 1993, when Warner Music acquired Fazer Musiikki, the leading Finnish record company. Since then, they have been remarkably successful, and in 2010, 82 per cent of all records sold in Finland were produced by the four multinationals. How and why did this happen?

In fact, the right to represent international labels had been important to local companies since the 1950s. About half of the recordings sold in Finland were international repertoire. There are considerable economies of scale in record production, and a steady supply of tested international repertoire helped record companies to build effective distribution networks. The success of a new recording is notoriously difficult to predict, but it was easy to sell records by the Beatles or other international celebrities who received a lot of free publicity even in the local media. Once the market had grown sufficiently, the multi-nationals, who had supplied much of the best-selling international repertoire, were ready to remove the middleman and take over the entire production and distribution chain.

To succeed in Finland, however, they also needed an attractive domestic catalogue. It was not enough to make new recordings; a strong back catalogue was also needed. During the past ten years, the record industry has been undergoing a difficult period of transition from CDs to digital distribution. In Finland, the value of annual record sales declined by 37 per cent between 2001 and 2010. Higher losses have been reported elsewhere, and it is possible that the Finnish market was again protected by the consumers' preference for domestic music, but the decline is real.

However, a closer look at the fiscal reports of the multinationals in Finland shows that they have adapted to the crisis remarkably well, and most of them have shown good annual profits. They have been able to expand their market share by acquiring successful independent companies and invest in new, related fields such as music publishing, merchandising and artists agencies. The economies of scale have also become important in the rapidly growing sector of secondary rights where income is derived from many sources. The money collected from radio play is divided on the basis of actual playlists, but compensation for home taping, for instance, is by necessity based on estimates, and the size of the catalogue becomes important.

The continuing growth of the multinationals has left little space for middle-sized regional companies, but there is no reason to believe that smaller independent record companies will disappear. With the introduction of affordable digital technology, recording costs have actually decreased, so the threshold of entering the record market is low. The reliance on economies of scale means that the multinationals have a higher break-even point for new productions than small companies. Independents still thrive in niche markets which are not interesting to the multinationals.

At the moment, there seems to be no clear formula for successful independent record companies. Some are truly international, selling their brand of experimental music to a small but global audience. Others simply aim to promote one artist or the artists of a single agency. However, it is interesting to note that the economically most successful independents work in niches that are commercial rather than cultural, such as mail-order or budget-priced records.

A study of the recording industry in Finland shows that it has changed considerably during the past two decades. However, other mass-media consumption has also been changing. Radio listening is also down. Library lending has diminished since 2004. The explosive growth of the computer games market may well have had as much effect on record sales as file-sharing; they affect the same consumer groups. We may be seeing the emergence of a new generation which no longer has the same interest in records as those which grew up in the period from the 1960s to the 1980s. But music is not dying: the demand for live music has continued to grow (Alanen 2011).

Sources

Except where noted, figures on record sales and market shares come from the excellent website of Musiikkituottajat ry, the Finnish Branch of IFPI (www.ifpi.fi, in English www.ifpi.fi/in-english). See especially the monthly statistics, total market estimate, yearly sales of IFPI Finland member companies and national top in Finland. Figures presented in this article were accessed on 10 October 2010; data for 2010 was revised on 15 September 2011.

Business information on record companies is based on annual statements submitted to the National Board of Patents and Registration in Finland, available to the public at the Board. In condensed form, the data is accessible from several online sources, such as Fonecta Finder, www.finder.fi/. For EMI Finland, for example, see www.finder.fi/Musiikkituotantoa/Emi%20Finland%20Oy%20Ab/ HELSINKI/taloustiedot/162458.

For data on royalties collected on public performance (including broadcasting) of sound recordings, see the website of Gramex ry, www.gramex.fi/fi/tietoa_gramexista/keratyt_ja_jaetut_korvaukset.

Information (in Finnish) on the rights owners' view of music piracy are from the website of Tekijänoikeuden valvonta- ja tiedotuskeskus ry, e.g. http:// antipiracy.fi/ajankohtaista/203/piratismin-avainlukuja-2010-valtiovallan.

Notes

1   It is worth noting that Finland is constitutionally bilingual, with Swedish as the second national language. Although the percentage of Swedish-speakers has since 1900 diminished from 13 to 5 per cent, Swedish popular music has been quite popular in Finland and there was a modest local production of records in the Swedish language. Music publishers and record companies used to have close contacts with their Swedish counterparts. Today, however, most Swedish records sold in Finland are in English and the demand for Swedish dance music is fulfilled by a few small regional distributors.

2   Traditional record piracy, the sale of illegally produced discs, was never widespread in Finland and was mainly limited to CDs bought by tourists from market stalls in Russia and Estonia, but this trade has largely disappeared.

3   However, it is worth noting that, unlike the UK and some other European countries, Finland has adopted an interpretation of the broadcasting right, which means that no compensation will be paid for the airing of American recordings, as the United States has not ratified the Rome Convention and thus American broadcasters do not pay for the use of European recordings.

Bibliography

Alanen, A. (2011) Elävän Musiikin Markkinat Käännekohdassa, *Tieto & Trendit*, 3: 32–7.

Aunola, M. (2009) Patrons and Pathfinders: Two Tales of Successful Strategic Evolution in the Finnish Music Industry. Dissertation, University of Tampere. Available online at: http://tutkielmat.uta.fi/pdf/lisuri00100.pdf (accessed 6 June 2012).

Gronow, P. (1983) The Record Industry: The growth of a Mass Medium, in R. Middleton (ed.) *Popular Music, Vol. III*. Cambridge: Cambridge University Press.

Gronow, P. (1984) Taistelu Kasetista, *Tiedotustutkimus*, 1.

Gronow, P. (1995) The Record Industry in Finland, 1945–1960, *Popular Music*, 14: 1.

Muikku, J. (2001) *Musiikkia Kaikkiruokaisille: Suomalaisen Populaarimusiikin Äänitetuotanto 1945–90.* Helsinki: Gaudeamus.

Vilkko, A. (2010) Soittolistan Symbolinen Valta ja Vallankäytön Mekanismit, Ph.D. dissertation, University of Tampere. Available online at: http://acta.uta.fi/pdf/978-951-44-8295-3.pdf (accessed 6 June 2012).

France

Population:	65.3 million (21st)
Languages:	French
Capital:	Paris (pop 10.4 million)
Currency:	Euro (€). $1 = €0.75
GDP:	$2.56 tn (5th)
GDP (PPP)/capita:	$33,820 (24th)
Median age:	39.9

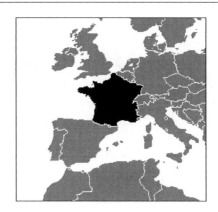

GDP data from World Bank

Population data from CIA world factbook

Exchange rate used by IFPI (2011) (source: Oanda)

2010 Recorded music market

Overall income:	$865.3m	
World ranking:	5th	
	Income	**World ranking**
Physical sales	$641.1m	5th
Digital sales	$146.1m	5th
Performance rights	$78.1m	5th

Historical recorded music market ($m, at IFPI's 2010 exchange rate)

	1999	2000	2001	2002	2003	2004	2005	2006	2007	2008	2009
Trade Value			1758.3	1830.9	1567.5	1354.0	1331.5	1270.6	1073.5	935.0	909.8
Retail Value	2482.3	2483.5	2818.7	2932.8	2509.5	2178.0	2122.7				

Proportion of domestic repertoire (market value, physical sales only)

1991	1995	2000	2005	2010
44%	47%	51%	61%	58%

Album certification levels

	2010	1999
Gold	Domestic – 50,000	Domestic – 100,000
	International – 50,000	International – 100,000
Platinum	Domestic – 100,000	Domestic – 300,000
	International – 100,000	International – 300,000

8   France

Hugh Dauncey and Philippe Le Guern

Introduction

To what extent is it possible to consider the French recording industry as in any way 'different'? Structurally, the French market is very similar to that of other major forces in the world recording industry such as the United States, Britain, Germany and Japan: the French recording industry is highly concentrated. Indeed, although this phenomenon is something of a constant in the global history of the record industry, in France it has recently reached new heights, with the 2000s seeing 95 per cent of music sales in France provided by the four major labels. Conversely, the influence of independent labels in France is increasingly small, with the 600 independent labels identified by the *Syndicat national des éditeurs phonographiques* (SNEP) accounting for the remaining 5 per cent of sales. Whereas in the 1960s and 1970s the French record-buying public was mostly familiar with the names of French independent labels such as Trema, Erato, Vogue and Barclay, nowadays there is not a single French recording company enjoying comparable levels of recognition.

Given the structural similarity of the French record industry to others across the world, its oligopolistic composition follows general patterns of industry structure imposed by the major labels worldwide with a small number of artists, often drawn from popular music outside France, dominating music radio station playlists and distribution channels, arguably to the detriment of emerging 'local' music and artists. And, given these similarities, the French industry has been no more successful in escaping the negative effects of the worldwide downturn in record sales, even if France was a little late in experiencing the crisis.

However, notwithstanding these structural similarities, if one looks more closely at the French music industry and French music in general, one can identify a certain number of features specific to the 'landscape' of French music, which suggest that although it may not be a complete exception to worldwide patterns, it nevertheless represents a relatively distinctive way of doing things. Thus in what follows, we will consider how the French state has – principally since the mid-1980s – been willing to intervene in the music industry through an array of taxes, levies, subsidies, and other mechanisms and bodies intended to stimulate the supply and regulate the demand of music by, for example, fostering independent record labels. We shall also consider the ways in which this supportive interventionism is informed by theories of French cultural policy which mobilise notions of the 'exceptional' nature of cultural goods and services in terms of international trade and of France's own particular cultural and linguistic identity within discourses of 'cultural diversity'. A further area in which French music 'organises things differently' is to be found in the government efforts to regulate ongoing crisis in the record industry by introducing controversial policies – known as the HADOPI law – to repress the unauthorised downloading of music.

Before considering contemporary developments in the French music industry, however, it is useful to reflect briefly on the way in which the industry has emerged in France, from its earliest days to the present.

The development of the French music industry

Academic approaches to the analysis of popular music in general vary somewhat between British and French traditions, as we have demonstrated in a recent study (Dauncey and Le Guern 2010) and this is indeed the case in terms of music as business. For example, the ethnographic study of record companies in France has been the exception rather than the rule. French research has focused strongly on the mediation of music through objects such as the phonograph or the record itself, rather than looking at the actual operation of record label companies (which are analysed only in terms of economics/finance). The work of Maisonneuve, for example – who investigated the development of the early market for music in France – emphasises the major role played by the Pathé brothers (key figures in the development of the cinema industry). It was the Pathé brothers – who set up a phonograph factory in Paris as early as 1894 and, two years later, created the first recording studios – who were arguably the initiators of the French music industry (Maisonneuve 2009). Pathé's strategy was predominantly centred around publishing song music (their catalogue contained some 2,500 titles in 1898) and the rise of such catalogues went hand in hand with the development, during the end of the nineteenth century and the first decades of the twentieth century, of a national distribution system for recorded music and ancillary products. Maisonneuve contrasts the situation in the late 1890s, when Pathé and the *Compagnie française du Gramophone* were the only distributors of gramophones and recordings sold from shops in central Paris, to that of the 1930s when, after a somewhat gradual expansion of the sector over the intervening decades, over eight hundred companies were supplying music, and musical goods and services in the capital and provincial cities (including dozens in Paris itself) (Maisonneuve 2009: 200).

At the turn of the twentieth century, Pathé exemplified the growing international success of the French music industry, as it progressively launched subsidiaries and opened factories and even recording studios across Europe, as well as in the US and the Far East (Maisonneuve 2009: 241). After 1927, however, Pathé's near monopoly over the industrialisation of the French record weakened, its turnover falling as a result of the global downturn. The company sold out to Columbia in 1929, which was subsequently absorbed by EMI in 1931 (Tournès

2002: 465–77). As the fortunes of Pathé waned, and eventually failed, its competitors and challengers grew in strength and number and, by the 1930s, the French industry was dominated by half a dozen or so companies, the most significant of which being Gramophone, Columbia, Decca, Ultraphone, Ducretet and Salabert.

During the troubled – politically, economically and culturally – period of the 1940s the development of the French music industry and of cultural consumption in general were somewhat inhibited by armed conflict and occupation, and then by political and economic reconstruction following liberation. Although, both culturally and economically, France after 1945 was a more open society, interested in and welcoming to (notably) American cultural forms, the music industry was forced to wait until the later 1950s before fully participating in France's growing post-war prosperity. Although agricultural and industrial production regained pre-war levels by the early 1950s, cultural consumption arguably only began to become truly significant in the middle years of what the French describe as the *30 Glorieuses* (the 30 glorious years of growth, 1945–75) as the post-war demographic boom combined with new-found prosperity and a changing international music culture. During the early years of this new growth, the record industry was still essentially dominated by the major recording companies of previous decades but was further stimulated by newcomers such as Disques Barclay.

During the 1950s, traditional francophone singer-songwriters such as Georges Brassens and Jacques Brel became increasingly commercialised as vinyl LPs and singles replaced the old 78s, and as radio and the press increasingly mediatised popular music, but it was the phenomenon of imported US rock music (and the appearance of its French version for adolescents, known as 'Yé-Yé') in the early 1960s which turned the vinyl record into a mass-market product of musical consumption. From 1960 to 1970, the sales of singles rose by 20 per cent (from 25 to 30 million), while the sales of LPs more than doubled to 20 million. A number of minor labels, such as Pacific, Bam and Ricordi, appeared at the time, and several independent labels, such as Barclay and Vogue, enjoyed key positions in the French record market and were able to compete with the majors until the 1970s (Verlant 2000), when they were bought out by Philips and Bertelsmann (Guibert 2006: 128).

The French music industry during the 1970s was usefully described in a groundbreaking study by Antoine Hennion (Hennion 1981), and this portrait allows us now, with the benefit of our contemporary perspective, to see quite how much things have changed. Analysing the structure and workings of the French music sector in the 1970s, Hennion concluded that increasing concentration of the world record industry was unlikely, and that the trend for hit records to be globalised was little affecting the world of French *chanson*. While accepting that the oligopoly of major record companies was exclusively 'Anglo-Saxon', he did not see this as automatic proof that the US and Britain were exercising any form of cultural supremacy, arguing instead that the success of the French subsidiaries of the majors had only become possible after they had effectively 'gallicised' their staff and operational methods or collaborated with French producers, such as in the case of Warner-Filipacchi and Phonogram-CBS France, whose success

Hennion saw as owing much to 'very French' policies of artistic management. Indeed, even though a company like Phonogram-France was foreign-owned, it was not preventing 70 per cent of its sales in France from being 'locally produced' (Hennion 1981: 206–7).

Developments in the 1980s seemed to support Hennion's argument that there would be increased fragmentation of the recording industry. Inspired by British independent labels such as Rough Trade, a number of new independent labels and distributors, such as New Rose and Dancetaria, entered the industry and shared an anti-capitalist and anti-imperialist rhetoric aimed against the majors. These genres and labels favoured the rise of alternative musics imbued with a 'subversive' ideology and strongly wedded to the expression of their ideas in the French language, leading to the rise of record companies such as Bondage, the Gougnaf movement, Boucherie productions, Lithium, New Rose and others, and the emergence of artists and groups among whom the best known are Négresses Vertes and la Mano Negra. The importance of the independent labels has been variously discussed (e.g. Lebrun 2006) and they have been examined mostly in terms of their 'resistance' vis-à-vis the majors. The rise of these independent labels had been made possible notably by the legalisation of free private radio stations implemented by the new socialist government in 1981, and their contribution to the industry was to introduce an ideological rejection of formatted and commercialised music, and to propagate a movement of intolerance towards the mainstream record industry in general. However, although this independent movement did indeed facilitate considerable changes in terms of genres and opportunities for different kinds of artists, it was short-lived and, by the early 1990s, the most significant artists who had been representative of this alternative music scene abandoned the independent labels in order to sign with majors (for example, Mano Negra left Boucherie productions for Virgin). The adventures of the alternative labels and distributors ended for the most part in commercial failure and/or their absorption by the majors. Even though most of the contemporary French 'independent' labels are now linked to the majors in terms of finance and distribution, like other major markets the history of the French record industry reveals a constant tension between these two types of agent. This can be witnessed, for example, in arguments concerning the HADOPI law, which will be discussed below.

By the 1990s, therefore, the French recording industry had considerably consolidated as the then six majors became commercially and culturally dominant. A study published in 1997 demonstrated that the independent labels were in severe difficulties (d'Angelo 1997). Taking the first half of 1993 d'Angelo highlighted that whereas the majors accounted for 'only' 64 per cent of records commercialised in France, 98 per cent of 'Top 50' hits were from majors and only the remaining 2 per cent from independents. This resulted in the majors achieving 88 per cent of total turnover in the French recording industry.

The difficulties experienced by the independent labels, coupled with their ideological significance in promoting French language music has resulted in the French state offering support to the recording industry. For example, 2005 saw the establishment of the *Club Action des labels indépendants français* (CALIF), an organisation intended to protect independent record shops, facilitate independent labels' access to the market, and has worked in partnership with the Ministry of Culture to strengthen the independent sector through grants, subsidies and various tax breaks. This state intervention is characteristic of the contemporary French industry and will be discussed below.

Trends and developments in the contemporary recording industry

In the 2000s, the French recording industry has, in common with the record business worldwide, been enveloped in a discourse of crisis as it has struggled to adapt to the online music environment. In this section, we set out some of the main trends and forces at work since the turn of the millennium, considering how the downturn has differentially affected the range of music formats, media and genres/repertoires.

First, it should be noted that the recession in record sales affected France later than most other territories, occurring only in late 2002. Despite global sales stagnating and then declining from 1995, in France industry turnover consistently increased between 1996 and 2002, before falling from its peak of €1.3 billion in 2002 to €1.1 billion in 2003. The later impact of the recession in the French market in particular could perhaps be explained in various ways, with one interpretation being that, given that piracy seems to have affected international mainstream hits more acutely, the French market was protected by its dependence on a signifi-cant catalogue of domestic artists. A second explanation, favoured by the SNEP (*Syndicat des éditeurs phonographiques*, the umbrella organisation of the French recording industry), is that France's adoption of the Internet and on-line services in the early 2000s was less developed than in the US or Britain, and this backwardness may have technologically limited the contribution of music piracy to the downturn in sales (Irma 2011). The SNEP argue that the decline in record sales can be explicitly linked to the adoption of high-speed broadband connections.

When it did hit, the downturn was at least as severe in France as elsewhere. Beginning towards the end of 2002, the French recording industry has seen a fall in the value of of physical sales of music of more than 60 per cent, with increasing digital sales failing to make up the shortfall. Declining numbers of physical sales have been experienced unevenly across different formats. Singles have been particularly hard-hit, falling sixfold between 2002 and 2009, from 784 million to a mere 125 million. According to the SNEP, album sales in this period fell from 2,535 millions to 973 million. Music DVDs also fell by a third in revenue terms.

In contrast to the decline in physical sales, digital income has been on the increase since the mid-2000s. In 2008–09, for example, legal Internet downloading of music increased by 56 per cent (32 per cent on the Web and 60 per cent on mobile phones), and income from streaming subscription services increased by 143 per cent (although income from mobile phones ringtones fell by more than 40 per cent).

However, the rise in digital income is still relatively small and not enough to offset the decline in physical income. Income from digital sales is still only roughly 15 per cent of that of physical sales (€75 million compared to €512 million in 2009), while income from online streaming totalled 11 per cent of overall income in 2009.

A final point to be made is that sales of different kinds of music were affected to differing extents by the overall crisis: classical recordings were the worst hit (down 14 per cent in 2008–09), whereas sales of French pop music remained strong at over half the overall turnover of the record industry (reaching a high point of 62 per cent in the first half of 2010) compared with 30 per cent of market share for non-French artists. In 1998 French music represented 50 per cent of turnover, and in 2000, 58 per cent. This ratio between French and overseas music is relatively stable, and reflects both the strengths and weaknesses of a French market strongly attached to, and dependent upon, a musical repertoire produced by indigenous artists. The fortunes of French-language music and of the international repertoire have been relatively comparable in terms of the overall downturn in the industry, although in terms of the long-term trend in record sales, figures suggest a general resilience – and even occasional upwards movement – in the percentage of French-language production in overall record sales. Considered in terms of the 'hit-parade' of singles sales and album sales, this essential resilience – varying from year to year, but evident as an ongoing trend – can be seen from the fact that in 2009, 5 of the top-ten singles in terms of sales were French-language (compared with 5 also in 2008, 9 in 2007, 10 in 2006 and 8 in 2005). In 2009, 5 of the best-selling albums were likewise francophone (compared with 5 in 2008, 8 in 2007, 10 in 2006 and 8 in 2005). As we have discussed in a recent study (Dauncey and Le Guern 2007), emerging artists in France and the UK face differing challenges in breaking into the music industry, to which public policies in the two countries are bringing different responses, but which in France often centre around the promotion of French-language creativity.

Numerous explanations can be advanced to make sense of the almost uninterrupted crisis in the recording industry, and it is interesting to see to what extent some of these interpretations are specific to the French market itself. Some hypotheses have been both discussed theoretically and put to empirical testing: the end of the life-cycle of the CD as a product; record prices reaching levels that influence negatively on consumers' willingness to pay (though SNEP argues that the CD is the only cultural product whose price in France has declined in the last few years); insufficient variety of music on offer; and so on. There are also explanations that emphasise the declining opportunity to purchase CDs: although the concentration of sales points in hypermarkets and general superstores has effectively brought about the near-extinction of independent record shops, these stores have themselves been reducing space devoted to music sales and refocusing activities on other products. Currently, the market for music is led by the specialised music stores, which are FNAC, Virgin Megastore and the Espaces culturels Leclerc. In fact, between 2002 and 2008, the turnover of record labels generated by the generalist hypermarkets and superstores fell by 70 per cent.[1] It is thus clear that channels of distribution are becoming more concentrated, at the same time as the variety of music offered through them is also being reduced.

As in other territories, the SNEP has pinpointed illegal downloading as the primary explanation for declining sales. The issue of the impact of file-sharing on record sales has given rise to plentiful research, whose conclusions are far from being unanimous (see Moreau and Curien 2006 for an overview). Supporters of the thesis that illegal downloading is to blame for falling music sales suggest that French people spent an average of 512 minutes per month sharing files, compared with 301 in Germany and 227 in Britain, at equal bandwidths (Tera Consultants 2008). Conversely, a range of analyses contest the significance of illegal file-sharing to the decline in record sales. These interpretations have been usefully summarised by Waelbroeck (2010) and point out that daily numbers of individuals who download are remaining constant while sales continue to fall, and that many file-sharers remain significant purchasers of music.

Given that the record companies have been unable to take full advantage of the new digital opportunities available to them, it is plausible that at least part of the decline can be explained by the shift from physical to digital music rather than mere piracy. In 2009 the SNEP itself recognised that the crisis was caused more by a problematic transfer of value between the 'physical' market and the digital economy than by any fall in the number of units sold. A SNEP study suggested that sales of singles had in fact risen by 13.9 per cent in 6 years from 39.3 million to 44.3 million, and that declining turnover was in reality due not to an effect of volume but of value, given that each sale of a single in 2008 accrued €1.3 on average to the industry, compared to €3.4 in 2002. However, the SNEP also found that album sales in traditional distribution declined by 58 per cent in volume (73 million albums) between 2002 and 2008, and that only 1.2 per cent of this fall (1.5 million albums) had translated into purchases via the Internet (SNEP 2009). Such data indicates that there is no guarantee that the declining volume of physical sales of music can be compensated for by a rise in digital sales through a growing Web-based market. However, it also calls into question the idea that piracy is responsible for declining sales, and leads us to question the appropriateness and usefulness of the mechanism of the repression of music piracy currently in operation in France, known as the HADOPI law, which we will consider in detail in the following section.

As a result of the downturn, various structural modifications indicate the effort that has gone into adapting the industry to the changing market conditions which have occurred in the space of less than a decade: falling investment in marketing (halved between 2002–9 to €72 million); a growing proportion of artists who are released from their contracts (70 new contracts offered by a French record company in 2009 and 88 contracts terminated, whereas in 2002 the ratio was 171: 75).[2] In terms of specific job losses, a study published in 2006 suggested that more than 700 jobs wopuld be lost over a period of 3 years, amounting to 20 per cent of total employment (UPFI 2006), and the crisis in the music industry naturally has related effects on employment in related activities in other cultural industries.

Such changes to the structure of the market bear witness to the industry's willingness to try to adapt, but one of the most striking features of the French response to the problems in the record industry has been the implementation of supportive measures by the state. Among the range of policies and initiatives put in place by government, most recently it has been the HADOPI law against piracy that has assumed pride of place, even though it is, in fact, surrounded by other often more long-standing mechanisms of a less repressive character.

The French government's response to the crisis in the recording industry reflects a long-standing tendency within the French cultural sector. It is to a consideration of the different ways in which the French state has increasingly come to implement measures in favour of the music industry – either through incentivisation, 'protectionism' or repression of unauthorised consumption – that we now turn.

State intervention in support of the recording industry

While the French state has a reputation for interventionism in many fields, especially in high culture, historically, it has been not used to intervening in the running of the recording sector, as it was an activity considered to be the responsibility of market forces and private enterprise. Neverthelesss, in contrast to this past disinterest and disengagement, government initiatives since the 1980s and 1990s have belatedly recognised not only popular music as an economic activity but also as a cultural-linguistic artefact important to maintaining France's 'place in the world'. This 'new' interventionism in favour of a popular-cultural form reflected a broadening – initiated by socialist governments and culture ministers in the 1980s – of the definition of what French 'culture' actually was, and consequently, of what could actually benefit from state support.

In the following discussion we will consider first the ways in which French governments broke from previous disengagement with the music industry through landmark policies in favour of French-language music in broadcasting in the 1990s and show how this cultural-linguistic 'protectionism' fits with wider theories and issues surrounding 'cultural diversity' and economic activity and world trade. Second, we will review more briefly some of the most significant tax-breaks, incentives, subsidies and levies introduced by the French state in support of the music industry. Third, we will consider in some detail – as a case-study of current attitudes of the French state towards the music industry in crisis in the digital world economy – the application since late 2009 of measures intended to reduce digital piracy of recorded music.

French-language music quotas and the concept of cultural diversity

A much-discussed piece of French legislation in the 1990s imposed quotas for the broadcasting of francophone music. The Carignon law of 1 February 1994 obliged radio stations to programme a minimum 40 per cent of content by French or francophone artists during the daytime (6.30 am to 10.30 pm), of which half had to be new artists or new productions. Much criticised for being a dirigist protectionist measure in favour of the French music industry, the principal aim of the law was stated as being to protect 'cultural diversity' (in other words, to favour French-language songs over 'international' pop music). However, in response to ongoing protests from artists and commercial radio stations that considered these measures too restrictive and 'protectionist', the law was revised in August 2000, lowering the required threshold of francophone material to 35 per cent, with 25 per cent to emerging artists. The industry body SNEP welcomed these modifications in declarations made in 2001, judging that the law had indeed indirectly facilitated the French recording industry's strong performances: in 2001, 90 per cent of the top-twenty best-selling albums were French-language (a list of week-by-week album sales in France can be found at http://chartsinfrance.net/charts/0002/albums.php). A comparative study of France, New Zealand (where there is no requirement for 'local' content in radio broadcasts) and Australia (where there is) undertaken by Mason does seem to suggest that protectionist measures have had a beneficial impact on French music: between 1996 and 2001, the proportion of locally produced music rose from 49 per cent to 59 per cent in France, but in New Zealand fell from 9 per cent to 7 per cent (Mason 2003).

The quotas on French-language music and the various strictures intended to stimulate the entry of new artists into the industry imposed since 1994 have been a highly visible and highly debated example of interventionism, discussed by commentators outside of France in terms of what is often unavoidably seen as commercial protectionism. However, their logic goes beyond merely the music industry as they are examples of what the French state conceives of as legitimate 'defence' (the term is perhaps less emotive than 'protection') of French culture and language against encroaching Americanisation (for treatments in English, see e.g. Dauncey 2003; Hare 2003; Looseley 2003). In discussions in the 1990s over the traditional notion of French 'cultural exceptionalism' (or what is seen as France's unique contribution to world culture in literature, the arts and other domains) and the cultural and economic policies associated with fostering and promoting it internationally, it was often difficult to draw clear boundaries between 'culture' and 'economics'. Indeed, state support for activities considered as culturally important has become progressively conflated with the concept of the 'cultural exception', or the need for 'culture' to be treated differently in international trade than other goods or services (Dauncey 2010). Within the General Agreement on Tariffs and Trade (GATT) and – more specifically from 1995 – the General Agreement on Trade in Services (GATS) how to define 'culture' and what 'protection' should be afforded to French cultural activities became central themes of French politics during the mid and late-1990s. Negotiations on trade in audio-visual products within GATS included debates launched notably by France and Canada, that the audio-visual sector needed to be treated differently from other goods and services, allowing the notion of 'cultural exception' to come strongly to the fore. In the 2000s these were enhanced by the emergent concept of 'cultural diversity' as another principle of French state intervention in culture. 'Cultural diversity' is a more semantically neutral term which has developed in official discourse in an attempt to refocus debate on a more positive role for cultural policy – and related policy areas such as broadcasting – in terms of the pluralistic fostering of French creativity in its widest sense, including popular music. With French support and that of other non 'Anglo-Saxon' cultures/countries, the concept was developed by UNESCO, and in June 1999 the UNESCO conference '*La culture: une marchandise pas comme les autres?*' prepared what became, in November 2001, the *Unesco Universal Declaration on Cultural Diversity*, and the subsequent *Unesco Convention on the Protection and Promotion of the Diversity of Cultural Expression*, which was adopted in October 2005 and ratified by France in July 2006.

It is difficult to reach a definitive judgement on the success of the Carignon law. As demonstrated above, the market share of French records throughout the 2000s has been consistently increasing. This appears to represent a slight improvement since the mid-1990s, when the declining strength of 'local' French production prompted government action. Again, taking statistics discussed earlier in this chapter, but reinterpreted in another light here, SNEP figures show a similar attrition rate for French-language and English-language record sales in the industry slump recorded in the 2000s and that the ratio between French and overseas music in terms of market share is relatively stable over time (see the table at the start of the chapter: album and single sales 1995–2009, SNEP 2010). However, it can be argued that without the Carignon law the situation of French language music would have been far worse, given the pressures of a globalised market in music and the dominant place of English language expression in music. French groups and French-language music have remained viable during the 2000s although, increasingly at the time of writing, concerns are being voiced at the rising numbers of French artists and groups who are increasingly choosing to express themselves in English.

Taxes and levies

The legal requirements imposed on French broadcasting by the Carignon law of 1994 attained a high profile both in France and abroad, but in some senses are merely the tree that hides a forest of other mechanisms of legislative action which are much less debated in the media but whose nature and effects are worthy of discussion here in order to give a rounded view of how the French state intervenes in support of the music industry. Since the 1985 law on copyright, royalties and other related issues, French governments have undertaken a number of experimental initiatives in an attempt to create a supportive environment for the recording industry. The principal feature intended to foster this has been the establishment of funding bodies (financed by a levy of 25 per cent of tax on private copying of music) which provide 'indirect' subsidies to record production through financial aid to live music performance, training and education of musicians and a wide range of other funding initiatives which aim to stimulate 'creativity' in the music sector. Similarly, the state has created fiscal mechanisms such as a tax break for 'phonographic production'. This tax break (a *crédit d'impôt*) is available to all music labels except those that are 'non-European' or owned principally by radio or TV companies (such as M6 or TF1 Music). Its stated purpose is to foster the emergence of new artists and francophone-expression music (Irma 2008), and it is justified both by appeal to the notion of fostering 'cultural diversity' and supporting a struggling sector of the market in cultural goods and services.

The levy on private copying was set up by the 1985 law on the rights of authors of sound and audio-visual works. This law was an attempt to extend to creators of records legal protection similar to those traditionally enjoyed by the authors of books and other written works and was intended, in the eyes of the socialist government of the time, to reinforce a shift in cultural policy towards a broader definition of 'culture', including more popular and commercial activities than previously recognised by the Ministry of Culture. The Lang law (named after culture minister Jack Lang) of 1985 originally introduced a tax on audio and video cassettes, with digital recording media such as CD-R, DVDs, MP3s and satellite decoders with hard drives being added in 2000. According to the law's promoters, these technologies were being used to undermine the commercial bases of musical and audio-visual creativity. Subsequently subsumed within the French legal code on Intellectual Property Rights, since 2001, this levy now also applies to the private copying of graphic artistic products such as video games.

Three-quarters of the taxes levied on the various personal-use recording media are passed on to the authors, performers and editors of musical, video/film and other artistic works, through a complicated system of collecting bodies (SORECOP and Copie France), organisations representing copyright holders of all kinds and bodies that collect the revenues accruing from the taxes. The remaining 25 per cent of the revenues are then fed back into artistic creation through subsidies to music festivals, theatrical productions, cinema and television festivals, documentaries and other productions, and a wide range of other activities. In 2009, some €183 million from audio and audio-visual recording media were thus allocated through this levy on private copying (see for various details the industry site www.copieprivee.org). The fact that fully three-quarters of the tax goes to the 'creators' of music, one quarter is fed back into 'creativity' and nothing goes to the record labels themselves is an interesting and significant demonstration of France's strong attachment to authors' rights, embodied in complex and robust legal mechanisms, and defended tenaciously by bodies such as SACEM.

As well as national policies, regional goverments in areas such as Provence-Alpes-Côte d'Azur, Rhône-Alpes, Aquitaine and Paris have also been active in developing subsidies for the local music industries. This is also the case for the project *Labels en Ville* which targets local economies and aims to help small labels and their surrounding networks of economic activity such as record shops. It is motivated by the threefold objective of protecting employment in a sector undermined by a crisis which is nevertheless highly visible in terms of promoting the image of the locality and helping 'cultural diversity'. The tools for such support to the music industry vary between regions but, to take Rhône-Alpes as an example, the initiatives grew out of a 2003 study of the regional recording sector which identified 200 labels, 15 or so distributors, 15 or so publishers and almost 80 record shops, but which also concluded that the sector was lacking in funding and financial support. Acting on these conclusions, the regional government voted to support the Rhône-Alpes recording and music industry through a varied system of subsidies for the production, distribution and marketing of recorded music, support for local companies at international trade fairs, an on-line music forum collating information and activities helpful to the sector and other facilities (Irma 2007). This regional funding reached €388,000 in 2006.

A final government initiative in support of the recording industry which it is useful to consider here is the recent *Carte musique jeune* or young person's music card. Launched in October 2010 and funded by a budget of €74 million over 3 years, this aims to encourage young consumers (12–24) to purchase music, and is the product of recommendations made by the Zelnik report on creativity and the Internet (Zelnik 2010). The card's principle is that of indirect subsidy, through a system which allows young music fans to pay only half the price of their purchases, the rest being underwritten by the state (the €25 card thus buys €50). Although the government has planned for a million cards, initial take-up by early December 2010 was disappointing, with only 22,000 sold in the whole of November (Fabre 2010; Torregano 2010).

Although the overall range of measures implemented in France to support the recording industry can clearly be seen to represent strong involvement in the sector, the real effects of this involvement and support are more difficult to see. The restructuring of some areas of the industry and the collapse of other activities in the sector has made identifying the impact of new government initiatives rather complex. Moreover, doubt remains surrounding the capacity of these measures to affect a consuming public already so influenced by the concept of 'free music' and by the practices of illegal downloading. Indeed, most recently, alongside their array of subsidies, promotions and levies – just some of which have been briefly discussed here – French governments have become increasingly preoccupied not only with the deleterious effect on the music industry of 'traditional' practices of private copying, but with the newer problem of digital piracy, perceived in the digital economy of musical goods and services to be undermining the sector's chances of prosperity. It is thus to a consideration of the 2009 law on the protection and encouragement of creativity on the Internet that we now turn.

Government approaches to digital piracy: the HADOPI Law and High Authority (2009)

As we have been reminded by Beuscart's recent analysis of the music industry (2008: 70), the issues raised by the rise of the digital economy are very different from those traditionally arising in the pre-Internet age. Music copyright holders argued very early in the growth of Internet file-sharing that downloading was reducing record sales but, until very recently, the measures available to prevent illegal downloading in practice were considered unlawful by the French national computing and freedom watchdog, the *Commission nationale de l'informatique et des libertés* (CNIL), and the state's attempts to manage the sector were thus often contradictory and conflicting. In 2009, however, the centre-right government of François Fillon moved to simplify and clarify matters by passing a law creating a new official body charged with monitoring and regulating the licit and illicit trading of digital culture – especially music – on the Internet. This law is universally known as the HADOPI law, so-termed because of the name of the body which it set up: *Haute autorité pour la diffusion des œuvres et la protection des droits sur Internet.*

This 'high authority' for digital diffusion of cultural products and protection of copyright aimed, in summary, to reduce the illegal downloading of music and films through a system of escalating warnings and penalties (warning email, then registered letter, then cancellation of service provision). This transfer of the policing of downloading from the legal system alone to a dedicated body was intended to improve the responsiveness of the system to piracy. The HADOPI body worked closely with ISPs, whom it required to help 'police' activities which were in contravention of the new law.

Drafting and passing the HADOPI law created considerable debate and reaction in France. It was only after lengthy debates and negative judgements rendered by the CNIL and by the *Autorité de régulation des communications électroniques et des Postes* (ARCEP) and an initial invalidation of the law of 10 June 2009 by the Constitutional Council (on the grounds that, because of conflicts between rights to privacy and private property, the HADOPI was not empowered to terminate Internet connections) that peer-to-peer downloading was finally declared illegal in French law.

The nature of the debates around HADOPI highlight that the recording industry is not a coherent unity that speaks with one voice. Essentially, two main groups were in conflict: on the one side 'mainstream' artists (PC INpact 2008) the major labels, big independent record labels, bodies representing companies in the sector (SNEP), and organisations representing copyright and royalty holders (SACEM, SACD etc.); and on the other, a number of small independent labels and 'rebelling' artists, alongside telecoms operators and some of the more radical Internet users. In fact, the unity of the 52 mainstream artists who signed a pro-HADOPI charter broke down somewhat during the following months (PC INpact 2010).

Within the lobby of small independent labels (grouped together in associations or federations such as the CD1D unifying 100 labels, or the FEPPIA, (*Fédération des Producteurs et Editeurs Indépendants d'Aquitaine*)), an open letter addressed to members of the French parliament in 2009 defined the terms of the lobby's rejection of the thinking behind the HADOPI. This letter pointed out that the more than 600 small independent labels in France collectively producing more than 3,000 items a year were, if considered together, in effect (as suggested by the *Syndicat de l'Artisanat*, or artisan workers' trades union) the biggest recording company in France, responsible for 90 per cent of original creation of music by artists of all kinds of genres and backgrounds, despite their often very small scale in terms of employees (0–5 on average). The letter explained how these labels were the creators and defenders of the 'cultural diversity' that France was so keen to protect, but were weakened in their creative role because the HADOPI law's protection of copyright and royalty owners' entitlement to recompense neglected to take into account the difficult situations of many independent artists and labels, as well as posing grave threats to individual freedoms. Essentially, in the eyes of these independent labels, HADOPI measures focused too closely on the interests of the major labels and their ongoing policies of digital distribution which – in the view of the minor labels – contributed too much to both lower and lower prices for recorded music, and a reduced importance for CDs. The independents argued that their contributions to musical creativity were thus threatened by HADOPI as much as protected.

In summary, the points raised by the independent producers related to the destruction of the physical marketplace for music by the major recording companies through their lack of interest in the fate of record shops, cut-throat competitive pricing policies, interest in new business models based on digital media and abandoning CDs, and partnerships with music streaming sites such as Deezer. In referring to the concept of 'cultural diversity', a central notion in many debates in France (*Mouvements* 2005), the independent producers made the most of their position as 'scouts' on the fringes of the oligopoly of labels in order to criticise the central monopoly enjoyed by the majors, asking the falsely naive question of whether the aim of the HADOPI law was actually to create a situation where music would soon be produced only by the majors and distributed by a handful of websites entrusted by them with the task, in a context where the independents, as 'artisans of music' and talent scouts of cultural diversity, would no longer exist. For the independents, HADOPI was focused too much on the majors' model of business in the music industry – characterised notably by high and rising marketing costs – and was therefore obscuring consideration of their own concerns.

The divided opinions over the HADOPI law were similarly revealed by the reactions of the telecoms operators (ZDNet 2010). The law required that Internet users whose service provision was terminated for piracy were nevertheless still obliged to pay their subscription, and that service providers were held to communicate the details of suspected pirates to the HADOPI. The telecoms/service provider Free was quick to point out the shaky legal framework of these responsibilities, as well as complaining about the lack of compensation for companies undertaking the task of providing information to the HADOPI. For Free, the law was a 'bad' law, resolving nothing, easily evaded and ignoring recent changes to the nature of piracy, and the company called for a new consulation between the state and agents in the sector, intended to produce a real solution rather than the previous fake discussions of 2007 which had merely allowed the major recording companies to impose their own solutions to the problem (ZDNet 2010). The response of the government to this was to institute a fine of €1,500 for any case of piracy not signalled by operators to the HADOPI, thereby forcing Free to comply.

The final version of the HADOPI law was adopted on 15 September 2009. What effects of the HADOPI law on the real behaviour of consumers and on the overall regulation of the market for music goods and services can be ascertained? The question seems hard to answer, given the little time separating us from the changes put in place (and a fuller analysis of the HADOPI can be found in Le Guern and Bastit (2011)). The market in recorded music in France remains in a state of upheaval and the analysis that can be made of the most recent trends offers little in terms of a clarification of the overall situation. Taking the summary of business during the first half of 2010 provided by the SNEP, figures demonstrating growth of 4.1 per cent per annum and a turnover of some €293 million seem to contradict somewhat the acute crisis often diagnosed within the industry. Similarly, digital sales growth is calculated at 12 per cent (€43 million) and conventional business is bucking the trend of decline since 2003 with growth of 2.5 per cent (€196 million). These figures are interpreted by the SNEP as the effect of the HADOPI law and as proof of the efficacy of anti-piracy legislation. The SNEP's willingness to link these figures with the new law is somewhat ironic given their criticism of a survey conducted in late 2009, which suggested that HADOPI would have little impact on downloading (Dejean *et al.* 2009). This poll of behaviour was undertaken in late 2009 through a telephone survey of 2000 representative Internet users consuming music and video in the French administrative region of Brittany, and aimed to evaluate the dissuasive power of the HADOPI measures among a population of people well aware of the law and its workings. Overall, the main conclusion of this survey was that the law has limited effects, serving mainly to encourage the modification of techniques of piracy. Only 15 per cent of peer-to-peer users have abandoned these practices as a result of the HADOPI law, and two-thirds of these reformed peer-to-peer downloaders still continue with piracy through different techniques. Of the Internet users who still persist with peer-to-peer sites, 25 per cent have similarly modified the ways they illegally access music. All in all, the survey concluded that the number of pirates has actually slightly increased since the implementation of the law, and that 'repentant pirates' make up only 5 per cent of the total numbers of legitimate Internet users (Dejean *et al.* 2009: 13). Nonetheless, during 2010, the SNEP was happy to link rising trends in business to the HADOPI, despite it being equally still too early to see the full picture, and in 2011 a SNEP report on the state of the music industry reported an apparent decline in peer-to-peer activities and greater uptake of legitimate downloading. Overall, gross digital sales rose by 14 per cent in 2010 and physical sales declined by 8.9 per cent within the wider context of a 5.9 per cent fall in the market for recorded music overall, and the SNEP at least interpreted the decline in P2P and rise in legal downloading directly to the HADOPI (SNEP 2011). A study published in May 2011 by the HADOPI examined the first effects of the new law (HADOPI 2011), concluding in a highly positive way that the new measures had significantly reduced piracy, claiming, for example, that 50 per cent of Internet users described themselves as now more likely to consume cultural products legally rather than through piracy. But these conclusions have been the subject of substantial debate, and criticisms have been made of the methodology used to gauge perceptions and the effects of the law (PC INpact 2011).

Concluding remarks

The HADOPI law has thus represented a concerted effort by the French state to intervene in the music industry in order to protect creativity and profitability. The emphasis placed on piracy as a central malaise of the French music sector has focused attention significantly on the Internet and on the activities of 'rogue' consumers, and the state's central involvement in setting up the mechanisms of repression has continued previous interventionism. But such a reading of the crisis and of the need for the HADOPI may amount purely and simply to a denial of reality. At the very least, other interpretations of events are possible, notably the hypothesis that the recording industry has been simply too slow to react and adapt to evolving changes in market conditions and consumer behaviour. Additionally, despite the battery of measures put in place by the governments in terms of taxes, tax-breaks, subsidies to creativity and so on, negative changes in the nature of the supply of music can be observed, such as fewer new artists signed, fewer albums commercialised, reduced marketing budgets, and so on, which are described by the major labels as *effects* of the crisis in the industry, but which can equally be interpreted as self-fulfilling phenomena (for instance, sales are falling because supply is diminishing, and not the reverse). The attention focused on the HADOPI and on the more financial dimensions of piracy's undermining of the music industry through lost revenues has perhaps, for once, distracted the French state from more long-standing preoccupations with France's cultural distinctiveness and exceptionalism, and from her ongoing need to 'protect' the French language.

Despite the difficulties experienced by the French recording industry, positive successes still occur (for example, Charlie Winston, produced by the independent label Atmosphériques). However, in a context in which it is difficult to envisage a stable overall future for the French recording, it would seem likely that state intervention will become increasingly important, working through mechanisms of subsidy and support to production and consumption such as those we have considered here. Nationally, French public policy is concentrating principally on helping producers or discouraging piracy. However, although state support and intervention in the recording sector have never been so extensive, more and more French artists are, following the examples of famous predecessors such as Air, Phoenix, Cocoon and many others, currently choosing to sing in English and to target success in the international market for popular music.

Notes

1   In 2008 the relative importance of the different channels of distribution for music as physical product was as follows: Internet and mail order (4 per cent); general hyper- and super-markets (41 per cent); specialised superstores (54 per cent); others, including independent record shops (1 per cent).
2   Studies of the French music industry rely heavily on SNEP data, principally because major labels and their related record companies only make their figures available to the SNEP and disclose them to no other organisation.

Bibliography

ARTMONEY (2010) Rapport annuel 2009 – Marché de la musique enregistrée. Available online at: www.artmony.biz/t3267-rapport-annuel-2009-marche-de-la-musique-enregistree (23 April) (accessed 16 December 2010).

Barreiro, E. (2005) Crise de l'industrie musicale ou obsolescence du CD? Available online at: www.numerama.com/magazine/1724-crise-de-l-industrie-musicale-ou-obsolescence-du-cd.html (accessed 27 October 2011).

Beuscart, J.-S. (2008) L'industrie du disque: bilan et perspective, in P. François (ed.) *La musique – une industrie, des pratiques*. Paris: La documentation Française, pp. 65–79.

Bourdieu, P. (1998) *Contre-feux 1*. Paris: Liber.

Bourdieu, P. (2001) *Contre-feux 2*. Paris: Liber.

Cheyronnaud, J. (2003) *Musique, politique, religion: De quelques menus objets de culture*. Paris: L'Harmattan.

D'Angelo, M. (1997) *Socio-économie de la musique en France: Diagnostic d'un système vulnérable*. Paris: La Documentation française.

Dauncey, H. (2003) The French Music Industry: Structures, Challenges, and Responses, in H. Dauncey and S. Cannon (eds) *Popular Music in France from Chanson to Techno: Culture, Identity and Society*, Aldershot, Hants., and Burlington, VT: Ashgate, pp. 41–56.

Dauncey, H. (2010) L'Exception culturelle, in T. Chafer and E. Godin (eds) *The End of the French Exception? Decline and Revival of the 'French Model'*, Basingstoke, Hants., and New York: Palgrave-Macmillan, pp. 72–84.

Dauncey, H. and Le Guern, P. (2007) De la difficulté d'émerger sur les scènes de 'musiques actuelles': les exemples de la France et de l'Angleterre, in J.-M. Seca (ed.) *Musiques populaires underground et représentations du politique*. Paris: InterCommunications/EME, pp. 56–83.

Dauncey, H. and Le Guern, P. (2010) *Stereo: Comparative Perspectives on the Sociological Study of Popular Music in France and Britain*. Aldershot, Hants., and Burlington, VT: Ashgate.

Fabre, C. (2010) Démarrage laborieux des mesures contre le piratage des œuvres sur Internet. Available online at: www.lemonde.fr/technologies/article/2010/12/18/demarrage-laborieux-des-mesures-contre-le-piratage-des-uvres-sur-internet_1455370_651865.html (18 December) (accessed 20 December 2010).

Guibert, G. (2006) *La Production de la culture: le cas des musiques amplifiées en France*. Paris: éditions Seteun/Irma.

Guibert, G. and Le Guern, P. (2010) Charting the History of Amplified Musics in France, in H. Dauncey and P. Le Guern (eds) *Stereo: Comparative Perspectives on the Sociological Study of Popular Music in France and Britain*, Aldershot, Hants.: Ashgate, pp. 59–73.

HADOPI (2011) *HADOPI, biens culturels et usages d'internet: pratiques et perceptions des internautes français*. Paris: Hadopi: 2011.

Hare, G. (2003) Popular Music on French Radio and Television, in H. Dauncey and S. Cannon (eds) *Popular Music in France from Chanson to Techno: Culture, Identity and Society*, Aldershot, Hants., and Burlington, VT: Ashgate, pp. 57–76.

Hennion, A. (1981) *Les Professionnels du disque: une sociologie des variétés*. Paris: Editions Métailié.

Irma (2007) Labels en ville: Les dispositifs locaux de soutien à la filière discographique. Available online at: www.irma.asso.fr/LABELS-EN-VILLELes-dispositifs (3 September) (accessed 14 December 2010).

Irma (2008) Labels: l'Etat fait crédit! La relance du disque par le crédit d'impôt. Available online at: www.irma.asso.fr/LABELS-L-ETAT-FAIT-CREDIT-La#nb1 (3 March) (accessed 12 December 2010).

Irma (2011) La Révolution 360° a-t-elle eu lieu? Les stratégies de diversification du disque. Available online at: www.irma.asso.fr/LA-REVOLUTION-360-A-T-ELLE-EU-LIEU (4 January 2011) (accessed 10 January 2011).

Lebrun, B. (2006) Majors et labels indépendants: France, Grande-Bretagne, 1960–2000, *Vingtième siècle*, 92: 33–45.

Le Guern, P. and Bastit, P. (2011) Crise de l'industrie musicale et politique anti-piraterie en France. Hadopi: internet civilisé ou politique répressive? in H. Dauncey and C. Tinker (eds) special issue on 'Popular Music and the Media in France', *Contemporary French Civilization*, 36(1–2): 141–60.

Looseley, D. (2003) *Popular Music in Contemporary France: Authenticity, Politics, Debate*. Oxford: Berg.

Maisonneuve, S. (2009) *L'Invention du disque, 1877–1949: genèse de l'usage des médias musicaux contemporains*. Paris: Editions des Archives Contemporaines.

Mason, P. (2003) Assessing the Impact of Australian Music Requirements for Radio. Available online at: www.mca.org.au/research/research-reports/research-reports/637-assessing-the-impact-of-australian-music-requirements-for-radio (accessed 9 January 2010).

Moreau, M. and F. Curien (2006) *L'industrie du disque*. Paris: La Découverte.

Mouvements (2005). Special number on Menaces sur la diversité culturelle, *Mouvements*, 37 (January–February).

OPSIS (2010) *L'enquête Marsouin* (Enquête 'Résidentiels 2009' de l'Observatoire). Available online at: www.marsouin.org (accessed 3 January 2011).

PC INpact (2008) Loi HADOPI: 52 artistes soutiennent la riposte graduée. Available online at: www.pcinpact.com/actu/news/44327-artistes-appels-hadopi-riposte-graduee.htm (23 June) (accessed 4 January 2011).

PC INpact (2010) Calogero: HADOPI ne marchera pas, la solution? Tout verrouiller. Available online at: www.pcinpact.com/actu/news/60657-calogero-hadopi-verrouiller-deezer-vol.htm (accessed 8 January 2011).

PC INpact (2011) Enquête de la HADOPI: tous les détails et le document. Available online at: www.pcinpact.com/actu/news/63510-enquete-sondage-hadopi-document-telechargement-illegal.htm (11 May) (accessed 26 October 2011).

Powdermaker, H. (1950) *Hollywood, the Dream Factory: An Anthropologist Looks at the Movie-Makers*. Boston, MA: Little, Brown and Co.

SNEP (2010) Rapport sur l'économie de la production musicale 2009. Available online at: www.Disqueenfrance.com

SNEP (2011) Rapport sur l'économie de la production musicale 2010. Available online at: www.Disqueenfrance.com

Sylvain Dejean, Thierry Pénard et Raphaël Suire (2009) Une première évaluation des effets de la loi HADOPI sur les pratiques des internautes français. Available online at: http://www.marsouin.org/IMG/pdf/NoteHadopix.pdf

Tera Consultants (2008) Report on the *Impact économique de la copie illégale des biens numérisés en France*. Paris, November.

Torregano, E (2010) Echec de la Carte musique et déroute de la gestion collective. Available online at: http://electronlibre.info/Deroute-de-la-carte-musique-et-de, 00993 (13 December) (accessed 14 December 2010).

Tournès, L. (2002) Jalons pour une histoire internationale de l'industrie du disque; expansion, déclin et absorption de la branche phonographique de Pathé (1894–1936), in J. Marseille and P. Eveno (eds) *Histoire des industries culturelles en France, XIXème-XXème siècles*. Paris: ADHE, pp. 465–77.

UPFI (2006) Les principaux Enjeux du dispositif crédit d'impôt à la production de phonogrammessynthese. Available online at: www.upfi.fr/index.php?page=actions &action=dossier&dossier_id=1&doc_id=3&PHPSESSID=42a069fdd5 (accessed 26 October 2011).

Verlant, G. (ed.) (2000) *L'Encyclopédie du rock français*. Paris: Hors Collection.

Waelbroeck, P. (2010) L'industrie musicale face au téléchargement. Available online at: www.laviedesidees.fr/L-industrie-musicale-face-au.html (21 September) (accessed 14 December 2010).

ZDNET (2010) HADOPI: Free accepte de relayer les emails d'avertissement à ses abonnés. Available online at: www.zdnet.fr/actualites/hadopi-free-accepte-de-relayer-les-emails-d-avertissement-a-ses-abonnes-39755458.htm (18 October) (accessed 1 January 2011).

Zelnik, P. (2010) Rapport de la Commission 'Création et Internet'. Paris: La Documentation française.

Japan

Population: 126.5 million (10th)
Languages: Japanese
Capital: Tokyo (pop 36.5 million)
Currency: Yen (JPY). $1 = JPY87.63
GDP: $5.46 tn (3rd)
GDP (PPP)/capita: $33,994 (23rd)
Median age: 44.8

GDP data from World Bank
Population data from CIA world factbook
Exchange rate used by IFPI (2011) (source: Oanda)

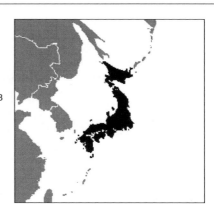

2010 Recorded music market

Overall income: $3958.5bn
World ranking: 2nd

	Income	World ranking
Physical sales	$2885.2bn	1st
Digital sales	$979.0m	2nd
Performance rights	$94.3m	2nd

Historical recorded music market ($m, at IFPI's 2010 exchange rate)

	1999	2000	2001	2002	2003	2004	2005	2006	2007	2008	2009
Trade Value			5460.5	4953.8	4581.7	4650.3	4677.0	4799.8	4798.2	4840.7	4316.6
Retail Value	8366.7	7926.8	7889.2	7115.7	6495.3	6742.4	6852.6				

Proportion of domestic repertoire (market value, physical sales only)

1991	1995	2000	2005	2010
72%	76%	78%	74%	81%

Album certification levels

	2010	1999
Gold	Domestic – 100,000	Domestic – 200,000
	International – 100,000	International – 100,000
Platinum	Domestic – 250,000	Domestic – 400,000
	International – 250,000	International – 200,000

9   Japan

Masahiro Yasuda

Introduction

According to Recording Industry Association of Japan (RIAJ 1991, 2001, 2011a), Japan remains the world's second most lucrative record market in 2010, with CD, DVD and other music-related goods worth ¥411.9 billion produced in the year. A closer examination reveals that its market importance in the world has grown from 16.5 per cent in 1999 to 22.8 per cent in 2009, whereas the US market share has shrunk from 37.3 per cent in 1999 to 24.5 per cent in 2009. According to the IFPI (2009, quoted in MacClure 2009), Japan's physical market has superseded the US counterpart in 2008 with total market value of $3.22 billion (¥316.5 billion) in Japan that year as opposed to $3.12 billion in the United States.

Apart from the consumers' attachment to physical formats, one of the most notable features of the Japanese market is the strength of its domestic repertoire, which has grown from 72 per cent in 1991 to 81 per cent in 2010. However, whereas a strong local repertoire is often interpreted as a sign of a thriving independent music scene, in Japan the situation is not so clear-cut. Another survey (Oricon 2011) suggests that 70.8 per cent of the Japanese record market in 2010 is dominated by so-called J-pop; localised (and, some would say, sterilised) versions of the Anglo-American popular styles such as folk, rock and hip hop. This means that the Japanese market today has a relatively conservative consumer base for physical distribution and is dominated by domestic – J-pop – catalogue sales.

One of the reasons behind the strength of J-pop is the predominance of what can be called 'domestic major' labels. The so-called 'big four' – Sony (17.5 per cent), Universal (11.6 per cent), EMI (5.0 per cent) and Warner (3.6 per cent) – comprise only 37.7 per cent of the Japanese market, whereas domestic labels such as Avex (13.9 per cent), J Storm (6.5 per cent), King (4.2 per cent), Victor (3.9 per cent) or Pony Canyon (3.0 per cent) perform equally or even much better than the transnationals. This is perhaps one of the defining characteristics of the Japanese recording industry today: we cannot indiscriminately consider these domestic labels as 'local indies' given that their structure in, and impact on, local music production make them comparable to the transnational majors.

The market dominance of the domestic majors imposes a series of difficulties for the transnational majors, due mainly to a set of locally embedded commercial practices such as the so-called 'tie-up' production and the complex web of consumer services, including the record rental and karaoke businesses. The tie-up is a widely employed commercial strategy based on sharing the production cost of a master record, and subsequent synergetic profit derived from its exploitation, among record companies, advertisement agencies and media corporations, most notably TV broadcasters. The tie-up has become a crucial determinant for both a record company and its artists to attain commercial and popular success, at the expense of the dissipation of creative control. Along with this, the record companies would be eager to 'plug' the song to transnational megastores, record rental stores and karaoke boxes, for they are regarded as important taste prescribers in Japan where the number, and diversity, of radio station is limited. It is these local particularities in music production that gave rise to J-pop in the 1990s.

As such, a commercially successful song in Japan is assembled in a series of localised, if not local, political, economic, cultural and technological mediations, to which even the transnationals have to adhere. It seems to have at least two implications. First, it furthers the discrepancy between domestic and international sales in the market. Indeed, even in the age of digital communication, it is difficult for international artists to reshape their songs or organise their release schedules according to the demands of such remote clients as Japanese advertising agents and/or television soap opera producers. Moreover, most of the international repertoires are excluded from the promotional operations involving record rental stores and karaoke boxes. This is due to a set of locally negotiated exceptions to authors' and phonogram producers' rights in Japan that are only applicable to domestic repertoires,

Second, if the local particularities served as a sort of informal barrier in favour of J-pop in the 1990s, today they have become increasingly seen as an internal structural weakness that impedes musical creativity, as the domestic record market shrank rapidly from ¥607.5 billion in 1999 to ¥283.6 billion in 2010. By this I do not simply mean that consumers are increasingly sceptical of the opaque nature of the tie-up business, but also that the labels are finding their business practices in contradiction with the recent shift in musical communication technologies and consumption styles, particularly so-called user-generated and participatory cultures in which music ought to be 'shared' rather than protected jealously. The point here is that in Japan there is no collecting society for phonogram producer's rights regarding online streaming of copyrighted recordings, like PPL in the UK. Thus, under the current Japanese copyright legislation, the streaming of commercial recordings on the Internet falls in the same legal category as P2P file-sharing, requiring prior consent from each and every right-holder.

As in most of the countries in this volume, the Japanese recording industry has been undergoing drastic changes since the turn of the century. While many point to the end of the 'physical' market, it seems to have more to do with the conservative business conventions of the recording industry and its complex web of interests shared with the neighbouring mass-media industries, and perhaps more importantly of the intellectual property politics of the government that determine the shape of the music business in Japan. It is an historical process: in order to grasp its possible future, we ought to situate the current state of the Japanese recording industry within a wider historical context of political, economic, cultural and technological socialisation of popular music production in Japan.

The history of the Japanese recording industry

1920s–30s: 'Tokyo Koshin Kyoku' and the senzoku-sei system

The first attempt to integrate dispersed music-related businesses by and around record production in Japan was made in the late 1920s and resulted from a series of seemingly unrelated incidents. In 1923, following the devastating Great Kanto Earthquake, the government introduced 100 per cent import duties on luxury articles, including phonographs, to encourage domestic economic recovery and to raise enough public funding for disaster recovery. In order to avoid paying these taxes, three globalising record companies established themselves in Japan and began to press their international catalogues locally. In 1927, Nippon Polydor was set up and started pressing its German catalogues. In the same year, Nippon Phonograph Company ceded its stocks to US Columbia to form Nippon Columbia Company, while US Victor launched an entirely new company for its Japanese operations, called the Victor Talking Machine Company of Japan Ltd.

However, the foreign record companies did not simply press and market their European and American catalogues but also began to develop and promote local repertoires, hand in hand with the rapidly growing domestic film industry. *Tokyo Koshin Kyoku* (1929) was the first song derived from a consciously orchestrated promotion between a record company (Japan Victor) and a film company (Nikkatsu Corporation) in that the record was produced simultaneously with a film of the same name. Played eagerly in cafés and bars in urban popular areas (though banned from the radio for being too indecent), the 78 rpm is reported to have sold about 2–300,000 copies (see Nakamura 1991). The unprecedented sales figure indicated the ripeness of the Japanese record market and a series of similar cooperative projects generated similar success over several years.

There are a few important consequences derived from the phenomenal success of *Tokyo Koshin Kyoku*. First, the division between a record company's international and domestic departments became solidified. Creative and production resources became almost exclusively allocated to the domestic department, whereas the international department would only select appropriate songs from a ready-made catalogue. Second, it accelerated the development of a nationwide distribution network controlled by the labels. As Azami (2008: 10) rightly points out, the direct networking of retailers was a prerequisite for a large-scale sales performance as it facilitated seamless and simultaneous exchange and sharing of sales information about hit songs nationwide.

Finally, and most importantly, the direct entrance of foreign capital coincided with the establishment of the *senzoku-sei* music production system. The *senzoku-sei* system resulted from an effort by the foreign record companies to realise a commercially efficient production system like Tin Pan Alley in the United States. However, in Japan there was little awareness of copyright law and professional musicianship (Wajima 2010: 25), and, therefore, unlike the Tin Pan Alley system organised around music *publishers*, in Japan it was *record companies* that employed composers, songwriters, performing musicians and singers, and exploited the rights for songs they composed, wrote, performed and sang. The exclusivity was maintained by a strict vertical, patronising hierarchy, in which a singer was an apprentice of a particular composer, often called *sensei*, or mentor. The apprentice was not allowed to sing songs composed by other composers not so much because of the contract but more because of an ethical obligation (25–6).

In this way, by the late 1920s to the early 1930s, the recording industry in Japan has realised a centralised vertical integration ranging from *senzoku-sei* production system to the nationwide direct distribution network. It also started to develop a horizontal integration of neighbouring media and entertainment industries so as to deploy multimedia cooperation strategies. This industrialisation of the recording businesses resulted in an oligopoly among Japan Victor, Nippon Columbia, Nippon Polydor, as well as King Records (founded in 1931 as a recording division of Kodansha book publisher) and Teikoku Chikuonki (founded in 1932 in Nara, in the southern-central region of Japan).

1950s–60s: phonogram producers' rights and production companies

The Asia–Pacific War of 1941–45, and the subsequent occupation by the US-led Allied Powers brought about a particular set of effects on the development of the recording industry in Japan. Most obviously, wartime politics drove out foreign capital; therefore the three foreign labels cited above came under control of native capital with nationalised trademarks. With their pressing plants destroyed during the war, however, the business took more than five years to recover the pre-war level of production. In 1947 annual production levels was as low as 12 million units, about a third of the figures in the 1930s. During this time almost 85 per cent of records were domestic music, of which about 75 per cent (that is, about 60 per cent of the total production) were popular songs produced with the *senzoku-sei* production system (Kurata 1992: 224). The international titles that were released tended to be old, as they were pressed from the dated masters imported before the war. As partnership deals with their former parent companies had expired during the war, Japanese record labels had no new international material to release. Ironically, however, the US-led occupation forces induced a mass craving for American popular music. The AFRS (Armed Force Radio Service) started airing the latest American jazz or country and western hits immediately after the end of the war. There were more than ten AFRS stations in Japan, including Tokyo, Osaka, Sapporo and Okinawa.

In an effort to catch up with the growing popularity of US, and later UK, popular songs, Japanese record labels had to negotiate licensing deals with US and UK labels. This international licensing business had a couple of definitive consequences in the way the Japanese recording business operated. First, the international department began exercising more creative and commercial influence on the local popular music scenes. Knowledge among international A&R staff about the latest music trends in the US and the UK became vital as the market share of international catalogues neared 50 per cent in the late-1960s. Second, it raised the consciousness among the local jazz, country and western and, later, rockabilly musicians – who would perform at a variety of entertainment and amusement venues for American GIs – of the phonogram producers' rights: simply, they realised that, thanks to the magnetic tape technology, they could make records without being employed by a record company. This resulted in the emergence in Japan of a form of music business based on the licensing of reproduction rights to master phonograms produced and invested in by entities outside the conventional record companies. This would challenge the *senzoku-sei* system whose repertoires began to feel more and more outmoded as the US and UK jazz, folk and rock attracted more and more Japanese youths.

The emergence of external production companies was seen as a sort of necessary evil by the labels. On one hand, they had to bear the domestic A&Rs' conservatism, deeply rooted in the *senzoku-sei* practices but lacking creative expertise in newer Anglo-American musical styles. On the other hand, it was felt necessary to respond to the growing youth market. The ways around this were, first, to accept the master licensing deals with emerging production companies and, second, to release domestic titles inspired by the Anglo-American styles under overseas labels, of which they were licensees, in order to avoid confrontation with the A&Rs and musicians employed under the *senzoku-sei* system.

Once the occupation came to end in 1952, the production companies, such as Watanabe Production (established by a bandleader Shin Watanabe and his wife Misa Watanabe in 1955) and Hori Production (established by a country and western guitarist Takeo Hori in 1960) would develop a strong partnership with emerging commercial television broadcasters that, in turn, found musical variety shows a very efficient way to attract audiences: the production companies produced television shows featuring their entertainers and their songs as a package. Their media exposure boosted the record sales whose masters were retained by the production companies. In this way, they managed not simply production but also marketing/promotion functions by themselves. Record companies were now obliged to pay royalties for the reproduction rights to the production companies.

1970s–80s: independent companies and transnational joint ventures

So far, we have seen chronologically two systems of record production that prevailed in Japan from the 1920s to 1970s. First, there was the *senzoku-sei* system that had come to be associated with *enka* genre. Second, I have described the production companies' master phonogram licensing business that predominated *idol pops*. In the 1970s, a third system emerged, based around a series of independent labels founded by small entrepreneurs and/or artists, with eventual participation by newly entered domestic record companies, whose songs were to be branded as *new music*.

The production companies' domestic licensing business was, as seen above, the first turning point in the decentralisation of the recording industry in Japan. Nonetheless, seen in terms of the division of labour, it was not very different from the *senzoku-sei* system: the song was planned and packaged by an external production company instead of a record company, but it was still composed, arranged, written, accompanied and sung by different people. Although the system was to prevail as the standard-bearer in the *idol pop* boom in the mid-1970s, it would become seen as incompatible with young people's growing interest towards Anglo-American rock and folk ideology, which suggested that music ought to be composed, written and performed by the same person.

The first attempt by the independent music makers to organise their creative activities into a recording business was Underground Record Club, or URC. URC was founded in 1969 by a folk music aficionado Masaaki Hata as an attempt to sidestep strict self-censorship often imposed by the major labels. His initial idea was to form a members club of underground folk music fans where they would receive a set of records in return for fixed-rate membership fees. However, as the membership grew at an unexpectedly high rate, he soon started distributing to select record retailers. Thus URC became, albeit in a restricted scale, a fully fledged record company that controlled not simply production but also marketing and distribution.

The success of URC was short-lived but encouraged some of the Japanese rock and folk musicians to set up their own record labels in order to gain creative and commercial autonomy (Azami 2004: 172). It also piqued the interest of a variety of domestic business entities conventionally external to the record production, ranging from commercial broadcasters to book publishers to audio hardware manufacturers, that sought to enter into the music business, as the market enjoyed an impressively rapid growth from ¥8,971 million in 1960 through ¥29,393 million in 1965 to ¥65,720 million in 1970 (RIAJ 2003: 8). Commercial broadcasters in particular were interested in retaining the rights to master recordings so as to realise an in-house synergy between televised music shows and sales of the songs featured in them. Even without expertise in music production, they simply needed to invest in and join forces with these small-scale labels and independent creators, who in turn lacked economic and/or human resources, for promotion and/or distribution. Reflecting this, the membership of RIAJ increased from 7 in 1960 to 22 in 1975.

It is interesting to note that the three systems described above were *all* inspired by the US business models while, at the same time, *all* deeply rooted in the local set of political, economic and cultural dynamics, each being associated with a particular genre of music, a differentiated ideology and a distinctive cultural taste. These localised practices, along with the governmental restriction on direct foreign investment put in place since the end of the occupation, meant that the transnational major labels were forced to form joint ventures with Japanese domestic labels. For the transnationals, it was vital to enter the rapidly growing Japanese market and to control directly their international repertoires that had previously been distributed by their respective licensees on a patchwork basis. However, at the same time, they found it equally crucial to take advantage of the increasing popularity of domestic catalogues so as to justify the investment: here again, the externalised production companies and independent labels turned out to be quite handy for them – all they needed was to reach out for the local producers.

In 1967, the Japanese government partially withdrew its protective measures against foreign capital investment and, in March 1968, American CBS entered a 50/50 joint venture with Japanese Sony to form CBS/Sony Records. CBS had had a licensing deal with Nippon Columbia that was its Japanese filial before the Second World War, but instead it approached Sony, a rapidly growing hardware manufacturer, who in turn was willing to enter into the software business to push further the hardware sales. In August the same year, CBS/Sony released its first records, including such prestigious acts as Simon and Garfunkel and Brother Four from the USA, and a Japanese male idol group, Four Leaves.

In the next year, Matsushita, Nippon Victor and Dutch Phillips (Nippon Phonogram) entered into a joint venture. Nippon Phonogram was to launch an affiliated label, Vertigo Japan, to release some of the leading Japanese rock and rhythm and blues acts of the time. It was followed by a deal among Japanese Pioneer, Watanabe Production and American Warner Group (Warner/Pioneer) in 1971, and Toshiba Music and British EMI (Toshiba EMI) in 1973. Watanabe Production had already established itself as one of the leading production and talent agency specialised in *idol pop*, whereas Toshiba Records was already been renowned for their commitment to the Japan's folk song boom in the 1960s.

Foreign direct investment had been totally liberated by 1975. Sony bought CBS in 1988 and renamed the entity as Sony Music Entertainment in 1991, whereas American Warner Brothers bought Warner/Pioneer in 1990 to become Warner Music Japan. Matsushita bought MCA in 1990 only to resell it to Canadian Seagram in 1995, whereas Toshiba withdrew from Toshiba EMI in 2007. As of 2010, the big four transnational majors, i.e. EMI, Sony Music Entertainment, Universal and Warner Music Group, are all present in the Japanese market with only SME being participated by Japanese capital.

The local particularities of the Japanese recording industry

Although the international major labels moved into Japan, the music industry in Japan presented different issues for them than in other markets. In this section I will outline the most important elements of what makes Japan a distinctive market, particularly in the light of that which would have a decisive impact on the structuring of what is called the 'J-pop industry complex' in the 1990s (Ugaya 2005: 93–4), and its repercussion on the current record market in Japan. I would like here to focus on three of the important aspects from the 1980s and into the 1990s: the emergence and legitimisation of record/CD rental business; the proliferation of compartmentalised karaoke boxes; and the nationwide deployment of Anglo-American megastore chains.

The first record rental shop was said to be launched in 1980 by a group of students in the western suburbs of Tokyo. The rental business grew quite rapidly thanks mainly to the popularity of portable cassette tape players among the youths. The recording industry immediately took civil actions against the leading rental traders for copyright infringement in 1981 while, in the meantime, the rental traders set up an industry group, Record Rental Commerce Trade Association of Japan, in 1984. The negotiation between the two parties settled in the same year to legalise the rental business in exchange for royalty payment to the right holders. In the following year, the copyright law was reformed to recognise rental rights to the authors, performers and phonogram producers of domestic catalogues. It was reformed again in 1992 to include international catalogues.

The settlement was not too disadvantageous to the labels, in that record rental shops, which increased from some 500 in 1980 to more than 6,000 shops nationwide by 1989, served as an ideal medium for notification of new releases in the Japanese context where the number of radio stations is limited. This is why the recording industry decided that singles could be authorised in rental shops only three days after their release date as opposed to up to three weeks for albums. This also explains, at least partially, the market domination of domestic repertoires from the 1980s: international repertoires are refrained from rental exploitation for one year after their international release date.

Karaoke took its initial commercial shape in the early 1970s as an entertainment in bars and nightclubs in which middle-aged business men would sing their favourite repertoires – almost exclusively limited to the *enka* genre – in front of a not necessarily acquainted audience. This perception of karaoke was to change dramatically in the 1990s with the compartmentalised and individualised karaoke box business. The first karaoke box was set up in 1986, and, according to All-Japan Karaoke Industrialist Association (JKA 2010), the number of karaoke boxes increased from 52,578 in 1989 to 160,680 in 1996. This was accompanied by technological advances, notably the MIDI synthesiser and sequencer, digital file storage and online distribution of karaoke tracks, which has enabled a massive list of repertoires not limited to *enka* but increasingly *idol pops* and *new music* produced by domestic and/or transnational majors. The prescriptive role of karaoke became so significant that songwriters would need to restrict the melody to be a certain voice range in order for a song to be commercially successful.

Another institution that characterised the shift in record consumers' tastes in the 1980s and 1990s was the nationwide establishment of parallel import megastore chains, notably US Tower Records (which entered Japan in 1981), UK HMV and UK Virgin Megastore (both in 1990). Although parallel importers existed in the 1970s, they became more and more central to the youth musical cultures in the course of the 1980s and 1990s, as they began to deploy their retail network nationwide. Initially dealing exclusively with the international records imported from the USA and the UK, they would embody some kind of 'authenticity' among the likes of subcultural elites and students.

For the recording industry, the parallel importers were problematic in two accounts. On one hand, the imported records were considerably cheaper than domestic ones as the former were not subject to the industry-wide resale price maintenance system. This also meant that the transnational majors became unable to take the initiative in creating and managing the image of their international artists in Japan, as the range of international products available in these shops was far wider and cheaper than those officially released through the Japanese branches of the transnationals. In order to justify the domestic pricing, the labels pursued a set of value-adding strategies, such as supplementing some bonus tracks or advancing Japanese release date.

On the other hand, the perceived hipness of the foreign megastores meant that their domestic catalogues became less attractive to the eyes of a growing number of young opinion leaders. The breakthrough was to have domestic catalogues available from these megastores. It was not an easy negotiation, but there was a mutual interest in that, ultimately, the parallel importers needed to deal with domestic catalogues in order to attain a certain level of space efficiency as their stores were getting bigger and bigger while the market share of the international catalogues never exceeded 30 per cent in the 1990s.

Consequently, by the 1990s, most of the transnational majors developed a closer cooperation with the parallel importers. The labels' international divisions began considering the parallel importers' sales performance as a means of monitoring the popularity of their international acts, while the domestic divisions started taking advantage of the exotic image of megastores to add cutting-edge values to their domestic catalogues. The foreign-owned, trend-setting stores on high streets, with their rapid nationwide growth and vast shop size previously unimaginable as a record shop in Japan, offered domestic producers a culturally invested space that would bridge Japanese artists to 'international' – Anglo-American – music scenes.

Tie-up strategies and the J-pop industry

Along with the wholesale shift that involved not simply the recording industry but also its neighbouring music-related industries, the independent *new music* creators and entrepreneurs were experiencing an unprecedented growth of their market thanks to carefully controlled exposure to mass media. Unlike the forceful and inhuman manipulation of the singer's image and song's content in the *idol pop* genre, the cooperation – known as 'tie-up' – was perceived as respectful of a musician's creative autonomy and musical quality. Certainly, the *new music* artists, largely influenced by the Anglo-American folk and rock ideology, were very sceptical of mass media, and television in particular. However, at the same time, the featuring of songs by some of the prominent American folk/rock artists in influential films such as Mike Nichol's *The Graduate* (1967) and Denis Hopper's *Easy Rider* (1969) were sensational enough for the Japanese artists to consider visual expression in regard to their music.

Therefore, at least initially, a tie-up deal was mediated by a limited number of respected producers who could go between advertisers and *new music* creators. Their differentiation strategy for reclaiming *new music*'s creative distinction was very simple: if the *idol pop* artists expose and exploit their physical appearance, ingratiating the mainstream television audience, the *new music* artists only provide songs that would accompany the televised images without appearing on the small screen themselves. Unlike advertisement jingles that would repeat the product name or the trademark, tie-up songs did not contain them: as the market matured, the advertisers preferred less obvious – more sophisticated and artistic – advertising strategies in which *new music* artists found their creative niche. Ultimately, at least in the beginning, an advertising agency never dictated the song to be written – it had to look for an appropriate song among those already written.

The first successful advertisement tie-up of the kind was said to be *Kimi no Hitomi wa Ichiman Boruto* ('Your pupils are worth ten thousand volts') by Takao Horiuchi in 1978. The song title was the exact catch phrase of an autumnal publicity campaign for a prominent cosmetics maker. Released in August, it topped single charts for more than a month and sold over 900,000 copies. By the end of the 1980s, television broadcasters also began approaching the *new music* creators so that their songs were featured as theme songs for television soap operas. The first successful case of a drama tie-up was Kazumasa Oda's 1991 double-platinum hit, *Rabu Sutôri wa Totsuzen Ni* ('Unexpected Love Story'), featured as the theme song for a TV drama entitled *Tokyo Love Story*.

By the beginning of the 1990s, the tie-up had become organised into a large-scale institution. The 'formalisation' of tie-up business, as Ogawa *et al.* (2005) argue, shifted the creative initiative from the independent creators and their labels to the advertising agencies. In the mid-1990s, Being, a production company established in 1978 by a producer/entrepreneur Daiko Nagato, gained momentum mediating the advertising and recording industries. Being was arguably the first professional production company optimised for a tie-up business, seeking to intervene in creative processes to meet advertisers' needs while maintaining artistic quality, so that the songs could simultaneously be advertisement jingles and autonomous musical works (ibid.: 73). In 1993, the groups contracted to Being dominated the number one position of single charts almost every week for over six months from January.

The term 'J-pop', signifying such songs, became widespread at this time. Stylistically, it resembles a lot of *new music* in that it draws on Anglo-American popular styles such as rock and hip hop. However, in the course of the 1990s, J-pop drove *idol pop* off the market to become *the* mainstream popular music in Japan. By then, J-pop tunes would reach audiences through television advertisements and/or soap operas, karaoke-boxes, foreign import megastore chains and/or rental CD shops. It became so banal that even recording industry insiders would denounce that J-pop was transforming music from a 'work of art' to a 'consumable commodity' (Ugaya 2005: 60–1). J-pop repertoires were increasingly being seen as sanitised, standardised and predictable.

The flipside of this J-pop boom was the historically unprecedented expansion of the record market in Japan. From an annual production of 290 million units (¥387.8 billion) in 1990, it attained in 1997 an annual production of 481 million units (¥588 billion) with 17 million-selling singles and 27 million-selling albums (RIAJ 1998). The million-selling titles were almost entirely domestic acts (except for Mariah Carey's *Butterfly* album). Only 5 out of the 17 singles and 10 out of the 27 albums were produced by the transnational majors, such as BMG Japan, Epic/Sony Records, Toshiba EMI and Warner Music Japan, while the rest were products of domestic major labels such as Avex D.D., B-gram Records, Johnny's Entertainment, Rooms Records and Toy's Factory. According to Ugaya (2005), 47 out of the annual top 50 singles of the same year were product of tie-up strategies.

The decline of J-pop

The empire of J-pop did not last long. As the century turned, record sales declined constantly from 481 million units (or ¥588 billion in value) in 1997 to 256 million units (or ¥283.6 billion in value) in 2010. The number of million-selling titles in the same year also plunged to only three albums and one single, as well as ten titles digitally distributed. J-pop, certainly, remains dominant in the Japanese market today, yet the cultural, economic and technological environment that surrounds it has been transformed drastically to expose the vulnerability inherent in the tie-up system. The situation seems more complicated in Japan than a simple 'end of the physical' rationale being presented by some Western commentators, for the 'physical' remains quite central to music consumption in this market. It would be more reasonable, rather, to look at a set of shifts in locally specific elements that altogether shrinks the distribution network and deflates the value of musical recordings.

First, television advertisements, J-pop's central medium of communication, are experiencing a drastic shift in viewing behaviours. As NHK's latest survey on daily practices (2011) suggests, the percentage of people who view television at least once a day decreased from 93 per cent in 1995 to 89 per cent in 2010. The trend away from television was sharpest in younger age groups: teenage female and male viewers decreased respectively from 91 per cent and 92 per cent in 1995 to 83 per cent and 82 per cent in 2010, while female and male viewers in their 20s decreased respectively from 87 per cent and 81 per cent to 78 per cent and 72 per cent. The tendency seems to be reflected in the regression in advertising expenditure on television. According to Dentsu (2011), annual advertising expenditure on television diminished by 12 per cent from ¥1,967 billion in 1998 to ¥1,732 billion in 2010. Television is no longer an efficient means to reach a young audience while, at the same time, broadcasters, who retain a significant stake in the phonogram production tie-up system, have so far been rather hesitant to embrace a shift to the Internet as the consumers' source of entertainment.

On the Internet, however, at the same time, the shift into commercial digital distribution has not been as successful as expected in Japan, due largely to the parent companies' stake in the global competition for technological standards, which hinders more than benefits the consumers. This is particularly the case for labels like SME and Toshiba EMI (although Toshiba has been detached from EMI since 2007), while the other transnationals are no longer owned by hardware manufacturers in Japan. In 1999, Bitmusic, Japan's first substantial digital distribution platform, was launch by SME, synchronised with the release of the first

Net Walkman, NW-MS7, equipped with in-house compression and DRM standards, followed by several other platforms including Avex's @music service.

SME also took the initiative in 2000 to start Label Gate, a joint capital corporation to build a foundation for legal, commercial, online music distribution in Japan. Bitmusic, @music and other distribution platforms of partner labels were then integrated under Label Gate's Mora music portal service in 2004. However, Mora's problem was that the catalogue proposed online was rather limited (about 40,000 titles at the time) because of other labels' reluctance to license their songs. Moreover, on top of the fact that Label Gate was one of the protagonists of Copy Control CD formats, consumers' response to Mora service – which required a dedicated in-house player with patented DRM standards – was divided. Equally, the pricing policy of Mora, initially set at around ¥350 per song (approximately $3.20 at the time), was considered too expensive compared with that in record rental shops which would let an album of ten songs for a day for the same price.

The launch of iTunes Music Store (iTMS, today's iTunes Store) in 2005, two years after its original US launch, further exposed the discrepancy between Mora and iTMS Japan in terms of the pricing policy and the richness of catalogue (see Tsuda 2004; Yagi 2007). iTMS Japan offered a catalogue of 1 million songs from 15 labels including Universal Music, Toshiba EMI and Avex, as opposed to Japanese Mora's 40,000 titles. At iTMS a song could be bought for ¥150 (approximately $1.36 at the time), even if Mora had reduced the pricing to ¥200 (approximately $1.82). Apple's 'generous' and 'flexible' DRM policies were also often celebrated in comparison with Sony's 'greedy' and 'rigid' ones. Although BMG Japan joined in 2006 and Warner Japan in 2007, as of January 2011 SME still refuses to participate in iTunes platform in Japan as it continues to operate the Mora service and considers iTMS's pricing irrational.

Mobile download service known as *chaku-uta*, or 'ringtune', has, on the contrary, had a better consumer reception in Japan (*chaku-uta* is a registered trademark of SME). Conceived as a means to draw cashflow back into the labels out of the use of songs they invested in but distributed as a MIDI-based mobile phone ringtone, the ringtune distribution service called *Rekochoku* – an abbreviation of 'directly sold by the record companies', was initiated in 2002 by Lable Mobile, another joint capital company financed by SME, Avex Network and Victor Entertainment, to which other leading labels, such as Toshiba EMI and Universal Music Japan, joined later. It introduced full-length *chaku-uta full* service in 2004, which means that the users could download an entire song/ recording directly to their mobile phones through cellular networks.

Unlike the slow catch-up of the PC download market, which remained below the ¥10 billion level until 2009 (¥10.2 billion that year according to RIAJ), the mobile download market in Japan grew rapidly from ¥32.34 billion in 2005 to ¥74.75 billion in 2010 (RIAJ 2011a). This can be explained by the fact that the *Rekochoku* service was an integral part of young people's expenditure on mobile phones (it would be charged with the mobile phone bill) and that the mobile network operators took advantage of music's capability on the new mobile phone terminals to attract young users. In the end, *Rekochoku* seems one of the main channels for the record companies to communicate their J-pop acts to the young population. Indeed, an annual music media user survey conducted by RIAJ (2011b) depicts that the use of physical, PC and mobile phone for music listening is clearly generational: if those in their 50s and 60s prefer purchasing CDs (26 per cent), to PC downloading (13.2 per cent) and mobile downloading (10.7 per cent), those in their 30s and 40s prefer PC downloading (48.9 per cent) to CD (41.3 per cent) and mobile (41.5 per cent) and the youngest age group from 13 to 29 prefer mobile downloading (47.7 per cent) to CD (32.7 per cent) and PC (37.8 per cent).

That said, even in 2010, the mobile phone download market occupies only 20 per cent of the entire record market that is shrinking anyway. The service has an inherent weakness, that a song purchased on one mobile phone cannot be transferred on to a PC or another mobile phone if the user decided to replace it. Also, the pricing of *chaku-uta full*, from ¥200 to ¥400, remains way above the iTMS service and, above all, record rental shops. According to the same user survey by RIAJ (2007, 2009, 2011b), the ratio of musical expenditure among CD purchasing, CD rental and online downloading was respectively 33.7:24.6:9.3 in 2006, 40.9:34.3:6.4 in 2008, and 33:24.5:9.3 per cent in 2010. While the growth and decline between 2008 and 2010 of the online downloading and CD purchasing can be understood as a direct impact of the entrance of Apple's iTMS, the constantly high frequency with which users rent CDs ought to be noted. The CD rental store chains, concentrating in number while gaining ground against the weakened parallel import megastore chains, is another element that deflates the value of music recordings while imposing a difficulty on the rapid growth of commercial digital distribution.

The case in point here is the leading nationwide chain Tsutaya, whose flagship shop in Shibuya, Tokyo, launched in 1999, sports a total of nine floors (seven stories above ground and two below) and boasts its range of cultural commodities as the nation's largest. Started in 1982 in Osaka, Tsutaya gradually extended its activities in the 1990s to not only renting but also retailing almost every cultural commodity, ranging from books, magazines, video games, CDs and DVDs. In its effort to improve the retail network and to attract customers with an ever stronger cultural edge, it engaged in an aggressive M&A operation in the 2000s while acquiring Virgin Megastores Japan in 2005 and 2009, entering into a takeover negotiation with HMV Japan, although it did not succeed (HMV's flagship Shibuya shop was closed down in August 2010). As of January 2011, Tsutaya has a network of some 1,400 shops nationwide and extends its activities even to online CD and DVD rental and retail services. The diversification of products in a Tsutaya shop means, above all, that CD rental has become little more than a loss leader to attract customers: they can rent a single for about ¥120 and an album for about ¥350 a day.

Clearly, the J-pop industry is trapped in a negative spiral. There is less and less opportunity for television tie-ups as there are fewer potential J-pop audiences watching television and lower advertising budgets on television. The Anglo-American megastore retailers that would prescribe an added value to J-pop repertoires have either disappeared or been absorbed into a CD/DVD rental giant that instead deflates music recordings' value (only Tower Records Japan, taken over from its US parent company in 2002, manages to survive).

In the meantime, the take-up of the commercial digital distribution platform has been rather slow in Japan, apart from mobile ringtune download services that are not free from the issues of interoperability resulting from a complex web of stakes invested in by the labels, the mobile phone manufacturers and mobile network operators. It is also facing the Apple's iTunes Store services that is beginning to show its impact on the market. Unlike Sony, Apple does not have a stake in the production of the contents it distrbutes, which works for its advantage in online culture.

The future of the Japanese industry

To face the downward spiral, the majors desperately throw more and more new talents to the Japanese market, but fail to catch up with new musical trends. According to RIAJ (2011a), the number of debutants has increased from 257 in 1999 to 502 in 2009 despite the constant sales decline. In order to do this, the majors are increasingly looking into various (sub)cultures on the Internet. However, it turns out that the current copyright system in Japan, which had been functioning in favour of J-pop's tie-up strategies until today, could hamper rather than facilitate their talent-picking activities.

Outstanding features of the recent rush of new releases are compilation CDs of songs originally available on the Internet, most notably those derived from an increasing number of non-profit net labels, such as Maltine Records and Bunkai-kei Records, that propose selections of artists and songs free of charge, and those from what is called the *Hatsune Miku* craze – a participatory online subculture based on a vocal synthesiser of the same name where songs featuring 'her voice' could sometimes attract more than a million viewers on video-sharing sites. In August 2008, Victor Entertainment picked up one of the leading *Hatsune Miku* producing units, livetune, and released a full CD, *Re: Package* (2008). It was the first ever attempt by a major label to include *Hatsune Miku* related music to their catalogue, and reached the number 5 position on national weekly charts.

The Internet also offers an experimental opportunity for musical mediation: content sharing services such as SoundCloud, Youtube and *Niko Niko Dôga* are essential for net labels and *Hatsune Miku* producers to communicate with their respective audiences, whereas live video streaming service such as Ustream provides musicians with an accessible means to expose their songs to public. The case in point here is a Ustream channel called Dommune (www.dommune.com), with D signifying that it is ahead of C for commune. It was launched by a visual artist Naohiro Ukawa in March 2010 and is delivered live from its studio in Tokyo from Monday to Thursday, from 19:00 to midnight, containing topical debates and non-stop music mix by renowned DJs. As in any other Ustream-based programmes, the audiences can join in the debate or comment on the music via Twitter service – it is not uncommon that the programme attracts more than 8,000 simultaneous viewers.

So these new musical cultures are attracting a fair amount of people today. Certainly, it is misleading to see them as having a massive public impact like the television tie-up that characterises the J-pop strategies. Yet it would be fair to say that they constitute what Jason Toynbee calls 'proto-markets' (2000: 25) that propose not only new kinds of music, but also new ways of mediating music and culture, thanks to the broadband technologies. Dommune does hint at potential future forms of televised media – more interactive and social, globally accessible and locally meaningful at the same time. The problem here, however, is that the major labels in Japan cannot overtly take part in these potentially productive proto-markets for a technical reason – the use of copyrighted recordings on the Internet is currently illegal without prior consent from the right-holders. Under the current Japanese copyright law, Internet streaming is considered as telecommunication, not as broadcasting. For a broadcaster to programme a recorded song on the radio or television, it simply does it without prior consent, which automatically generates the remuneration right to the song's author(s), as well as the performer(s) and the phonogram producer(s) who participated in the recording of the song in question. Namely, broadcasters can use whatever songs they need to, while fees are collected by JASRAC, JRC or e-license for the authors, and those for the secondary use by broadcasters are collected by RIAJ (Recording Industry Association of Japan) for the phonogram producers and by CPRA (Centre for Performers Rights Administration) for the performers.

For an Internet streaming service provider to do so, however, it will need obtain prior consent not only from the author(s), but also from the performer(s) and the phonogram producer(s). Under the current regime, while the author(s) can be represented by collecting societies such as JASRAC, JRC and e-license that offer a blanket right clearance scheme, the rights of making transmittable on the Internet – neighbouring rights for performers and phonogram producers instituted in the copyright law amendment in 1997 so as to tackle the problem of illegal file-sharing – has to be cleared beforehand. This means that, if one wants to launch a music streaming service on the Internet, she or he needs to negotiate with each and every neighbouring right holder of all the songs to be used in the programme.

It is for this reason that any attempt for Internet users to legitimately launch their own Internet radio services have been hampered in Japan so far. For the same reason, most of the social networking and/or cloud services based on music streaming such as Last.fm, Pandora, Spotify, Lala and Amazon Cloud Player could not deploy their services in Japan. Streaming video-sharing services such as YouTube, *Nico Nico Dôga* and Ustream are facing difficulty clearing master phonogram rights with each individual right holder, although they have managed to conclude a blanket agreement with author's rights-collecting societies such as JASRAC, JRC or e-licence. Technically, this means that we could stream copyrighted songs if, and only if, they are performed by ourselves. By the same token, DJ performances using copyrighted recordings on online programmes like Dommune are technically illegal in Japan.

Today, then, record companies, particularly the domestic and transnational majors, are in an ambivalent position where they cannot actively set and develop new trends in popular music, while the Internet is proposing unprecedentedly accessible, interactive and geographically disperse means of musical and cultural exchange to constitute a variety of proto-markets. The point here, however, is that legal framework impedes the bridging between proto-markets and the mainstream market in Japan under the current copyright system. The labels, obviously, are not willing to ignore these potential markets. However, the complex web of political, economic and cultural interests that they have structured with not only neighbouring media and culture industries but also legislative institutions has put them in circumstances in which they have difficulties in taking the initiative.

Conclusion

The recording industry in Japan is currently standing at a crossroads. It is facing two contradictory trends. On one hand, there is a centralising dynamism, which pulls the situation back to the order favourable to the conventional practices of the recording industry. As we have seen, in the face of diminishing physical retailing channels for J-pop, the majors have been quite actively taking initiatives in launching digital distribution platforms and mobile ringtune services to maintain its controlling position in the market despite the divided market receptions. Additionally, so-called 360 deal, i.e. a type of contract that allows a record company to receive income from all the activities that exploit the artist's branding power, not limited to record sales but also from live events, fan club or merchandise, etc., can be argued as the latest of their efforts to reintegrate the various functionalities that they had outsourced throughout its century-long structuration.

On the other hand, there is a decentralising tendency, which pushes the situation further to negotiate a new expedient order favourable to a more diffuse, participatory creativity. While the recording industry tries to harness the collapse of the conventional business model, new musical movements do not cease to emerge in a collaborative and participative cultural space enabled largely by the Internet technologies. These can be regarded as proto-markets, or experimental laboratories of popular music – net labels, *Hatsune Miku* and Dommune, among many other small and web-based music (sub)cultures, all take advantage of 'realtime' or 'communal' interactions enabled by the broadband technology to the extent that might be called *secondary liveness*, as in Ong's (1982) notion of 'secondary orality' (p. 136). However, the particularities (and problems for the recording industry) of these proto-markets are that their access to the mainstream market is mediated not only by cultural and economic investment (the 'sell-out'), but more rigidly by a locally specific regime of copyright.

Whether the 360 contract reintegrates the recording industry or the web-based participatory cultures transform it remains to be seen. Although we still cannot clearly foresee what the recording industry will be like in the decades to come, it seems fairly safe to say that its future shape now depends at least partially on how the government goes about reforming the copyright system and, in particular, the phonogram producers' right collection scheme and the legal status of converging broadcasting and telecommunication platforms. For the time being, we need to keep an eye on the recording industry's further development in Japan.

Acknowledgement

This work is a part of the research project supported by Grant-in-Aid for Scientific Research (KAKENHI) (B) 22320044, 'Comparative Study on Local Identity through Popular Music in Japan and the United States' from MEXT (Ministry of Education, Culture, Sports, Science and Technology) of Japan.

Bibliography

Azami, T. (2004) *Popyurâ Ongaku wa Dare ga Tsukuru Noka: Ongaku Sangyo no Seiji gaku (Who Makes Popular Music: Political Studies of the Music Industry).* Tokyo: Keisô Shobo.

Azami, T. (2008) Shôwa Shoki ni okeru Ôbei Mejâ no Honkakuteki Kousei to Nihon no Rekôdo Sangyô no Hatten (Western Majors' Fully Fledged Offensive and the Development of the Japanese Record Industry at the Beginning of the Showa Period), *Hiroshima Keizai Daigaku Keizai Ronbun Shu*, 31(2): 1–18.

Dentsu (2011) *News Release 23*, February. Available on line at: www.dentsu.co.jp/ news/release/2011/pdf/2011019–0223.pdf (accessed February 2011).

IFPI (2009) *Recording Industry in Numbers*. London: IFPI. (See also MacClure (2009).)

JKA (2010) *Karaoke Hakusho 2010 (Karaoke White Paper 2010)*. Tokyo: JKA.

Kurata, Y. (1992) *Nihon Record Bunka Shi (Cultural History of Records in Japan)*. Tokyo: Tôsho Sensho.

Kusek, D. and Leonhard, G. (2005) *The Future of Music: Manifesto for the Digital Music Revolution*. Boston, MA: Barklee Press.

MacClure, S. (2009) Japan Now World's Biggest Physical Music Market: IFPI, *MacClure's Asia Music News*. Available online at: http://mccluremusic.com/article/ Japan_now_world_s_biggest_physical_music_market__IFPI (accessed October 2011).

Nakamura, T. (1991) Early Pop Song Writers and Their Backgrounds, *Popular Music*, 10(3): 263–82.

NHK (2011) *2010 nen Kokumin Seikatsu Jikan Chôsa Hôkokusho (Report on the Inquiry into Daily Practices of Japanese 2010)*. Available online at: www.nhk.or.jp/ bunken/research/life/life_20110223.pdf (accessed February, 2011).

Ogawa, H. *et al.* (2005) *Media Jidai no Kôkoku to Ongaku: Henyô suru CM to Ongakuka Shakai (Advertisement and Music in the Age of Media: Transforming Advertisement and Musicalised Society)*. Tokyo: Shinyo Sha.

Ong, W.J. (1982) *Orality and Literacy: The Technologizing the World*. New York: Methuen.

Oricon (2011) *Entertainment Market Report 2010*. Tokyo: Oricon.

RIAJ (1991) *RIAJ Year Book 1991*. Tokyo: RIAJ.

RIAJ (1998) *RIAJ Year Book 1998*. Tokyo: RIAJ.

RIAJ (2003) *RIAJ Year Book 2003*. Tokyo: RIAJ.

RIAJ (2007) *Ongaku Media Yûzâ Jittai Chosa Hôkokusho 2006 (Report on Annual Survey of Music Media Users 2006)*. Tokyo: RIAJ.

RIAJ (2009) *Ongaku Media Yûzâ Jittai Chosa Hôkokusho 2008 (Report on Annual Survey of Music Media Users 2008)*. Tokyo: RIAJ.

RIAJ (2010) *RIAJ Year Book 2010*. Tokyo: RIAJ.

RIAJ (2011a) *RIAJ Year Book 2011*. Tokyo: RIAJ.

RIAJ (2011b) *Ongaku Media Yûzâ Jittai Chosa Hôkokusho 2010 (Report on Annual Survey of Music Media Users 2010)*. Tokyo: RIAJ.

Toynbee, J. (2000) *Making Popular Music: Musicians, Creativity and Institutions*. London: Edward Arnold.

Tsuda, D. (2004) *Dare ga 'Ongaku' wo Korosu Noka? (Who Will Kill the 'Music'?)* Tokyo: Shôei-sha.

Ugaya, H. (2005) *J-pop toha Nani Ka: Kyodaika suru Ongaku Sangyô (What is J-pop?: The Swelling Music Industry)*. Tokyo: Iwanami.

Wajima, Y. (2010) *Tsukurareta 'Nihon no Kokoro' Shinwa: 'Enka' wo meguru Sengo Tishû Ongaku Shi (Invented myth of 'Japanese Spirit': a History of Post-War Popular Music around 'Enka')*. Tokyo: Kôbun-sha.

Yagi, R. (2004) *Nihon no Ongaku Sangyô ha Dou Kawarunoka: Posuto iPod Jidai no Shintenkai (How will the Japanese Music Industry Change?: New Development in the Post-iPod Era)*. Tokyo: Tôyô Keizai Shinpô Sha.Jn.

South Africa

Population: 49.0 million (25th)
Languages: 11 official languages
Capital: Pretoria (pop 1.4 million)
Currency: Rand (ZAR). $1=ZAR7.34
GDP: $363.7 bn (28th)
GDP (PPP)/capita: $10,486 (77th)
Median age: 25.0

GDP data from World Bank

Population data from CIA world factbook

Exchange rate used by IFPI (2011) (source: Oanda)

2010 Recorded music market

Overall income: $123.4m
World ranking: 18th

	Income	World ranking
Physical sales	$114.5m	14th
Digital sales	$6.4m	34th
Performance rights	$2.5m	35th

Historical recorded music market ($m, at IFPI's 2010 exchange rate)

	1999	2000	2001	2002	2003	2004	2005	2006	2007	2008	2009
Trade Value			90.8	103.2	103.3	124.7	137.6	142.1	145.4	135.0	133.1
Retail Value	151.0	142.2	145.2	165.1	165.2	199.6	220.5				

Proportion of domestic repertoire (market value, physical sales only)

1991	1995	2000	2005	2010
41%	20%	23%	46%	46%

Album certification levels

	2010	1999
Gold	Domestic – 20,000	Domestic – 10,000
	International – 20,000	International – 25,000
Platinum	Domestic – 40,000	Domestic – no award
	International – 40,000	International – no award

10 South Africa

Tuulikki Pietilä

Introduction

For all of the countries in this volume, the demographic, economic, ethnic and cultural composition of the country plays a large part in shaping the musical cultures and industries within it. Nowhere is this more true, however, than in South Africa. It has a population of 50 million people, but this is highly fragmented by wealth (almost half live below the poverty line[1]) and ethnicity (79.4 per cent of the population are African, 9.2 per cent White, 8.8 per cent Coloured and 2.6 per cent Indian/Asian[2]). There are eleven official languages, and many unofficial languages. It is also a country shaped by a long-run development trajectory of racial inequality and segregation that was systematised and legalised as apartheid policy in 1948 before being officially dismantled in 1994.

The structure, and the potential, of the South African recording industry are shaped by the wide socioeconomic and cultural differences created in the course of its history. Due to the ethnic and cultural diversity, as well as the economic disparities, the music market is fragmented into several segments according to consumers' musical taste and spending power. This is seen, among other things, in the way that formats have changed and are changing. The CD is currently the most common format, but the high-end market is shifting to the digital format, while a number of people at the lower end still rely on cassettes. Another characteristic of the South African market is the relative strength of the local repertoire during the early twenty-first century – its popularity has contributed to the increasing music sales in the country amid the globally more common trend of decreasing sales (although the latest statistics show some decline in the overall record sales). The overall value of record sales in 2010 was R906.2 million ($123.4 million), down from a 2007 high of R1.067.5 milion ($145.4 million) (IFPI 2011: 85).[3] The majority of the revenue comes from physical product (93 per cent in 2010, compared to just 5 per cent from digital (ibid.)). Most of the digital sales come from mobile use; online music sales accounted for only 11 per cent of the digital sales in 2009.[4] The quality of South African broadband services is ranked near the bottom of international surveys (Muller 2009, cited in Primo and Lloyd *et al.* 2011: 117), although the situation has improved somewhat in recent years with the arrival of new high-capacity cables.

While the official statistics do give a sense of the size and the changes in the South African record market, they do not give a complete picture. The official figures are bound to belittle the size of the market somewhat since they lack some independent record labels' sales and, obviously, the purchase and use of unauthorised recordings that play a relatively large role in the country's musical culture. Furthermore, the statistics do not account for the popularity of the South African live acts both domestically and internationally. According to industry insiders, the live music scene has been increasing in importance as record sales have started to show signs of a downward trend. Unfortunately, there are no reliable sources of data as for the size of the South African live music market within or without Africa. The live music events are important occasions also for record sales, but at least part of these sales remain unrecorded.

Historical development of the South African recording industry[5]

The South African recording industry is the most advanced one in Africa, with a long history of multinational corporations' entwinement with local companies. The beginnings of the industry can be traced back to the turn of the twentieth century when British and American companies started distributing their labels in the market through local agents or through establishing their own local branches. Recordings of local music started soon after. These were made by Zonophone, Columbia Graphophone Company, HMV and Brunswick Records (Stapleton and May 1987: 259, 264). There were several local operators early on in the South African market; the one that remains important today is Gallo Records. It was initially a small shop, opened by Eric Gallo, in Johannesburg in 1926, and named the Brunswick Gramophone House after American Brunswick Records, whose releases it sold (Andersson 1981: 38). Eventually, Gallo started recording local music, first by sending artists to record in London and, from the 1930s, in their own studio in Johannesburg. Several other powerful local labels and companies arose during the first half of the twentieth century; among these were GRC, Trutone, Teal, Troubadour, RPM and Tusk. However, all but one of these became eventually incorporated either with Gallo or EMI, who emerged as the main competitors in the local market.

Of all the multinational companies, EMI has had the strongest presence in South Africa. It was also the only major label not to disinvest from South Africa during the most intense years of struggle against the apartheid regime. It is the only multinational company ever to have operated a recording studio in the country, which it did from 1951 until the early 1990s. At the end of the 1970s, EMI acquired the CCP Record Company which specialised in producing local Black music, and remains an important producer of local music today. In addition to the CCP subsidiary, EMI maintains an office in South Africa.

During the era of anti-apartheid struggle, the other multinational companies scaled back their presence in South Africa, either by closing their wholly owned branches and forming subsidiary companies or by arranging licensing deals with local producers. For example, in 1986 Warner Elektra Atlantic (WEA, what became Warner) sold the company to its local employees, who renamed it Tusk Music Company. Tusk continued distributing WEA records in South Africa, as well as releasing local music.[6] Upon the dismantling of the apartheid regime in 1994 all of the majors, except for Warner, began to re-enter the country: BMG had opened its office in South Africa in 1993, and in 1995 Sony opened its office in South Africa and PolyGram established its own subsidiary, PolyGram South Africa (later to become Universal).

However, although the majors began to return to South Africa, Gallo remained a significant part of the South African recording industry. It had benefited from the majors' withdrawal as it appeared as a respectable local partner for many of the international companies' licensing agreements.[7] In 1997 Gallo Record Company bought Tusk and thus obtained the rights to distribute the Warner Music International's catalogue.[8] At the time, Gallo itself was part of the huge South African media and entertainment conglomerate Johnnic Communications (Johncom). In the mid-2000s Johncom and Warner Music International (WMI) entered a joint venture and formed Warner Music Gallo Africa (WMGA). The new entity is the licensee for WMI's roster of international acts in sub-Saharan Africa and holds worldwide digital rights to Gallo's domestic repertoire (Brandle 2006: 15).

In 2007 Johncom was renamed Avusa Limited, of which Gallo remains a part. Avusa is a huge media and entertainment conglomerate that owns a wide array of newspapers and magazines, book stores, cinemas, a countrywide logistics system for music, films and videos. Additionally, Avusa distributes films and videos for cinemas and home entertainment. Today, the Gallo music group includes WMGA, Gallo Music South Africa (Gallo's old and new catalogue) and RPM Record Company (a dance label).[9] The company reportedly owns over 75 per cent of all recordings ever made in South Africa and the publishing wing is said to represent more than 80 per cent of South African songs (as well as many international music publishers, including Warner Chappell Music).[10]

CDT (Compact Disc Technologies), which is part of Avusa, is the leading CD and DVD manufacturer in South Africa: in 2005, it manufactured about 80 per cent of the CDs and all of the DVDs in the country. Avusa owns also the most important logistics system through which most major companies' and small labels' products are warehoused and distributed in the country. This is called ELS (Entertainment Logistics Services), and it reportedly manages logistics of approximately 70 per cent of the music industry and about 75 per cent of the VHS and DVD products in South Africa. It also services all retail and rental outlets countrywide.[11] Another distribution system is owned by EMI, but it is less used than ELS. There are also some independent distribution systems, such as the Select Music Distribution, specialising in Afrikaans music, and IRIS (Independent Record Industry Solutions). The independence of IRIS is, however, compromised by the fact that it uses the manufacturing services of CDT and the warehousing and distribution facility of ELS.[12] Avusa is thus very dominant in both the manu-facturing and logistics sectors; the sheer size of the country hinders efforts to set up alternative logistics systems.

Thus, even though Gallo Music is usually posed as the biggest independent record company in Africa, the affiliation with Avusa and the joint venture with Warner Music International make Gallo comparable to a major record company. An already high degree of integration and concentration in its operations is strengthened through Avusa. Vertical integration is achieved through the control of a good part of the music chain from the recording company, publishing and manufacturing (CDT) to warehousing and distribution (ELS). As a media and entertainment conglomerate, Avusa also provides a good degree of horizontal integration for its constitutive brands: Gallo Music products' visibility and marketing can be enhanced in a number of newspapers and magazines, book stores, cinemas and rental outlets for DVDs and videos that Avusa owns.

Market overview: the major labels

While in most regions in the world, recorded music sales revenues were decreasing in the early 2000s, in South Africa they were increasing annually.[13] The generally positive sales development in past two decades has been particularly due to the vibrant local music market, in contrast to international repertoire sales, which have remained relatively static. Local music sales have consistently increased during the post-apartheid era. International repertoire accounted for 65 per cent of units sold in 1999, but this had dropped to 46 per cent by 2010 (RiSA statistics). In value terms, the international repertoire fell from almost 80 per cent of revenue in the late 1990s to 54 per cent of trade value in 2010 (RiSA unpublished statistics for 2010).[14]

The growth in local repertoire sales is partly explainable by the fact that the CD format was increasingly replacing the cassette format during this time. In the international repertoire side the shift from cassettes to CDs started almost a decade earlier: the peak in the international CD unit sales took place in 1998–99.[15] However, according to the Managing Director of CCP, as much as 70 per cent of their music was still sold on cassette in 2003 (interview with author). The owner

Table 10.1 Sales of units: millions of South-African rands (RiSA 2007: 11)

	International				Local			
	CD	CD single	MC	DVD	CD	CD single	MC	DVD
1997	9.8	2.2	2.4	–	2.0	0.1	6.0	–
1998	10.7	1.8	1.7	–	2.3	0.2	5.6	–
1999	10.2	1.8	1.5	–	2.2	0.1	5.0	–
2000	9.0	0.9	1.0	–	2.2	–	4.4	–
2001	7.7	0.6	1.1	(0.1)	2.3	–	4.5	–
2002	7.7	0.7	1.2	0.2	3.0	–	4.2	–
2003	7.0	0.1	1.2	0.3	3.7	–	4.5	–
2004	7.9	–	0.7	0.6	6.5	–	4.7	0.2
2005	9.5	–	0.4	0.9	7.6	–	3.4	0.6
2006	8.5	–	0.3	1.0	9.7	–	2.9	1.1

Table 10.2 Units by average value: South-African rands (RiSA 2007: 12)

	International				Local			
	CD	CD single	MC	DVD	CD	CD single	MC	DVD
1997	41.22	17.12	21.18	–	27.03	15.98	15.26	–
1998	42.05	17.55	20.71	–	29.51	20.13	15.47	–
1999	46.72	19.21	23.18	–	31.67	18.70	15.33	–
2000	48.16	20.97	18.90	–	33.51	21.19	15.13	–
2001	53.96	19.79	18.81	91.11	38.07	18.42	14.98	–
2002	57.61	21.88	18.34	114.53	40.32	22.69	15.34	89.50
2003	59.51	24.65	16.98	114.95	40.52	20.89	15.18	87.05
2004	58.72	12.45	17.55	99.88	39.89	8.41	15.80	77.47
2005	52.91	24.72	17.24	88.11	37.36	19.33	15.84	69.57
2006	54.28	25.32	14.92	73.42	34.95	17.30	15.21	67.09

of Reliable Music, at the time one of the most important wholesalers catering for the less well-off Black market, said that CDs accounted for less than 5 per cent of their local sales in 1999, but almost 50 per cent of the local music was sold on CD by 2004 (interview with author). The number of local music cassettes sold clearly exceeded that of CDs until the end of 2003, after which time CD sales have exceeded cassette sales (see Table 10.1). In trade revenue terms, however, local repertoire CD sales exceeded cassette sales for the first time in 2000 and, by 2010, CDs accounted for 81 per cent of the local repertoire sales value (and 86 per cent of the international repertoire sales value). Cassettes contributed 2.3 per cent and 0.1 per cent respectively (RiSA statistics).[16]

Although domestic repertoire sells more units than international repertoire, international repertoire still brings in more money, because international repertoire is sold for higher prices than the local repertoire.[17] The major companies have been rather unwilling to reduce the prices for the international product. They would not even consider doing that in the case of relatively new releases and with music that attracts the better-off audience. With international genres that are popular especially among Blacks, at least some of the local subsidiaries have experimented with formats and packaging to make the music available more cheaply. This is done, for instance, by releasing the content of a CD on cassette, and by dropping the price of older catalogue music by packaging two CDs together and selling them for less than what they would cost separately.[18] With the local product, however, there has always been more flexibility and effort to meet the local purchasing power levels. In 2006, international music CDs were, on average, 55 per cent more expensive than local music CDs (see Table 10.2). Between 1997 and 2003, the average CD prices for the local repertoire increased by about 50 per cent and for the international repertoire by about 44 per cent, but after that the average prices started to decrease. Cassette prices in the local repertoire remained the same between 1997 and 2006, and fell by 30 per cent in the international repertoire.[19]

The fact that international repertoire is more lucrative, in value terms, than local music means that, for all of the major companies' South African subsidiaries and for Gallo, international repertoire remains a key interest and focus. The exact shares fluctuate from month to month, with Easter and Christmas being the strongest seasons for local music sales. In my interviews with representatives from the labels in 2004, at Gallo the local and international repertoire shares of their revenue from sales were estimated to be around 30 per cent and 70 per cent respectively;[20] at Sony, international music constituted 70–80 per cent of their sales;[21] at BMG, local music's share was said to be 25 per cent at best, but more commonly below 10 per cent;[22] Universal did not provide an estimate but a representative said that its focus was on international repertoire.[23] As in many countries, Universal was the market leader in international repertoire, although it did maintain a roster of local artists, with a focus on rhythm and blues, and hip hop.

As the local repertoire started to increase its share of sales in the 2000s, most of the major companies tried to capitalise by entering into licensing deals with independent labels. Gallo Music was the exception, as it focused more on signing local musicians on an artist deal basis, thus building its own catalogue of local music. A licensing and an artist deal differ in the way that they structure the tasks and the rewards of the parties and the ownership of the product. A licensing deal means that an artist or a record label (licenser) gives a finalised record or a whole catalogue of records to a record company (licensee) that promotes and distributes it. The licenser thus only uses the services of the licensee, and retains the proprietorship of the recording. The usual split of the proceeds is that 70–80 per cent goes to the licensee and 20–30 per cent to the licenser. An artist contract means that the record company produces the recording of an artist, and thereafter owns it for good. The artist is entitled to a royalty share, typically 8–18 per cent of the wholesale price of the record. However, the royalties start accruing only after the record company has deducted the production-related costs[24] from the record revenues; this is called the break-even point. Unless the artist is relatively popular, the sales are often not enough to reach this point and the artist is thus left without royalties.

Despite Gallo Music's ownership of a deep back catalogue of South African music, EMI's South African subsidiary CCP had the largest market share in the local repertoire in the mid-2000s. CCP's market leadership derived from them having on their list some of the bestselling stars in the bestselling genres, such as gospel and *kwaito* (urban youth music). Additionally, they have strong names in the African jazz and African pop genres. Gallo Music's catalogue is stronger in gospel, traditional African music and urban popular music of earlier decades, and Gallo was working on strengthening its contemporary urban and jazz catalogue.

Although it focused on international repertoire, Sony had a relatively good reputation among local Black artists in the mid-2000s. This was because, in comparison to BMG and Universal, Sony had a number of Black executives on board who were able to attract some of the cutting-edge local music to the company. For instance, Sony managed to strike a licensing deal with the Kalawa Jazmee record label, the most successful *kwaito* label in the country at the time. In 2004, Sony Music Entertainment merged with BMG, which had released some local music, especially in the areas of jazz, Afro-jazz and some *kwaito*, but mainly focused on international repertoire. The restructuring caused by the merger, and the consequent uncertainties concerning the future directions of the company, led some of the local artists and labels to leave and, today, Sony is most often considered by artists as just another major company.

According to music industry journal *The View* (2009), the major companies have recently started to move into the niche domestic repertoire markets. This is logical given the consistent growth demonstrated by the local repertoire during the post-apartheid era. The earlier focus on licensing deals with the local artists and labels has thus slightly shifted towards an interest in artist and multi-rights deals. So far, however, the most significant interests of the major companies – including Gallo – and their revenues continue to lie in the international repertoire.

The rise of local music and the independent sector

The major labels' focus on international repertoire means that most local music in South Africa is released by smaller independent labels. Their number has increased remarkably during the post-apartheid era. The main trade association, the Recording Industry of South Africa (RiSA) reportedly has around 1,400 members.[25] However, some independent labels do not belong to RiSA because they consider it a body controlled by the major companies.[26] In 2006, after a joint effort by several music industry-related bodies, an independent labels' association was formed, called AIRCO (the Association of Independent Record Companies).[27] In April 2011, the website of AIRCO lists some 200 members.

Today, the independent labels usually focus on releasing local music, even though the biggest of them also distribute foreign labels through licensing deals. An especially significant and historically unprecedented development has been the appearance of a number of Black-owned record labels. These are often owned by relatively famous producers, artists and industry insiders who are on the pulse of the emerging trends in the Black communities, especially in the areas of urban music (*kwaito*, hip hop, house music), gospel and jazz. This is significant because, in the apartheid era, ownership was mostly a White prerogative. In addition to the sense (and reality) of expanded post-apartheid freedom, these new labels are often fuelled by disappointments with major record companies' lack of transparency and their ways of dealing with issues of ownership and control. However, the working principles and practices of the majors and independents cannot be viewed in any dichotomous way. An increase in the number of small labels does not mean that the older, sometimes dubious, recording industry practices are now over and belong to the past.[28] Even though the rise of the Black-owned labels has been a remarkable development, the independent sector is currently quite diverse. Some of the new labels are owned by Asians and Coloureds. Additionally, a good proportion of the small labels are owned by Whites, many of whom have previously worked in a large record company and decided to go independent after amassing industry experience and networks, often having become tired of their limited room for manoeuvre in a big company.

Assessing the market share of the independent sector is complicated. AIRCO claims that its members account for almost 30 per cent of the domestic music sales and 60 per cent of South African music releases (*The View* 2009), but some other industry actors consider this an overestimation.[29] The overall validity of the market share information is limited by the nature and the coverage of the available recording industry data. RiSA gathers the sales data from its members and these numbers are utilised by the IFPI in compiling the annual worldwide statistics for the book *Recording Industry in Numbers*.[30] These figures do not give a completely correct picture of the South African market, however, because some independent labels do not belong to RiSA and thus do not report their sales to it. On the other hand, some of the small labels belong (and report their sales) to both RiSA and AIRCO, while some labels do not belong to any industry association. Additionally, apparently in their reported sales the record companies do not always distinguish between artist and licence deals – a distinction that is crucial with regard to the money returns and ownership. Naturally, the sales of pirated music are not included in the statistics either. Although piracy in South Africa is considered to be less severe than in the other African countries, it does exist and, it is argued, affects official sales. In the mid-2000s, the IFPI (2006: 96) estimated the physical piracy level in South Africa to be between 25 and 50 per cent. For 2009, RiSA estimated the street value of pirated music in South Africa at $6.2 million and, had the titles been sold officially, an equivalent retail value of $30.2 million (Primo and Lloyd *et al.* 2011: 109).[31]

Notwithstanding the flaws in the official data, the sales statistics do give some impression of how the independent sector has become more prominent in the last few years. According to the *Music & Copyright* trade magazine (2005: 8), the market leader in South Africa in 2004 was SonyBMG (32.3 per cent), followed by EMI (23.6 per cent), UMG (20.6 per cent) and Gallo (18.2 per cent) (2005: 8). This meant that the combined market share of these major companies was 94.7 per cent, leaving only a 5.3 per cent market share for the small producers. Move forward to 2008/09, however, and we see a significant growth in the independent sector. *The View* (2009) estimated that, in the first nine months of 2009, Sony was still the market leader (23 per cent), closely followed by UMG (22 per cent), EMI (18 per cent) and WMG/Gallo (15 per cent). The total market share of these companies was subsequently 78 per cent and that of the others 22 per cent.[32] Independent companies' market share of music publishing has also been increasing: for the first eleven months in 2009 their market share was reported to be 4 per cent (*The View* 2009).

The growth in the local music sales and the emergence of the independent sector cannot be explained merely by the format shift from cassette to CD discussed above. Like elsewhere in the world, technological advances have boosted local music production by making home and other small recording studios affordable and viable. This has contributed to the emergence of a large number of independent labels. There has also been an attempt to offer institutional support for local music by the radio quota system, stipulating that 25 per cent of the music played on the public and commercial radio stations and 40 per cent of the music played by non-profit broadcasters, has to be local (although enforcing this rule has not been very successful and many broadcasters do not meet the quota (*The View* 2009)).

Probably even more than the technological and the administrative innovations, the demand for the local music is boosted by the ongoing political and socio-economic developments in the country. In the post-apartheid era popular music has become an ever-more important vehicle for imagining and expressing emerging identities as the society undergoes major political transformations. Different Black music genres, such as gospel and urban youth music especially, have been important growth areas in the local music market. Other important Black genres are jazz, Afro-jazz, Afro-pop, traditional and neo-traditional music. Simultaneously, the Afrikaans music sector[33] has experienced an immense growth. The major genres in the Afrikaans music are country-rock, pop, rock, folk and punk.[34] The increased demand for Afrikaans music has made labels specialising in it important players in the market. The key labels in this sector are Select Music, Hoezit and Rhythm Records, all from Cape Town. According to Coetzer (2007: 16), the share of the domestic repertoire shipments by Select Music and its affiliate Select Music Distribution was as high as 21.4 per cent in 2006, behind only EMI/CCP with its 27 per cent share of the domestic shipments.

The segmented market

As the above discussions have intimated, South Africa contains what those in the recording industry describe as a 'highly segmented market'. The historical roots of such segmentation run deep. The segregation policies of the apartheid era extended to the broadcasting media and music recording. State support was directed primarily to White classical music institutions and musicians. In radio, special hours were set for Africans by the South African Broadcasting Corporation and, gradually, these were divided along linguistic lines with special programmes for different ethnic groups (Ansell 2004: 87). In the early 1960s this division was strengthened by the creation of separate Afrikaans and English stations as well as Radio Bantu, which consisted of thirteen different stations, each for a particular 'tribe' (ibid.: 109). In this way, radio was used as an instrument in the attempt at retribalisation and this forced artists to make monolingual recordings of distinct 'tribal' musics in order to get radio play. This policy fragmented the music market and listeners artificially to distinct, small niches, although in towns and townships especially people were accustomed to mixing different musical traditions, and local and global genres.[35]

It is most common to distinguish 'White' and 'Black' market segments and recently much of the focus of the industry has been in trying to tap into the gradually improving buying power of the large Black population, referred to as an 'emergent market'. However, labels such as a 'White market' and a 'Black market' conceal the fact that social class is currently as important a factor as race or ethnicity in influencing consumption habits and potential. The range in the affluence and spending power of the urban Blacks especially is wide: the poorest live in shacks in informal settlements, while some live in houses with electricity in the government housing areas and the wealthiest have moved into luxurious homes in the most upmarket neighbourhoods. The low-income Black population in the townships and, especially, in the rural areas can only afford to buy cassettes or lower price CDs. Many of these get their music from friends or vendors who sell pirated copies.[36] Middle- and upper-class Blacks have been buying CDs and DVDs for some time already, with more recent experiments with the digital use.

The buying habits of the wealthier Blacks, especially with regard to the music formats and shopping venues, are thus closer to those of the middle- and upper-class Whites than the poor Blacks. In terms of musical taste, however, things are less clear. The musical tastes of Blacks of different economic means can often be closer to each other than to those of Whites, but social class and location still play a differentiating role in the musical tastes among the Blacks as well. Jazz and Afro-jazz, for instance, are especially favoured by the urban middle- and upper-class Blacks, while the urban lower classes and those living in the rural areas often lean more towards, for instance, gospel, Afro-pop, urban youth music and traditional or neo-traditional music. This means, for example, that South African jazz is mainly sold on CD, whereas some of the traditional Black music, gospel and urban youth music are still sold on cassette. The demand for 'international Black music' – especially for the older African American music – among the South African Blacks has always been and remains relatively high, regardless of class. The genres of this music are typically rhythm and blues, soul, jazz and gospel, and they are often imported and sold (on CD and cassette) by small specialised labels that do not report their sales to RiSA. As mentioned above, Afrikaners have their own distinct music market. The English-speaking population with British and Irish ancestry does not form a distinct market segment to the extent that the Afrikaners do, but pop and rock are the major domestically produced genres.

Ethnicity and class do not completely determine musical taste; there are Blacks and Coloureds who perform and listen to classical music, Whites who perform what is considered traditional or neo-traditional African music, and Asians who like to rave to European house music. Western pop music is listened to across all the ethnic and language categories in the urban areas especially, and the local urban youth music genres and Afro-pop do cross over the ethnic and racial boundaries to some extent. Nevertheless, to a large extent the musical tastes of the different population groups do follow a recognisable pattern and the segmented market is not a fallacy.

In the twenty-first century the recording industry has been busy trying to find ways to make their product available to the whole range of the Black population in particular. The dream of many companies is to find music that crosses over to various audiences, but the wider structures do not easily lend support for it. Even though broadcasting has been reorganised in the post-apartheid era, contemporary public and commercial radio stations still target rather specific audiences. There is thus a station for jazz, classical music, urban Black music, adult contemporary, pop music, rock, and so on, as well as nine African-language stations. The record companies and labels thus always know on which radio stations their records can and must get airplay. The fact that there is no radio station catering to all or many kinds of audiences is seen by the recording industry representatives as one of the major problems perpetuating separate markets and delimiting the sales.[37] While many people who work in the recording industry consider the segmented market a fact that cannot be changed, others blame the industry itself for sustaining the market segmentation by not even trying to capture diverse audiences.

Opportunities for musicians in South Africa and beyond

The segmentation of the market means that most of the artists and musicians struggle to make a living. Kevin Stuart, running a label called Ready Rolled, summarised the fragmented market situation in 2004 by highlighting that, in a country of nearly fifty million people, no record has ever managed to sell one million units (interview with author).[38] The biggest album sales of local music have been around 400,000 units, and such figures are attained only by the most famous artists, such as the gospel singer Rebecca Malope or the late popular music artist Brenda Fassie. Sales of 80,000–200,000 units are considered very high and have been reached by several big names in various genres. Units of 10,000–20,000 are regarded good sales, and many of the small labels are happy with 5,000–6,000 unit sales.[39] The break-even point depends on the genre; while in traditional or popular music this can be at 5,000, in jazz it can be as high as at 25,000 units.

It is not impossible to earn a living by making music, however. The most popular artists can live on their royalties, record sales and live gigs.[40] However, even they often have to augment their earnings with additional tasks, such as producing and writing music for other artists, renting out personal studios, writing music or doing other work for the radio, TV, commercials, and documentary and other films. Typical additional tasks are also playing in the studio sessions and live gigs of other artists. The festival circuit is relatively well established, especially for the Afrikaans music and jazz music. However, the number of artists who can be accommodated in these events is limited, and complaints about the same few artists circulating in the festivals are common. The bigger names usually receive a good amount of money for a festival appearance. Government and corporate functions are among the best sources of income for musicians. Recently, some of the young artists in hip hop and popular music have expanded into merchandising by launching their own clothing or shoe labels. Corporate sponsorship also features relatively prominently in the South African music market, either sponsorship of individual artists or various live music venues, events, festivals and awards. Among the common sponsors are Coca-Cola, PepsiCo, Red Bull, Levi's, Standard Bank, Nedbank, ABSA Bank, South African Airlines, the National Lottery, Volkswagen, Old Mutual, and the telephone network operators MTN and Cell-C.

The corporate sponsorship is especially important in the live music scene given that, for a country with such a pool of great musicians and well-established recording industry, there are strikingly few regular live music venues, even in the largest cities, although the situation may be slowly improving. One often hears the relatively poor live music scene being explained by the argument that the South African population is not used to paying for live music and are, therefore, unwilling to pay, which results in the weak scene. The reasons for the situation are more complex, however. The persisting segregation of the whole society extends to the live music scene. Whites and some of the better-off Blacks are not comfortable with attending events in townships, where there is music in taverns, park jams, stadia and the community halls. Many Whites are wary of attending the city-centre clubs, too; these gather Blacks with disposable incomes and the more adventurous Whites, as well as artists and other cultural industry enthusiasts and insiders in general. Any attempts at clubs in the up-market areas (inhabited mostly by middle- and upper middle-class Whites and Blacks) tend to create complaints from the neighbours regarding noise and are soon closed or turned down. Township people often do not have the transport or the money to attend the city centre clubs or festivals of several days, even if they wanted, nor would they be seen in the few suburb venues.[41] Thus, there are perhaps more opportunities for a Black musician to play in a township, but these are often in venues with no proper equipment or other facilities. The fees for a musician for these events are little, if any. The artists of the more 'sophisticated' genres, such as jazz, would seldom perform in townships but rather in the city-centre clubs and the jazz festivals. White artists play in clubs and festivals, as well, either in their own or mixed bands. The Afrikaners have their own strong festival circuit. In addition to these socio-geographical strictures, the live scene is delimited by what many aspirant venue owners have described as a rather cumbersome procedure for applying for entertainment and liquor licenses.

Consequently, for most musicians the live scene does not offer as reliable or regular source of income as one might expect. The chances vary seasonally, as well, with Christmas and Easter being the peak seasons, in addition to the times of the various annual music festivals and other festivities (e.g. the annual Youth Day and Freedom Day, together with the more random events, such as the Soccer World Cup in 2010). The Cape Town International Jazz Festival gathers audiences of 33,000 and the Joy of Jazz Festival attracts around 20,000 visitors. The largest Afrikaans festival is the seven-night Huisgenoot Skouspel, held at the 6,000-capacity Sun City Superbowl. The capacity of the major regular live music clubs varies from around 100 (e.g. Zula Bar in Cape Town) to 1,000 (Bassline in Johannesburg).

The frequency of and the earnings from live performance thus vary a lot both seasonally and according to the popularity of the artist. At best a band of some popularity can earn approximately R20,000–60,000 for a gig. For festivals the fee can be R30,000–75,000, for a corporate gig R30,000–100,000 and for a club gig R4,000–15,000. Typically, however, the revenues from a club gig are based on a rather low flat fee or depend on the door takings, from which the venue first deducts a certain percentage. Thus, a musician can end up earning around R500 or less for a gig of three or four sets in a club. One cannot emphasise too much the wide range of fees and rewards among the musicians.

Despite these challenges in the home country, there are also opportunities beyond the border for some South African musicians. Obviously, at the highest level, several groups have become popular in the World Music market and tour regularly in Europe and beyond. Among these are Ladysmith Black Mambazo, Mahotella Queens and Johnny Glegg.[42] Several other artists and bands have attained international success, such as, for instance, Hugh Masekela and the late Miriam Makeba in jazz or Afro-jazz, Vusi Mahlasela in 'folk', Prime Circle in rock and the late Lucky Dube in reggae. There are several other smaller successes and numerous ongoing collaborations that involve recording and live touring especially in the Netherlands and Germany (both in Black music genres and Afrikaans music), as well as Switzerland, Austria, France, United Kingdom and the United States. More generally, however, although South Africa is a relatively small part of the global record industry, contributing just 0.8 per cent of the global value (IFPI 2011: 20), it is by far the biggest musical economy in the African continent. Therefore, it continuously attracts musicians from other African countries to move in and try their feet in the industry. The flow runs both ways: many South African musicians are very popular and they tour and perform in other African countries.

Whether a gig takes place within or without Africa, records are usually made available for the audience to buy at the event. There are no estimates about the number or the value of the South African records sold in the international markets outside the country. Some of these records are sold by the foreign licensees of South African music. However, because of problems caused by piracy and the lack of adequately functioning collection societies in most African countries, South African labels seldom seek licensing or distribution deals for their records in these countries.[43] The official statistics do not capture the popularity and the size of the South African live music market locally, continentally or globally. Many of the accompanying record sales remain unaccounted for, and, although these figures would most probably not change decisively the South African portion of the global music sales, they are important for the artists.

Conclusion

Most probably the South African recording industry will eventually encounter the technological and other challenges that the global music industry has been facing for some time already. It will take some time before the digital format fully impacts the South African market, however. The disparity in the economic means of the population will make the expansion of online downloading a slower process than in many Northern regions of the world. At the same time, there are some signs of the live scene becoming more vibrant as record sales have started decreasing. The overall pace and the specific trajectories of the recording industry change will continue to be shaped by the country's socioeconomic and cultural features, especially the wide disparity in the spending potential and the divergent musical tastes among its population.

Notes

1 In 2005–06, 33 per cent of households and 47 per cent of all individuals were estimated to live below the absolute poverty line (Armstrong *et al.* 2008: 8); 93 per cent of these individuals were Blacks (ibid.: 12; see also Leibbrandt *et al.* 2010a: 227).

2 These are the mid-2010 population estimates given by the government's Statistics South Africa (SSA 2010). The current statistics continue to use the population categories created by the apartheid regime. In this chapter I will use the words White, Black and Coloured with upper-case letters to indicate that these labels are social constructions created to classify and differentiate people artificially.

3 The fall is actually slightly steeper than indicated by the figures as, by 2010, the IFPI had begun to include revenue from performing rights in the overall value of the South African Market. However, in 2010 the revenue from performing rights was just 2 per cent of the overall value.

4 Different sources give somewhat different numbers for mobile and Internet users. According to *Music & Copyright* (2010, 404: 20), there were about 817,700 broadband subscriptions and 49.5 million mobile subscriptions in South Africa in 2009. According to IFPI (2010: 77), in 2009 there were 45 million mobile subscriptions, 3.9 million broadband HH (up from 400,000 broadband lines in 2008 (IFPI 2009: 89)) and 4.6 million Internet users.

5 For a more comprehensive account of the history and the developments in the South African recording industry, including the independent sector, see Pietilä (2009).

6 Interview with Benjy Mudie, the owner of Fresh Music and former Marketing and A&R Director at WEA Records/Tusk Music, 22 April 2004.

7 See Allen (2007: 267).

8 Interview with Benjy Mudie.

9 In 2009 Avusa sold the legendary Downtown Studios that Gallo used to own.

10 Available online at: www.avusa.co.za/businesses/entertainment/gallo-music-group. However, a significant percentage of the recording copyrights that Gallo holds are not accessible to the company because they lack master tapes and library copies of the published records. The reasons for this situation are several: the master tapes were not always regarded as important and were thrown away both at Gallo and in some of the companies it acquired; some of the kept tapes went missing in fires and moves into new premises; and some companies that Gallo acquired did not deliver all of their assets to Gallo (Allen 2007: 270).

11 Available online at: www.avusa.co.za/businesses/entertainment/entertainment-logistics-services

12 Available online at: www.irisdistribution.co.za/services.asp. According to Ansell *et al.* (2007: 42) IRIS reports to represent over fifty independent companies.

13 This was the situation until 2008, after which the sales value has been decreasing for three consecutive years: by 7.2 per cent in 2008, by 2.9 per cent in 2009 and by 8.8 per cent in 2010. These figures are based on the RiSA unpublished sales figures; the IFPI (2011: 85) reports somewhat smaller declines for the year 2009 (1.4 per cent) and for the year 2010 (7.3 per cent). Several factors have contributed to the decline, the most important ones being the economic recession, digital use and competing entertainment products (such as games). Some record labels maintain that piracy has also increased in recent years.

14 International repertoire sales in South Africa follow the global pattern. In 2009, UMG's greatest successes were Lady Gaga and Black Eyed Peas, SME's was Michael Jackson, EMI was successful with Coldplay, and WMG with Green Day and Madonna (*The View* 2009).

15 The figures are based on the RiSA report: available online at: www.risa.org. za/downloads/risa_2007_annual_report.pdf, p. 11. No consistent figures of the international and local repertoire unit sales by format are available for 2007–08. *The View* (2009) provides the change in sales by format and repertoire for the first eleven months of 2009.

16 I would like to point out that the available data do not include the sales of some small operators. Some of these operators focus on the cassette market and import

from the US and Europe genres such as soul, rhythm and blues, jazz and world music mostly for the Black consumers.

17 Also, some local repertoire is still sold on cassette, which has a much lower price.

18 The Strategic Marketing Director, Duncan Gibbon, from SonyBMG, explained that there is no point in reducing the price of a Bruce Springsteen or any White rock artist record, but that it makes a lot of sense in the case of Miles Davis or another jazz artist or an urban hip hop artist's record (interview with author, 20 May 2005).

19 RiSA report: available online at: www.risa.org.za/downloads/risa_2007_annual_ report.pdf, p. 12. It should be noted that these are average prices. The Managing Director of CCP mentioned that they have 25 different price categories for physical formats (interview with author, 2004). No data is available on the average price development since 2006. To contextualise these price fluctuations, the average wages for Africans rose between 1993 and 2005 by 48 per cent, for Coloureds by 29.5 per cent, for Indians by 28 per cent and for Whites by 11 per cent. By the year 2008 all but the Indians experienced rather decisive decreases in the average wages. In 2005 the average wage for Whites (R12,026) was almost four times the average wage of Africans (R3.118), and by 2008 the difference had increased (Leibbrandt *et al.* 2010a: 217, 225–6). However, the average personal income (including also earnings other than wages) of an African were only 13 per cent of those of a White person in 2008, while a Coloured earned 22 per cent and an Asian 60 per cent of a White's income. The average amount of wages and incomes hides the wide disparities in income, employment opportunities and poverty within the groups. While inequality has increased between the population groups, it has increased even more within each group during the post-apartheid era (the greatest inequality being within the African population (Leibbrandt *et al.* 2010b: 13, 16)).

20 Interview with the CEO of Gallo, 19 April 2004.

21 Interview with the Legal and Business Affairs Director of Sony, 26 April 2004.

22 Interview with the Artist Development Manager in BMG, 2 April 2004.

23 Interview with the Legal and Business Affairs Director of Universal, 17 March 2004.

24 What exactly is included in the recoupable costs is often an unclear and a moot issue for the artist. In addition to the recording and mastering expenses, the packaging and various promotional costs, such as a music video and touring costs can be included.

25 According to the RiSA website, in 2007 it had over 800 members. Today, the website lists 1,395 members (www.risa.org.za). In March 2011, David du Plessis, Operations Director of RiSA, said they have around 1,500 members (interview by the author).

26 The major companies are dominant in the management of RiSA and they have more votes than the smaller companies. All members have one primary vote in the general meetings. In addition, votes are allocated to RiSA members on the grounds of their direct financial contribution to the organisation through levies on units manufactured or imported. Much of RiSA's activities are funded by these levies (see www.risa.org.za/downloads/risa_2007_annual_report.pdf, p. 3).

27 AIRCO was formed by the Department of Arts and Culture, Business and Arts South Africa, the Moshito Music Conference and local authors' society SAMRO (*Music & Copyright* 2010).

28 See more on the independent sector in Pietilä (2009).

29 During my interviews in March 2011, Nick Motsatse, the CEO of SAMRO, estimated AIRCO members' market share at around 5 per cent, David du Plessis of RiSA considered it even lower. No one from AIRCO was at the time available for an interview or a comment.

30 The IFPI figures for the record sales in South Africa are annually somewhat higher than those given by RiSA. This is partly because the IFPI add a weighting to the raw data in an attempt to reflect the overall market (see Chapter 4 in this volume). Nowadays, the IFPI additionally includes digital sales and performance rights that are not counted in the RiSA figures.

31 According to a recent study (Primo and Lloyd *et al.* 2011: 100–01), in South Africa textbook piracy has been more ubiquitous and caused larger losses than film or music piracy during the 1990s and 2000s. In comparison to many other emerging economies, claims of losses to piracy have not been very high. The RIAA (Recording Industry Association of America) claimed $8.5 million in losses in the South African music market for the USA in 2005 (ibid.: 109). Any definitive data on the losses does not exist.

32 The full year data for 2008 provided by *The View* (2009) were virtually identical.

33 This is music of Afrikaners, who are descendants of Dutch, German and French settlers and who speak Afrikaans. In addition to the Afrikaners, the population category Whites includes English-speaking people of mainly British and Irish descent.

34 According to the report by Ansell *et al.* (2007: 29), gospel (59.8 per cent) and KWAITO (26.3 per cent) dominate in both urban and rural areas nationwide. Within the Western Cape province, however, Afrikaans music is the most popular music sector, and in Cape Town city rock/pop is the most popular genre. The national support of hip hop/rap is reported to stand at 20 per cent and that of jazz at 18.3 per cent (Ansell *et al.* 2007: 35). The source for these figures is not entirely clear, and apparently some of them date back to 2003.

35 The outcomes of this policy were not unequivocally negative. Radio Bantu did help some more rural styles and performers survive, and its compiled archives remain a rich resource for the nine African language radio stations that remain today (Coplan 2007: 251). Additionally, according to several industry long-timers, the restrictive government policies also gave an impetus for Black and White artists and audiences to disobey the restrictions and find ways and spaces to play and party together. In these people's views, objection to the repressive politics resulted in a music scene being much more exciting and vibrant in the 1970s and 1980s than today.

36 According to *Music & Copyright* (2010: 21), RiSA lists several local artists as the most pirated ones in the country. Primo and Llloyd *et al.* (2011: 109) cite a report by RiSA stating that 65 per cent of the products seized in 2009 were local repertoire. This is likely to reflect the spending power of those who buy local music. Several music industry insiders suggested to me that the lower prices for local repertoire were a means to combat piracy by making records more affordable.

37 Interviews with Andrew Rees, the Merchandise Manager of Johnnic Com-munications (25 March 2004); Kevin Stuart of the Ready Rolled label (30 March 2004); the MD of CCP (18 March 2004); the GM of Gallo Music Production (10 March 2004); artist and record label owner Don Laka (5 April 2004); Benjy Mudie (22 April 2004); and Harvey Roberts, the owner of Bula Music (16 March 2004).

38 More recently, the *Now* music compilations of international music are said to have sold around one million each (*The View* 2009).

39 For the sake of comparison, the best-selling foreign album (before the *Now* compilations) is said to be of Celine Dion with over 500,000 sold units. One of the international albums considered a good seller for an independent label was *Buena Vista Social Club*, which sold somewhat over 20,000 copies. I have compiled these and the above sales figures from a number of interviews.

40 In the future, the performing artists as well as the record labels stand to benefit from the 'needletime' rights (or what elsewhere are called 'neighbouring rights'), that is, public performance and broadcast royalties. The law on these rights has been in place for some years, but it is not fully implemented yet.
41 In 2011, the entrance fee for a concert in a city-centre club in Johannesburg (Bassline) is on the range of R40–200. A concert in the annual Joy of Jazz festival costs R350–450 and the weekend ticket R850. The Cape Town jazz festival day-pass costs R400 and the weekend ticket R550. For comparison's sake, in an urban area a domestic worker earns R1,500–3,000 per month, and a shop assistant R2,500–5,000 per month. A secondary school teacher earns about R9,000–25,000, an accountant R8,000–50,000 and an IT professional R12,000–50,000. These salary scales apply for the urban areas; the salaries are decisively lower in the rural areas, where the lower end of the above salaries drops by some 50 per cent and the upper end by 30 per cent at least.
42 More about the South African music in the world music market in Pietilä (2008).
43 To improve the situation, SAMRO (the Southern African Music Rights Organisation) has been giving instruction and training to several African countries' administrators for building and strengthening their collection societies (interview with Robert Hooijer, the Secretary of SAMRO, 5 April 2004).

Bibliography

Allen, L. (2007) Preserving a Nation's Heritage: The Gallo Music Archive and South African Popular Music, *Fontes Artis Musicae*, 54(3): 263–79.

Andersson, M. (1981) *Music in the Mix: The Story of South African Popular Music*. Johannesburg: Ravan Press.

Ansell, G. (2004) *Soweto Blues: Jazz, Popular Music, and Politics in South Africa*. New York and London: Continuum.

Ansell, G., Barnard, H. and Barnard, P. (2007) Final Report on the Micro-Economic Development Strategy for the Music Industry in the Western Cape. Prepared under tender for Department of Economic Development and Tourism, Western Cape Provincial Government.

Armstrong P., Lekezwa, B. and Siebrits, K. (2008) Poverty in South Africa: A Profile Based on Recent Household Surveys. A Working Paper (No. 4) of the Department of Economics and the Bureau for Economic Research at the University of Stellenbosch.

Brandle, L. (2006) WMI's Joint Venture Boosts Africa Presence, *Billboard*, 118 (23): 15.

Coetzer, D. (2007) The Voice of Afrikaans, *Billboard*, 119 (10): 16.

Coplan, D. (2007) *In Township Tonight! South Africa's Black City Music and Theatre* (2nd edn). Chicago, IL, and London: The University of Chicago Press.

IFPI (International Federation of the Phonographic Industry). The Recording Industry in Numbers, 2006, 2008, 2009, 2010 and 2011. London: IFPI.

Leibbrandt, M., Woolard, I., McEwen, H. and Koep, C. (2010a) Better Employment to Reduce Inequality Further in South Africa, in *Tackling Inequalities in Brazil, China, India and South Africa: The Role of Labour Market and Social Policies*. OECD: OECD Publishing.

Leibbrandt, M., Woolard, I., Finn, A. and Argent, J. (2010b) *Trends in South African Income Distribution and Poverty Since the Fall of Apartheid*, OECD Social, Employment and Migration Working Papers, no.101: OECD Publishing. Available online at: http://dx.doi.org/10.1787/5kmms0t7p1ms-en (accessed 7 June 2012).

Muller, R. (2009) Broadband: SA Versus the World. mybroadband, 27 May. Available online at: http://mybroadband.co.za/news/Broadband/8208.html (accessed 7 June 2012).

Music & Copyright (2005) Market Survey: South African Music Market, 289: 8–11.

Music & Copyright (2010) South African Authors' Rights Collections Remain Positive in 2009, Despite Continued Falls in Recorded-Music Sales, 404: 17–24.

Pietilä, T. (2008) Singing in the dark? World music and issues of power and agency, in *Globalization and Restructuring of African Commodity Flows*, N. Fold and M. Nylandsted Larsen (eds), Uppsala: Nordic Africa Institute, pp. 241–66.

Pietilä, T. (2009) Whose works and what kinds of rewards: The persisting question of ownership and control in the South African and global music industry, *Information, Communication and Society*, 12(2): 229–50.

Primo, N. and Lloyd, L. (2011) South Africa, in *Media Piracy in Emerging Economies*, J. Karaganis (ed.), SSRC (Social Science Research Council), USA.

RiSA (Recording Industry of South Africa, Johannesburg) (2007) Annual General Meeting (AGM). Available online at: www.risa.org.za/downloads/risa_2007_annual_report.pdf (10 June 2012).

RiSA, unpublished annual statistics, 1999–2010.

Stapleton, C. and May, C. (1987) *African All-Stars: The Pop Music of a Continent*. London and New York: Quartet Books.

SSA (2010) *Mid Year Population Estimates*. Pretoria: Statistics South Africa. Available online at: www.statssa.gov.za/publications/P0302/P03022010.pdf (accessed 9 January 2012).

The View (2009) Overall Recorded Music Sales Set to Fall in South Africa in 2009, But the Digital Potential Looks Significant, 22.

Interviews by the author

(For those who have wanted their identity concealed, only their title and position are given.)

Andrew Rees, the Merchandise Manager of Johnnic Communications, Johannesburg 25 March 2004.

Benjy Mudie, Owner of Fresh Music and a former Marketing and A&R Director at WEA Records/Tusk Music, Johannesburg, 22 April 2004.

David du Plessis, Operations Director of RiSA, Johannesburg, 30 March 2011.

Don Laka, an artist and Owner of Bokoni Music label, Midrand, 5 April 2004.

Duncan Gibbon, Strategic Marketing Director at SonyBMG, 20 May 2005.

Faizel Dajee, Owner of Reliable Music Warehouse, Johannesburg, 8 April 2004.

Kevin Stuart, Owner of Ready Rolled label, Johannesburg, 30 March 2004.

Harvey Roberts, Owner of Bula Music and a former GM of CCP (EMI), Johannesburg, 16 May 2004.

Nick Motsatse, CEO of Samro, Johannesburg, 28 March 2011.

Robert Hooijer, Secretary of SAMRO, Johannesburg, 5 April 2004.
Artist Development Manager in BMG, Johannesburg, 2 April 2004.
MD of CCP, Johannesburg, 18 March 2004.
CEO of Gallo, Johannesburg, 19 April 2004.
GM of Gallo Music Production, Johannesburg, 10 March 2004.
Legal and Business Affairs Director of Sony, Johannesburg, 26 April 2004.
Legal and Business Affairs Director of Universal, Johannesburg, 17 March 2004.

Ukraine

Population:	45.1 million (28th)
Languages:	Ukrainian (67%);
	Russian (24%)
Capital:	Kyiv (pop 2.8 million)
Currency:	Hryvnia (UAH).
	$1 = UAH 7.85
GDP:	$137.9 bn (51st)
GDP (PPP)/capita:	$6,658 (97th)
Median age:	39.9

GDP data from World Bank

Population data from CIA world factbook

Exchange rate used by IFPI (2011) (source: Oanda)

2010 Recorded music market

2005 was the last year that Ukraine was included in the IFPI's *Recording Industry in Numbers* yearbook.

Historical recorded music market ($m, at IFPI's 2010 exchange rate)

	1999	2000	2001	2002	2003	2004
Trade Value						
Retail Value	8.0	9.1	8.5	21.4	28.6	28.2

Proportion of domestic repertoire (market value, physical sales only)

1991	1995	2000	2004 (not 05, as others)
Not available	Not available	43%	32%

11 Ukraine

Adriana Helbig

The dramatic changes in political and economic structures since the fall of the Soviet Union in 1991 have influenced ideas about music's roles in people's lives. In Soviet times music was censored but recordings were cheap and accessible. The government's monopoly on music made intellectual property issues moot. New market economy practices have contributed to understandings of music as a commercial product to be sold and consumed for profit. Piracy, understood as the illegal reproduction and distribution of copyrighted music, is viewed by Western rightsholders and lawmakers as one of the greatest detriments to the development of music industries, globally and domestically. While piracy in Ukraine has significantly limited the revenue musicians have been able to generate from their products, black market channels have facilitated the spread of artists' music well beyond the reaches of formal music industry networks. Throughout the former Soviet Union, cheap access to music via illegal Internet sites and through pirated CDs has become the norm. Ukraine, alongside Russia, has some of the highest levels of media piracy in the world.

According to a report by the IE Market Research Corporation, annual online digital music download retail revenues in Ukraine rose from $1.5 million in 2010 to $10.2 million in 2011 (IEMR 2011).[1] Increased access to technology and faster Internet speeds account for much of this growth. Yet such statistics do not tell the whole story because only 18 per cent of people in Ukraine pay for downloaded music (ibid.). More than 80 per cent of digital music is pirated (IIPA 2011). Ukraine is considered by the IFPI as a 'top priority' nation as regards piracy. The nation is a distrusted economic zone among world music markets, due to a lack of regulation and law enforcement against copyright infringement.

Drawing on more than ten years of ethnographic work among musicians, cultural figures and influential players within Ukraine's music scenes, this chapter puts forth preliminary understandings of how capital, politics and piracy have influenced ideas about music's roles in people's lives, as well as the ways in which these overarching issues have shaped Ukraine's music industries during the first two decades of independence. It is divided into three parts, beginning with an analysis of the Soviet Union's monopoly over music distribution, showing how the state's control over musical expression created a cultural and political milieu that positioned popular music as a means to express anti-government and pro-Ukrainian sentiments. In the second part, the chapter considers continuities between popular music in the Soviet era and the years of independence, focusing on particular on the ongoing links between music and nationalist politics and on piracy. Finally, the third section analyses Kyiv's central role in the contemporary Ukrainian music industry.

Music, monopoly and censorship in the Soviet Union

Contemporary trends in Ukraine's popular music industries are rooted in a complex history of popular music's relationship to the state that changed dramatically from the Soviet era to the present. The scant data pertaining to music production in the Soviet Union and in independent Ukraine shows that a strong relationship between music and politics was set in place during the Soviet era. Music's ability to generate national and civic consciousness made the realm of popular music a highly contested domain in Soviet government, among audiences and among musicians themselves. The centralised model of governing in the Soviet Union was reflected in state-controlled music record production. From 1919 to 1921 the 'Revolutionary Central Agency for the supply and dissemination of printed products' (*Centropechat*) produced all audio recordings (Bennett 1981: ix). From 1922, when mass industrial production began, until 1965, record production was controlled by the Ministry of Culture through the All-Union Studio of Gramophone Records and the All-Union Firm of Gramophone Records (ibid.: x). The All-Union Firm of Gramophone Records was given the additional name *Melodiya* in 1964–65 (ibid.). *Melodiya* issued the majority of the music heard throughout the Soviet Union's fifteen republics. Recordings included classical, arranged folk music, children's stories, newly composed folk music, ethnic state ensemble recordings and locally produced popular music. Musicians who wished to record music had to submit their recording projects for approval from censoring committees. These political processes occurred because of the generally held view that music had the power to influence sociopolitical norms. Throughout Soviet history, therefore, various musical genres were subject to censorship, although, due to changes in the political environment, at other times the same genre could be celebrated. For example, inconsistent forms of censorship regarding jazz throughout Soviet history reveal that Soviet policy makers could not agree on whether jazz was an expression of 'decadent, bourgeois individualism' or should be supported as a struggle of Black people against imperialism (Culshaw 2006). Under Stalin in the 1930s, the saxophone was banned as an instrument of social protest (Starr 1983). By the late 1990s, jazz lost its widespread association as a genre of social protest. Today, jazz has become a voice against the new materialism in post-socialist society (ibid.).

During the Soviet era, limited access to musical information and subjective forms of censorship reinforced a network for musical creation via unofficial channels. An informal, personal network of exchange was one of the primary ways in which citizens circumvented Soviet control over musical production, consumption and dissemination. For example, in terms of creation, singer-songwriter Vladimir Vysotsky (1938–80), one of the most widely recognisable musical figures in Soviet popular music culture, used allegory and satire to criticise the Soviet regime in his socially aware songs. In terms of dissemination, audiences recorded his music at small gatherings and live concerts on cassette tapes. These private recordings (*magnitizdat*) were passed along from person to person, circumventing state censorship and control (Lazarski 1992: 64). Much of the Soviet Union's rock 'n' roll was distributed via underground networks, as was Western rock music (Bahry 1994; Ramet 1994; Rybak 1990). Western rock music came into the Soviet Union through indirect channels, particularly via foreign tourists and citizens living in the Baltic republics who had greater access to foreign goods. Copies of Western rock music were pirated on cassettes as well as cut into human X-rays, referred to as *rok na kostiakh* (literally, rock on bones) and *rok na rebrakh* (rock on ribs) (Yurchak 2006: 181–84).

Most music produced by *Melodiya* was issued on LPs and had a wide-reaching audience throughout the Soviet Union. Locally developed LP technology was financially accessible to most citizens and the majority owned LP playback equipment. The radio continued to be the most popular and easily accessible form of music distribution. As a mouthpiece for the state, however, most people recognised the radio as a medium for political propaganda, as evidenced by the local name for the radio system that was built into Soviet-era apartment housing – *brekhunets*, the liar. Music continued to be used as a form of social critique, however, as in the 1989 song *Brekhunets* (1989), sung by Andriy Panchyshyn, a member of the musical theatre group *Ne Zhurys* (Don't Worry): 'Lying from birth/The end has come/My Soviet kitchen radio/Chokes on the truth.' The song publicly questions the types of information disseminated via state-sponsored media, an act of dissent that was punishable by the Soviet state. When certain musical genres were recast as social commentary, rather than pure entertainment, the act of playing, listening and distributing these genres became a political act. In this way, music became viewed as a vehicle through which information and sentiment could be shared beyond the radar of state control. In the post-socialist context, much of this sentiment remains strong in Ukraine (Helbig 2006). Equally significant, however, is that the means through which these recordings were distributed – *magnitizdat* shared within personal networks of exchange to avoid official censure – also retain cultural significance in the post-Soviet era.[2] The following section discusses these continuities.

Soviet collapse, post-socialist identity politics and the rise of black market music

The fall of the Soviet Union in 1991 brought about a structural collapse of professional musical production and distribution in Ukraine and the *Melodiya* label lost its musical monopoly. The disintegration of the banking system, the devaluation of the Soviet ruble and the massive socioeconomic restructuring that came about with movements for independence left most people without access to disposable income and musicians without physical or economic opportunities to create music. Live music performance came to a screeching halt as state-owned performance venues, restaurants and clubs went bankrupt. Lack of access to technology made public performances very difficult. Few producers had money to invest in formal infrastructure. Music conservatories and state-sponsored choruses, ensembles and performance troupes stopped paying out salaries and many musicians had to seek sources of income elsewhere. Average salaries in Ukraine in the early 2000s were $100 per month (Boulware 2002). Most people had very little income to spare for live entertainment and recorded music. In 2002, a ticket to the opera in Lviv cost $1 and only a handful of audience members could afford to go. Many musicians emigrated to the West, while others made it through the economic transition by trading at the bazaars.

Post-socialist economic collapse and widespread political corruption opened the market to illegally reproduced cassettes of local music and to contraband Western media including, but not limited to, pornographic magazines, B-rated Hollywood movies and cassettes of Western popular music. The most common Western popular music in circulation in the 1990s were cassettes of high-profile contemporary Western singers such as Madonna and Michael Jackson. By the 2000s, the primary modes of black market music distribution changed from audio cassettes to MP3 compact discs. Black market CDs continue to be sold at bazaar kiosks, metro stations and in stores. CDs of local and international popular music are sold alongside CD-ROMs, DVDs and audio/video cassettes (Boulware 2002). The largest bazaars for such activity include the Petrovka and Radiolubitel in Kyiv, Mayak in Donetsk, and the large bazaars in Kharkiv, Odesa, Lviv and other major cities (IFPI 2005).

In 2005, the IFPI identified Ukraine as one of ten 'priority countries' with 'unacceptable piracy rates' (IFPI 2005). According to the International Intellectual Property Alliance, more than 80 per cent of music and video discs sold in Ukraine are illicit (IIPA 2011). The rampant breaking of intellectual property laws prompted the United States to impose trade sanctions on Ukraine in 2001. In 2005, Ukraine put forward a new law that focused specifically on optical disc piracy and the government made highly publicised raids on pirate factories and warehouses (Haigh 2007: 169). There have also been high-profile lawsuits filed by rights holders against illegal CD production plants such as the Kyiv-based Rostok plant that made missile parts during the cold war and began making optical discs in 1995 (IIPA 2009: 333). In turn, the United States reinstated trade relations with Ukraine and repealed the Jackson–Vanik restrictions on Ukraine in 2006. Issues of piracy have not gone away, however. In the last five years, hologram labels have appeared on allegedly officially licensed CDs, although it is clear that many of the labels themselves are pirated as well.

Many musicians in Ukraine speak out about the loss of revenue with regard to piracy. They participate in press conferences and meet with politicians, urging them to enforce existing laws and introduce new legislature regarding copyright protection. The Ukrainian copyright watchdog site Ukrainian League of Musical Rights (www.musicliga.org) warns musicians of companies guilty of copyright infringement and publishes a list of production companies that sell music legally, including Universal Music Group, EMI, Warner and Ukraine-based companies such as CompMusic, Moon Records, Universal Media and Mama Music. According to Alexei Humenchuk, director of the musicliga website, it costs about UAH55,000 ($7,000) to record a song, promote it and issue a music video. In 2007, the cost of recording and promoting an album in Ukraine was UAH200,000 ($25,000) and the present piracy rates make it impossible for artists to earn their money back. Musicliga estimates that the loss of royalties for 2009 was $25 million.[3] The ignoring of intellectual property laws is not just a question of consumer attitudes, however, but is rather embedded in many business practices. The IIPA estimates that 90 per cent of broadcasting operations infringe, with cable operators and TV stations – as well as restaurants, bars, and shopping malls – refusing to pay royalties to collecting agencies (IIPA 2011: 353).

The persistence of piracy is thus one way in which the Ukrainian recording industry still reflects its historical backround in the Soviet era. Another way is through the continuing links between music and politics. In Ukraine, much officially produced and distributed music in the late 1980s and early 1990s was done with the help of Ukrainian diaspora organisations in the United States and Canada. Wanting to capitalise on the role that Ukrainian-language popular music could play in stirring Ukrainian ethnic consciousness, diaspora organisations invited many Ukrainian-speaking musicians to perform in community centres and at Ukrainian heritage festivals throughout North America. Similarly, diaspora musicians began taking part in politically organised festivals in Ukraine to show public support for Ukrainian-language music among audiences that feared overt nationalist expression due to a history of persecution by the Soviet regime.

In 1989, members of Rukh, the People's Movement for Restructuring in Ukraine, launched the Chervona Ruta Festival in Chernivtsi (Czernowitz), western Ukraine. The Chervona Ruta Festival was the first Ukrainian-language music festival held in independent Ukraine, named after the song *Chervona Ruta* (Red Rue) that won the Soviet Union's Best Song of the Year award in 1971. It was composed by Volodymyr Ivasiuk (1949–79), whose Ukrainian-language songs had a wide-reaching nationalist influence far beyond the musical realm (Sokolowki 2008). His outward support for a language that was censored and banned in the public sphere by authorities at various times in Soviet history made Ivasiuk a target for authorities and it is widely believed that he was murdered by the KGB.

Hosting the first Chervona Ruta Festival in Ivasiuk's birthplace was thus a symbolic gesture. Drawing on the musician–martyr Ivasiuk as a symbol of Ukrainian ethnic (and, by extension, anti-Russian) consciousness, festival organisers, independence leaders, diaspora community representatives, musicians and audiences used music to strengthen Ukrainian nationalist political platforms. The festival takes place every other year in a different Ukrainian city and continues to adhere to the policy of only featuring songs in Ukrainian.

The growth of ethnic Ukrainian consciousness and its influence on popular music production, and vice versa, temporarily halted the public performance of Russian-language music in the 1990s. Efforts by local Ukrainian nationalist leaders, particularly in western Ukraine, to control the types of music played in the public sphere based on language choice continued into the early 2000s. During the Ukraine

Without Kuchma anti-government protests in 2001, local officials in the western city of Lviv banned Russian-language rock music from public transport. That same year, Ukrainian-language singer Ihor Bilozir was murdered by ethnic Russian youths who provoked a fight with the musician when he sang a Ukrainian song at an outside café in Lviv. Pro-Ukrainian national media outlets compared his death to that of Volodymyr Ivasiuk by the KGB (Zhurzhenko 2002).

In many ways, the development of music industries in Ukraine reflects political tensions as tied to regional differences in culture and language. Based on my observations at numerous music festivals in cities and villages throughout Ukraine, it seems that language trumps genre in terms of musical choice among audiences. Ukrainian-language musicians are strongly supported by audiences in western Ukraine and in the predominantly second World War era diaspora communities throughout North America and Europe. Russian-language musicians have greater support in the more Russified central and eastern parts of Ukraine and gain access to Russian music markets via musical scenes in St Petersburg and Moscow.

The connections between music and language go beyond nationalism, however, and extend explicitly into formal politics. For instance, hip hop competitions in the eastern city of Kharkiv are sponsored by Ukraine's Party of Regions, *Partia Regionov*, the pro-Russian leaning political party in power that uses its funding to solidify youth support for its political platform. In the western city of Lviv, Orange Revolution supporters, such as Ruslana Lyzhychko and Oleh Skrypka, enjoy financial support from pro-Western, pro-ethnic Ukrainian opposition parties. Perhaps more significantly, performance contracts are tied into political networks. During election cycles, the most prominent artists in Ukraine are contracted by politicians to campaign for them. In such ways, candidates who win elections reward musicians with semi-exclusive rights to perform at public festivals and city-sponsored events. Currently, Ukrainian-language music is in a tenuous position because pro-Russian candidate Victor Yanukovych won the 2008 presidential election, defeating Victor Yushchenko (leader of the 2004 Orange Revolution). The changeover in power in 2008 has reflected itself in the choice of popular music groups – from Ukrainian-language to Russian-language.

Local politics, however, do not explain why the majority of popular music groups from Ukraine, whether Russian or Ukrainian-language, do not succeed within the international markets in the West. Ethnomusicologist David Emil-Wickström has identified East European diaspora-based music scenes in Germany that support artists from Russia and Ukraine (Wickström 2009, 2008a, b). The majority of musicians, however, depend on the expanding Russian market for more performance and recording opportunities. The fact that Anastasiya Prykhodko, an ethnic Ukrainian singer from Kyiv was voted as the Russian representative in the 2010 Eurovision contest in Moscow (with her bilingual Ukrainian-Russian song *Mamo*) suggests that the issue of language may play less of a role outside of Ukraine's borders than within the country itself. Nevertheless, most musicians from Ukraine who strive for the Russian market sing in Russian and are connected to a growing Russian music industry within Ukraine. In Kyiv, Moon Records, which has reissued many recordings done by Ukrainian-language artists in the 1990s, is reportedly a Russian-owned firm. The company has reissued numerous popular music classics from the 1970s to 2000s. The re-release of historical music helps listeners gain access to recordings that were not readily available due to limited quantities of production on outdated mediums such as LPs and cassettes. Lavina Music, the largest music distribution company in Ukraine to date, have released recordings of Ukraine's most popular musicians, including Ani Lorak, Tina Karol, Asiya Akhat, Alyona Vinnytska, Vitaliy Kozlovskiy, Esthetic Education, Druha Rika, Skryabin, Mandry, VV, Okean Elzy, and others. The company's success lies in meeting the growing demands for digital music in a variety of media formats and through cooperation with media partners in the US, England, France, Sweden and Russia.[4]

The emergence of a new music industry in Ukraine

The Orange Revolution, a series of protests that led to fair democratic presidential elections in Ukraine, established the nation's capital, Kyiv, as the home of a multiculturally professionalised music industry. It helped lift corrupt government censorship from radio and television, solidified a nationwide distribution network for CDs, validated home computer music-making and positioned the Internet as a way through which people in Ukraine share music (as the only uncensored domain during the Orange Revolution, the Internet was one of the primary ways that music and political information were shared). Media coverage of the Orange Revolution helped Kyiv attract musicians from all parts of Ukraine. Broader organisational events, such as Kyiv's hosting of the 2005 Eurovision contest (Wickström 2008a), and a series of free public concerts by Elton John in 2007 and 2012, and Paul McCartney in 2008, sponsored by oligarch-turned-cultural patron Viktor Pinchuk, elevated Kyiv to the status of a city that is now commonly included on Western artist world tours. Hip hop artist 50 Cent gave a concert in 2006 and the Rolling Stones came to Kyiv in 2007. Few major concerts by Western musicians have been sponsored in other cities to date and many musical talents from the western, southern, and eastern parts of the country have moved to Kyiv.

Despite the relative openness in Ukraine's public sphere, musicians continue to take great risks in participating in the local music industries, due to the lingering networks that are tinged by political ideologies regarding airplay and access to media coverage. Political elites with the greatest access to economic capital play an important role in shaping the local music industries in independent Ukraine. They finance the types of popular music that are consumed in the public sphere and influence the ways in which music is regulated and disseminated. Changes in political leadership reflect themselves in the types of musical genres that gain the greatest market share in the public sphere based on language choice, lyrical content, and, most importantly, on the political ideologies of the musicians themselves.

Television and radio offer increasing opportunities for musical access. Local musicians compete for airtime with international artists, particularly from the United States and the Russian Federation. A relatively small number of politically connected Ukrainian artists enjoy continued media exposure, although the types of musicians featured are directly connected to the election cycle. While the Orange Revolution did its part in overturning media censorship, politicians continue to have great influence over the types of information featured in media outlets. Musicians have also begun to rely on philanthropic support from oligarchs, the so-called white-collar mafia, who have begun to recast themselves as cultural benefactors to appease the continued criticisms from the majority of Ukraine's population who earn a very meagre income. Figures such as the aforementioned Victor Pinchuk, son-in-law of former President Leonid Kuchma, offer cultural grants for classical music events, ethnic music recording projects, and public concerts of popular music. The Ukraine 3000 International Charitable Fund,[5] founded by Kateryna Yushchenko, wife of former President Viktor Yushchenko, funds folk music projects. While tied in part to political ideologies, there seems to be a greater emphasis on cultural philanthropy that supports civil society discourses and on multicultural pluralism that aims to present a more balanced approach to the underlying ethnic tensions in Ukraine.

Although the post-socialist association between music and politics remains strong, Ukraine's music markets continue to feature and introduce fresh talents in a variety of musical genres. Networks of small recording studios have sprung up in all major cities for anyone willing to pay the nominal fee for recording. Local young producers versed in editing equipment help produce demo CDs and sign better young musicians to their small-scale labels. CDs produced by these studios have small production runs, generally numbering between a hundred and a thousand. Better produced CDs are often reissued by larger labels in Kyiv. In conversations with Ihor Melnyk, a Kyiv-based entrepreneur who sells made-in-Ukraine CDs over the Internet (UMKA),[6] there is great desire among consumers to keep up with the latest sounds and gain access to records within a few months of their release. Melnyk purchases newly released CDs from distributors and keeps them in his office to sell at the time of release and later, because CDs are not re-released and, once sold out, they become unavailable except in digital or pirated format.

The relationship between indie labels and larger labels in Kyiv is financially skewed. Large local labels in Kyiv that reissue CDs produced in other towns by smaller labels have garnered a greater percentage of the national market share and are at an advantage over smaller labels in terms of the quantity of CDs they can produce. International major companies such as EMI and Warner Music Group have issued CDs of major Ukrainian pop stars such as Ruslana Lyzhychko, winner of the 2004 Eurovision contest. Other labels based in Kyiv include Ukrainian Records, the representative office of the world's largest recording company, Universal Music Group in Ukraine. Regional artists whose music becomes popularised in Kyiv often move to the capital city. This system of production ensures a constant flow of talent to the capital but simultaneously drains other cities and towns of its better musicians and impresarios. This makes it difficult to maintain viable, genre-based scenes in smaller cities, unlike in Kyiv where genre-specific clubs and venues enjoy financial gain.

Small, locally owned music stores have opened in the major cities, as have small chain stores selling music and videos, such as the aforementioned Meloman. These stores predominantly feature US music artists, Russian-language films from the United States and the Russian Federation, and a small array of Ukrainian-language music and video discs. However, musicians working in Ukraine are at a great disadvantage due to the lack of outlets through which their products are marketed. There is little information available in music magazines or on the Internet about local artists, and there seems to be a lack of nationwide networks regarding music-related information about existing and emerging artists beyond Ukraine's urban centres. People in western Ukraine are not always aware of popular artists in eastern Ukraine and vice versa. Although this is due in part to differences in language and in political ideologies, it nevertheless reinforces the fact that Ukraine's music industries are not effective in promoting artists on a national, let alone an international scale. Furthermore, access to financial success in the popular music industries is not equal for musicians from all parts of the country. It is very difficult for musicians in Ukraine to make it professionally unless they live in Kyiv and are fully integrated into the music scenes in the capital city. The merging of styles, languages and political ideologies in Kyiv makes it difficult to speak of Ukraine's music industries as national. Rather, they are centralised in the capital in terms of broader distribution networks, media accessibility and performance networks.

Radio, particularly Internet radio, has to some extent helped widen the reach of a variety of local and world music genres. The Internet has also become a more widely used forum for the exchange of information, and many national and regional newspapers upload news to websites. Internet penetration remains quite low in Ukraine, however, as hardware is relatively expensive. Furthermore, the opportunities to legally purchase music online are limited for Ukrainians. Most international and local Internet sellers do not accept credit and debit cards issued in Ukraine, while global online corporations such as Apple do not have a presence in Ukraine's computer and music player industry, so very few people use iTunes or own iPods. Locally produced technology is not advanced enough to take advantage of all developments within the worldwide music industries. Despite these limitations, however, the cyber and digital black markets have flourished alongside the physical black market because pirated music, videos and software from Ukraine are aimed at Internet buyers in the West, and include pay-per-download and streaming services (IIPA 2011: 352). Music portals such as mp3fiesta.com have become common domains for accessing MP3s, although these have been listed by the IIPA as illegal music distributors and reinforce Ukraine's position as a tenuous market in which to conduct music-related business.

Mobile phone use, known locally as *mobilka*, has also become increasingly widespread in Ukraine. Mobile phone companies, such as Nokia and Samsung, promote their telephone communication products as gateways to wireless Internet access and digital music. The ever-expanding cell-phone market in the last decade, similar to the Internet boom in the last half-decade, has outpaced regulation, making law enforcement against musical piracy extremely difficult. Although not every cell phone model has the ability to play music, and not every consumer has the

Figure 11.1 A Samsung mobile phone advertisement featuring Beyoncé in Kyiv, 2009. The caption reads 'Imagine, from music to conversations – one step'. Photo © Adriana Helbig.

opportunity to download music, the cell phone has emerged as one of the main music-playing and storage devices among upwardly mobile youth in urban cities.

Images that invoke Western artists are used readily and without copyright enforcement in advertising technology within Ukraine's expanding market economy. Western artists bring cachet to products. In the advertisement on the preceding page, an extension of a US campaign, African-American singer Beyoncé holds a Samsung phone. The image of a dark-skinned celebrity invokes Western musical consumption through the association to widely marketed R&B and hip hop music from the United States on Ukraine's music television station M1, and reinforces the cultural association between English-language music, middle class identity and Western product consumption.

Conclusion

Despite the crackdown by international and national organisations on music piracy in Ukraine, music distribution continues to be predominantly a black-market activity due to the alleged lightness with which such crimes are treated in the Ukrainian court system. The International Intellectual Property Alliance has recommended that Ukraine be retained on the Watch List for 2010 and that such a listing be reinforced by a six-month US-Government out-of-cycle review (OCR) to assess whether the government of Ukraine has accomplished a series of prescribed measures. These include a crackdown on copyright enforcement, website operators that illegally offer copyright licences and holograms, increased border control against smuggling CDs and effective control of illegal CD-burning operations. In 2011, IIPA elevated Ukraine and Russia to the Prority Watch List, 'as a result of very severe enforcement problems', as well as numerous long-standing legal deficiencies' (IIPA 2012: 1). According to *Wired Magazine* journalist Jack Boulware, who conducted research in the early 2000s among black-market music vendors,

> Ukraine's piracy wouldn't be possible without government complicity, or at least complacency. The country's five CD factories have been among its most lucrative private businesses, and few officials have had the stomach to challenge them – not to mention their shadowy organized-crime customers.
>
> (Boulware 2002)

It appears that widespread corruption within the Ukrainian government itself makes laws against piracy very difficult to enforce.

The development of Ukraine's music industries must be viewed within broader political, economic and socio-cultural processes. The potential for growth is immense, considering the constantly rising economic status of the country's citizens. However, piracy rates continue to increase as a greater percentage of people gain access to digital technology. The majority of people do not view piracy as a crime (Haigh 2007) because it has not been presented as a crime to the general public through the systematic enforcement of international copyright law. The black market for music has become a part of everyday life, flowing over from Soviet era attitudes that prize the acquisition of information beyond government control and regulation. During the early years of independence, the lack of regulation regarding music distribution has resulted in the development of highly connected channels between music distributors and political officials that do not enforce intellectual property laws. Much research is needed among those involved in the black market to reflect the ways people relate to music as a commercial product. Ethnographic contextualisation will shed light on how actors within the music industries relate to issues of money and how they develop notions of trust among each other.

When analysing processes that facilitate various forms of piracy in countries such as Russia, where the piracy market value in 2005 was $332 million (Mertens 2005: 4), it is crucial to take into account the ways in which the black market developed parallel to emerging political and economic post-socialist transitions. Piracy in the former Soviet Union did not emerge within a developed market economy in response to expanding technologies, as in Japan, and as a form of file-sharing to circumvent the capitalist system as in the US (see Condry 2004). Rather, the primary motivations for music piracy are cultural and economic. Research shows that Ukraine's CD makers portray themselves as Robin Hood figures, protecting their country's consumers from high prices set by the avaricious US music and software industries (Boulware 2002). The price of official CDs has increased from UAH10 ($2) in the early 2000s to approximately UAH50 ($10) in 2010. CDs sold in bazaars continue to be cheaper ($6). Post-socialist black market dealings regarding the buying and selling of music are not perceived by the majority to be illegal, but rather as an offering of goods (music as commercial product) to consumers who initially had no access to local and international musical products. The black market and Internet piracy prevail because they have become a normalised form of musical reproduction, distribution, and consumption.

Acknowledgement

Special thanks to Kristina Miller and Isaac Gustafson, undergraduate research assistants at the University of Pittsburgh, for their assistance in analysing statistical data for this project.

Notes

1   In Eastern Europe, digital music retail revenues are expected to increase from $11 million to $192.4 million in 2014. By comparison, digital music retail revenues in Asia are expected to reach $13.5 billion in 2014 (IE Market Research Corporation 2011).
2   The song *Brekhunets* (1989) by Andriy Panchyshyn has been uploaded to various musical sites on the Internet, including YouTube. However, it reflects some *magnitizdat* recordings' poor sonic qualities tinged with distortion from its live recording on Soviet-era recording equipment.
3   Available online at: www.musicliga.org/ru/news/71.html
4   Available online at: lavinamusic.com

5 Available online at: www.ukraine3000.org.ua
6 Available online at: www.umka.com.ua

Bibliography

Bahry, R. (1994) Rock Culture and Rock Music in Ukraine, in S. Ramet (ed.) *Rocking the State: Rock Music and Politics in Eastern Europe and Russia*, Boulder, CO, and Oxford: Westview Press, pp. 243–96.

Bennett, J. (1981) *Melodiya: A Soviet Russian L.P. Discography*. Westport, CT: Greenwood Press.

Bilaniuk, L. (2006) *Contested Tongues: Language Politics and Cultural Correction in Ukraine*. Ithaca, NY: Cornell University Press.

Boulware, J. (2002) Pirates of Kiev, *Wired Magazine*, 10.03, March. Available online at: www.wired.com/wired/archive/10.03/ukraine.html?pg=1&topic=&topic_set= (accessed 8 June 2012).

Condry, I. (2004) Cultures of Music Piracy: An Ethnographic Comparison of the US and Japan. *International Journal of Cultural Studies*, 7(3): 343–63.

Culshaw, P. (2006) How Jazz Survived the Soviets, *The Telegraph*, 14 November. Available online at: www.telegraph.co.uk/culture/music/rockandjazzmusic/3656544/How-jazz-survived-the-Soviets.html (accessed 7 June 2012).

Haigh, M. (2007) Downloading Communism: File Sharing as Samizdat in Ukraine, *Libri*, 57: 165–78.

Helbig, A. (2011a) Brains, Means, Lyrical Ammunition: Hip-Hop and Socio-racial Agency among African Students in Kharkiv, Ukraine, *Popular Music*, 30/3: 315–30.

Helbig, A. (2011b) On Stage, Everyone Loves a Black: Afro-Ukrainian Folk Fusion, Migration, and Racial Identity in Ukraine, *Current Musicology*, 91: 7–24.

Helbig, A. (2006) The Cyberpolitics of Music in Ukraine's 2004 Orange Revolution, *Current Musicology*, 82: 81–101.

IEMR (2011) *Ukraine Digital Music Forecast for Online, Mobile, and Subscription Channels, 2010–2014.* Vancouver, BC: IE Market Research Corporation.

IFPI (2005) *The Recording Industry 2005 Commercial Piracy Report.* London: International Federation of the Phonographic Industry.

IIPA (2009) International Intellectual Property Alliance. Special 301 Report on Copyright Enforcement and Protection. Washington, DC: International Intellectual Property Alliance.

IIPA (2011) International Intellectual Property Alliance. Special 301 Report on Copyright Enforcement and Protection. Washington, DC: International Intellectual Property Alliance.

IIPA (2012) International Intellectual Property Alliance. Special 301 Report on Copyright Enforcement and Protection. Washington, DC: International Intellectual Property Alliance.

Khinkulova, K. (2005) Ukraine Cherishes Orange Sounds, *Ukraine Action Report*, 605, 22 November. Available online at: http://action-ukraine-report.blogspot.com/2005/11/action-ukraine-report-aur-number-605.html#a7 (accessed 7 June 2012).

Klid, B. (2007) Rock, Pop, and Politics in Ukraine's 2004 Presidential Campaign, *Journal of Communist Studies and Transition Politics*, 23(1): 118–37.

Lazarski, C. (1992) Vladimir Vysotsky and His Cult, *Russian Review*, 51(1): 58–71.

Mertens, M. (2005) Thieves in Cyberspace: Examining Music Piracy and Copyright Law Deficiencies in Russia as It Enters the Digital Age, *ExpressO Preprint Series*

Paper 663, The Berkeley Electronic Press. Available online at: http://law.bepress.com/expresso/eps/663 (accessed 7 June 2012).

PRNewswire (2010) 'Big Four' International Music Majors – Universal Music Group, Sony Music Entertainment, Warner Music Group and EMI Group License the Content for Just Launched First Russian Music Video Portal, iviMusic, *PRNewswire*, 5 October.

Ramet, S. (ed.) (1994) *Rocking the State: Rock Music and Politics in Eastern Europe and Russia*. Boulder, CO, and Oxford: Westview Press.

Ryback, T. (1990) *Rock Around the Bloc: A History of Rock Music in Eastern Europe and the Soviet Union 1954–1988*. Oxford: Oxford University Press.

Sokolowski, S. (2008) The Myth of Volodymyr Ivasiuk during the Perestroika Era. Master's thesis. University of Alberta.

Starr, F. (1983) *Red and Hot: The Fate of Jazz in the Soviet Union, 1917–1980*. New York: Oxford University Press.

Wickström, D.-E. (2009) The Russendisko and Music from and of the Post-Soviet Diaspora, in J. Fernandez (ed.) *Diasporas: Critical and Inter-Disciplinary Perspectives*, Oxford: Inter-Disciplinary Press, pp. 65–74.

Wickström, D.-E. (2008a) 'Drive-ethno-dance' and 'Hutzul punk': Ukrainian-associated Popular Music and (Geo)politics in a Post-Soviet Context, *Yearbook for Traditional Music*, 40: 60–88.

Wickström, D.-E. (2008b) Marusia Visits Russendisco: Cultural Flows Surrounding the Russendisco, *Musik & Forskning*, 31: 65–84.

Yurchak, A. (2006) *Everything Was Forever, Until It Was No More: The Last Soviet Generation*. Princeton, NJ: Princeton University Press.

Zhurzhenko, T. (2002) Language Politics in Contemporary Ukraine: Nationalism and Identity Formation, in A. Bove (ed.) *Questionable Returns*. Vienna: IWM Junior Visiting Fellows Conferences, Vol. 12.

Index

Page numbers in *italics* denote a table/figure/illustration